Practical Oracle Database Appliance

T0183682

Bobby Curtis

Fuad Arshad

Erik Benner

Maris Elsins

Matt Gallagher

Pete Sharman

Yury Velikanov

Apress·

Practical Oracle Database Appliance

ISBN-13 (pbk): 978-1-4302-6265-7

ISBN-13 (electronic): 978-1-4302-6266-4

President and Publisher: Paul Manning
Lead Editor: Jonathan Gennick
Technical Reviewer: Frits Hoogland
Editorial Board: Steve Anglin, Mark Beckner, Ewan Buckingham, Gary Cornell, Louise Corrigan, James T. DeWolf, Jonathan Gennick, Jonathan Hassell, Robert Hutchinson, Michelle Lowman, James Markham, Matthew Moodie, Jeff Olson, Jeffrey Pepper, Douglas Pundick, Ben Renow-Clarke, Dominic Shakeshaft, Gwenan Spearing, Matt Wade, Steve Weiss
Coordinating Editor: Anamika Panchoo
Copy Editor: Kimberly Burton-Weismann
Compositor: SPi Global
Indexer: SPi Global
Artist: SPi Global
Cover Designer: Anna Ishchenko

Distributed to the book trade worldwide by Springer Science+Business Media New York, 233 Spring Street, 6th Floor, New York, NY 10013. Phone 1-800-SPRINGER, fax (201) 348-4505, e-mail orders-ny@springer-sbm.com, or visit www.springeronline.com. Apress Media, LLC is a California LLC and the sole member (owner) is Springer Science + Business Media Finance Inc (SSBM Finance Inc). SSBM Finance Inc is a Delaware corporation.

For information on translations, please e-mail rights@apress.com, or visit www.apress.com.

Apress and friends of ED books may be purchased in bulk for academic, corporate, or promotional use. eBook versions and licenses are also available for most titles. For more information, reference our Special Bulk Sales–eBook Licensing web page at www.apress.com/bulk-sales.

Any source code or other supplementary materials referenced by the author in this text is available to readers at www.apress.com. For detailed information about how to locate your book's source code, go to www.apress.com/source-code/.

Contents at a Glance

Contents

Foreword

How did the Oracle Database Appliance (ODA) come into being? That's a good question, and I'd like to share some of the history, motivation, and thought-process behind the appliance's creation.

We in the the Real Application Clusters (RAC) development group at Oracle were striving to make RAC a more broadly adopted technology. Oracle RAC saw rapid adoption and growth in its first decade (2001 through 2011) in the market, but many mid-market customers were avoiding RAC for reasons of perceived complexity and cost. While RAC was common and accepted in large, enterprise environments, Oracle's mid-market customers did not have a simple and affordable RAC database solution.

In early 2010, Oracle acquired Sun Microsystems and a new world of possibilities opened up. Sun had a Cluster-in-a-Box hardware system that wasn't yet commercially available. It had server, storage, and networking in an attractive, 4U-size form factor. That system proved to be the simplest way to deploy RAC. Using it, we were able to deploy RAC in 55 minutes!

On went the light bulbs. This Cluster-in-a-Box was truly the answer to our "RAC for the Masses" dream. We developed the Appliance Manager software to simplify and automate deployment, patching, and storage management. That software together with the appliance made RAC implementation dead-simple. And that is how the ODA was born.

Our next challenge was cost. What's the use of inexpensive hardware if software costs break the bank? This is the challenge that we had to overcome in order to make our RAC-in-a-Box solution attractive to mid-market customers. Could cluster hardware and RAC database software be purchased and deployed for under $100,000? With the support of Oracle's executive management, the ODA became Oracle's first, capacity-on-demand system. In other words, customers could buy in at a low price, and then turn on more cores and add license features as their needs grew. That approach is what made sub-$100,000 Oracle RAC systems a real possibility.

Early customers raved about the simplicity of the ODA. Many RAC skeptics were converted. Several customers adopted ODA as a standard. But like it usually happens, customers soon wanted more! With each generation of ODA, the CPU, memory, and storage capacities grew. Customers wanted to also put their applications inside the ODA. And that's why we built the ODA Virtualized Platform. The database could run in its own virtual machine (VM), and customer applications could run in their own VMs. Customers could pay for what they used at each tier, with full application and database isolation security. Hence the concept of a Solution-in-a-Box was born. People started thinking of the ODA as a modern-day AS/400.

Fuad Arshad is one of the authors on this book, and it is my pleasure to say a few words about him. I first met Fuad when he was my customer. It was one afternoon in which Fuad deployed four ODAs end-to-end, and had Oracle RAC running on all of them. He literally couldn't believe it. He understood that he had just accomplished in one afternoon what his organization had previously taken months to do. He understood that this was a paradigm shift in deploying Oracle and RAC. For him and his organization, it changed the game, and the requests kept pouring in to him: "Can I have an ODA, please?".

Fuad and his team mates followed ODA with a fever that I have rarely seen among customers. Fuad quickly became one of the most knowledgeable people on the technology and our most valuable customer-feedback asset. He tested everything relating to ODA. He blogged about it. He spoke at user conferences. Fuad's fever has driven him to write about a subject for which he oozes passion. And that is true of his coauthors too. I wish them well, and every success with their book.

—Sohan DeMel
Vice President, Product Strategy and Business Development
Oracle Corporation

About the Authors

Bobby L. Curtis, MBA, has spent 18 years in information technology, 12 of which he has been using Oracle products. He specializes in database monitoring and data integration technologies, both aimed at making usability simpler and easier. Currently, he is working as a senior technical consultant focused on implementations and migrations of scalable databases while providing monitoring solutions for these environments. Bobby is a member of the Independent Oracle User Group (IOUG), the Oracle Development Tools User Group (ODTUG), the Georgia Oracle User Group (GOUSER), and the Rocky Mountains Oracle User Group (RMOUG). He lives with his wife and three kids in Douglasville, GA. Bobby is honing his technical skills at Enkitec (www.enkitec.com). He can be followed on Twitter at @dbasolved and his blog at http://dbasolved.com.

Fuad Arshad is a senior database architect who has worked with Oracle Database technologies for more than 16 years. He has experience in all aspects of Oracle Database, from management to tuning, and he is an Oracle Certified Expert. He frequently blogs about Oracle at http://www.fuadarshad.com. Fuad participates in online forums and social media. He is an active Twitter user, and you can find him there at http://www.twitter.com/fuadar. Fuad has presented at conferences such as Collaborate and Oracle OpenWorld on topics ranging from Oracle Real Application Clusters to Oracle Database Appliance. Fuad currently works for Oracle Corporation in its North American Sales organization. He is husband to Saba, and Father to Areej and Ammaar, whom he tries to spend all of his non Oracle related time with.

Erik Benner is a solution architect with BIAS Corp., where he focuses on solutions that meet the customers' business needs. Erik worked with the Oracle Database Appliance prior to its official release, and continues to discover new ways to leverage the technology as not only a database server, but also as an application system when virtualized. Erik is a common speaker at Oracle events, focusing on the areas of Oracle Database Appliance, Linux, and virtualization. When not working, Erik enjoys spending time with his family at their observatory, where the telescopes outnumber the people.

Maris Elsins is an experienced Oracle Applications DBA currently working as team technical lead at The Pythian Group. His main areas of expertise are troubleshooting and performance tuning of Oracle Database and e-Business Suite systems. Maris has led or taken part in numerous Oracle e-Business Suite implementation, maintenance, migration, and upgrade projects. He is a blogger and a frequent speaker at Oracle-related conferences such as UKOUG, Collaborate, and others. Maris is an Oracle Certified Master and a holder of several Oracle Certified Professional certificates. He's also a member of the board of the Latvian Oracle User Group.

Matt Gallagher is a lead database architect at a major Fortune 500 company. He has 17 years of Oracle experience. He specializes in developing enterprise-class database administration and architecture solutions. Matt's experience includes the Oracle Database Appliance, Exadata, Oracle RAC, Data Guard, and ASM. He has developed solutions for all types of database requirements, including high-availability, transactional, and decision support systems.

Pete Sharman is a principal product manager with the Enterprise Manager product suite group in the Server Technologies Division at Oracle Corporation. He has worked with Oracle for the past 18 years in a variety of roles, from education to consulting to development, and has used Enterprise Manager since its 0.76 beta release. Pete is a member of the OakTable Network and has presented at conferences around the world, including Oracle OpenWorld (both in Australia and the United States), RMOUG Training Days, the Hotsos Conference, Miracle Open World, and the AUSOUG and NZOUG conferences. He has authored a book on how to pass the Oracle8i Database Administration exam for the Oracle Certified Professional program. He lives in Canberra, Australia, with his wife and three children.

Yury Velikanov has more than 15 years of Oracle DBA experience. He is an Oracle Certified Master in 9i/10h/11g versions. For his involvement in the Oracle community, he has been recognized as an Oracle ACE Director. During the last few years, Yury has been involved in Oracle Database Appliance projects. He happily shares his experience with you in this book.

About the Technical Reviewer

Frits Hoogland is an IT professional specializing in Oracle database performance and internals. Frits frequently presents on Oracle technical topics at conferences around the world. In 2009, he received an Oracle ACE award from the Oracle Technology Network, and a year later became an Oracle ACE Director. In 2010, he joined the OakTable Network. In addition to developing his Oracle expertise, Frits works with MySQL, PostgreSQL, and modern operating systems. Frits currently works at Enkitec LP.

Acknowledgments

Special thanks to all of my friends and family who have supported me in this endeavor; especially my wife, Patty, and my children, Brendan, Patrick, and Addison. Love you guys!

—Bobby Curtis

Writing the acknowledgements is probably the hardest part of the book, This is part of the sheer amount of people that helped in the book and my fear that I will miss some of them in the process. I will however start with my family abd the tremendous support that I got from my Wife Saba and my two kids Areej and Ammaar who knew this was time I was taking away from them to focus on the book. I also want to acknowledge the whole Database Appliance team at Oracle, including but not limited to Sohan Demel, Ian Cookson, Sanjay Singh, Duane Smith, Ravi Sharma. The support I got from the whole ODA organization as we were trying to get the ODA off the ground and running was tremendous. I would like to like to put praise for Brian Bong, Brice Lahl, Jesse Hogan, Qin Huang and one of the my co-authors for the book Matthew Gallagher for the tremendous support system we built and the risks we took to make this a success. The Apress team including Jonathan Gennick , Anamika and Kimberly for putting us in the right path and helping us get thru the perils of writing a book. Last and not least the other co-authors for working as a team and getting it done. It was truly a pleasure working with all of them.

—Fuad Arshad

Thanks to my family for the patience and support that made this possible.

—Maris Elsins

I would like to thank Jonathan Gennick, the staff at Apress, Bobby Curtis, and Fuad Arshad for giving me the opportunity to work with them on this book project. It's been a great experience.

—Matthew Gallagher

I appreciate all the help received from Apress and the authors that collaborated on this book. I would like to say huge thanks to my lovely wife, Karina, and sons Max and Nik, who supported me a lot along the way. Without you I would have never made it.

—Yury Velikanov

Introduction

The world of information technology has changed rapidly since the inception of computers during the '60s and '70s. These changes have helped propel many different aspects of our economy to include what and how businesses conduct daily operations. With these changes to organizations, especially internally with information technology, faster and better ways of achieving business goals have been pushed and developed.

As businesses start to depend more on data stored within their systems, faster ways of processing and reporting data have developed. Over time, organizations have asked for ways to improve processing, achieve greater throughput, and report more quickly. This eventually led to the development of systems that could leverage both software and hardware resources together, leading to the development of engineered systems.

After the development of engineered systems, such as the Exadata, many organizations were left with a difficult choice of either a massive expense for an engineered system (Exadata) or to build their own. This decision affects a large number of small- to medium-sized businesses. Oracle recognized this, leading to the birth of the Oracle Database Appliance.

What Is the Oracle Database Appliance?

At a high level, the Oracle Database Appliance is a server and storage and network hardware, combined with network, cluster, and database software and templates. The Oracle Database Appliance is a fully supported, integrated system consisting of hardware and software components. Being that it is an integrated system, it is engineered to work at both the software and hardware layers, is simple to configure and maintain, and preconfigured to work with database workloads. Additionally, it is designed to help organizations minimize costs, increase adoption time, and lower risk in database deployment and maintenance.

How This Book Came to Be Written

The authors of this book have been in the information technology industry for many years. In that time, we have seen and dealt with many different platforms across a wide range of applications and databases. During this time, however, we have not seen a compact, engineered system that can be a benefit to organizations more than the Oracle Database Appliance. The idea for this book came about while many of us were implementing Oracle Database Appliances for a variety of customers. As we implemented the Oracle Database Appliance in various environments, we would run into a problem or two and realized there was not a single complete body of work for this appliance. Sure, there were Oracle documents, but at some level, finding information was a challenge. At that moment we realized, when there were issues, surely we were not the only ones hitting them. The desire to write this book grew even more when all of us met at a conference and began talking about issues with the Oracle Database Appliance. We all agreed that the industry needed a book about this complex yet simple engineered system. All of the authors of this book had a desire to share our knowledge, which we have gained from using the Oracle Database Appliance. Hence, the need for this book was kicked into motion!

Why Buy This Book

If you are a DBA or a manager who deals with databases on a regular basis, this book is going to provide you with information on using the Oracle Database Appliance. No matter how complex an environment your organization has, you will be able to use the information in this book to bring the Oracle Database Appliance, throughout its life cycle, within your organization.

An understanding of what the Oracle Database Appliance can do will radically improve your ability to quickly implement complex solutions, while ensuring rapid deployments of databases. At the same time, you will develop ideas on how to uniquely use this appliance when moving from homegrown solutions to out-of-the-box solutions.

CHAPTER 1

■ ■ ■

Oracle Database Appliance

The Oracle Database Appliance (ODA) is a newer member of Oracle's Engineered Systems family of products. It is meant as an entry-level appliance to provide a pain-free, Oracle Database implementation experience. An ODA implementation saves time and money by providing an easier path to deploying a highly available database solution using a combination of the Oracle Database Enterprise edition and Oracle Unbreakable Linux (OEL) clustered across two nodes.

Why an Appliance?

Traditional hardware deployments can take anywhere from weeks to months to implement, depending on the procurement and the deployment model that a company employs. Upgrades to Oracle database versions can also be a challenge because each hardware/software combination needs certification at various levels to ensure a smooth upgrade.

The evolution of the Oracle Database is very important to understand as we look at the engineered systems. Oracle has incorporated a variety of enhancements as it evolved the Oracle Database product. Through its evolution, the complexity of the software has increased. From a very simplistic relational database management system (RDBMS) in Oracle V4 to the reintroduction of Oracle Real Application Clusters, which was released as part of V9, Oracle has revolutionized the RDBMS and clusterware spectrum.

The database administrator (DBA) role has evolved as a result of the enhancements to the Oracle Database product line. Roles and responsibilities have increased, and coordination with multiple infrastructure groups that have a disparate goal has also increased. As Oracle introduced versions 10 and 11 of the database, the life of a DBA became more complicated, particularly with the addition of Automatic Storage Management (ASM) and Grid Infrastructure (GI). The DBA is now in charge of volume management and for ensuring that all aspects of the infrastructure meet the requirements of the Oracle stack.

Complexity has its own perils, and problem resolution time is greatly increased as the number of components increase. Virtualization of hardware and platform can also make things worse if all aspects of infrastructure are not fully evaluated properly. The infrastructure and software costs to ensure complete compliance can be very expensive for an organization, and innocently updating firmware in one piece of the infrastructure can cause turmoil in other aspects of the infrastructure or software.

The human element is very important as we talk about the advances in infrastructure and software. DBAs have seen their responsibilities increase with each release of the Oracle database stack. They are now expected to understand all aspects of the RDBMS, infrastructure, OS, and network to deliver a comprehensive and defect-free solution to the customer. Delivery of such a solution requires extensive coordination with various infrastructure groups, and may require costly upgrades or purchases.

The ODA is an entry-level appliance meant to help with infrastructure and software deployment, as well as upgrades. It comes as a complete, boxed solution meant for small- and medium-sized businesses, as well as enterprises, for rapid deployment of hardware and software. The ODA was introduced at Oracle OpenWorld 2011, with a second version, the X3-2, shipping in April of 2013. The ODA is the first appliance to support pay-as-you go licensing. It provides customers the ability to start with as few as 2 cores and move up to 32 cores (X3-2), as needed.

Management costs and build costs are significantly reduced because the ODA comes preconfigured with interconnect and storage, as well as a tuned OS. The ODA also includes the option to virtualize the appliance, which can result in significant savings to the organization by providing a complete boxed solution for virtualizing applications and the database.

Businesses and enterprises often struggle with deadlines, and by using a traditional model of deployment, which includes procurement as part of the project budget, it is often very hard to provide the agility that is required for a business to bring ideas to fruition quickly. A typical deployment cycle can range from 30 to 90 days, which can make a product that requires a database harder to get to market. Figure 1-1 shows a typical deployment cycle in a traditional system vs. that with an ODA, based on deployment experience with Oracle Real Application Clusters (RAC). This may vary by the deployment maturity model of an organization.

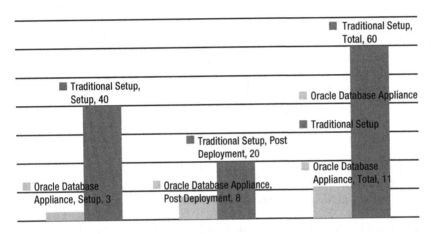

Figure 1-1. Traditional server vs. ODA with RAC

The disparity between a traditional setup and the setup of an ODA is huge. It may differ based upon the practices and processes implemented by an organization. Traditionally, the process to deploy hardware includes the following steps:

1. Procurement of hardware

2. Delivery of hardware

3. Setup of hardware

4. Network connectivity and switch setup

5. OS setup and tuning

6. Database software setup

7. Best practices post setup

These steps are just some of the many required to get a system up and running, and may differ based on the infrastructure model an organization uses. Organizations have always had the ability to pre-buy and pre-provision infrastructure, as well as build a shared model to support the business. This can be cost effective in some cases, but can also be problematic because continuous understanding of new business requirements is a must. Business requirements drive the complexity of the infrastructure according to the availability model. Requirements can drive the need to prepare an environment that can support various business initiatives and provide an on-demand framework that allows faster provisioning. The ODA can be used as an enabler for a private cloud-based framework or a simple provisioning model.

The ODA's unique licensing model, as well as the ability to provide virtualization out of the box, can help organizations build a scalable model for deploying applications and databases at a fraction of the time and cost. The ODA comes as a complete package, which makes Oracle responsible for all components. This allows the organization to focus on the business rather than the technology, and frees up the DBA's time to focus on design rather than setup and coordination. A traditional ODA deployment exercise consists of the following:

1. Procure hardware

2. Install hardware

3. Set up the database appliance

4. Implement organizational best practices

The steps needed to implement an ODA are significantly less than a traditional setup because Oracle bundles hardware and software as one unit and allows for management and maintenance of the stack as one, which is not how traditional infrastructure is managed.

The Appliance Hardware

ODA is marketed using the tagline "Simple, Reliable, Affordable." Currently, it is available in two hardware configurations: the original and the ODA X3-2. Billed as part of Oracle's strategy for "Hardware, Software, Complete," the ODA brings forward a simple cluster that includes two database server nodes, storage, as well as cluster interconnect and simplified management built into the appliance itself.

Oracle Database Appliance V1

To date, Oracle has shipped more than 1,000 Oracle Database Appliances.[1] The original ODA is a complete unified box solution that contains two 2U Sun M4370 servers, along with storage and networking components. The total size of the ODA V1 is 4U in datacenter rack terms. Figures 1-2 and 1-3 show the front and back of the appliance, respectively, and highlight the simplicity of the ODA's design.

Figure 1-2. *The front of the Oracle Database Appliance V1*

---

[1]Oracle, "Customers Worldwide Simplify Database Management with Oracle Database Appliance," http://www.oracle.com/us/corporate/press/1940385, April 29 2013.

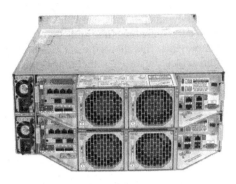

Figure 1-3. *The back of the Oracle Database Appliance V1*

Each ODA unit consists of two physical servers, and each physical server consists of a server node and an Integrated Lights Out Management (ILOM) component. Chapter 2 delves into detail about the ILOM and explains the importance of the ILOM in the ODA unit. Table 1-1 lists the specifications of the ODA V1 from the Oracle Database Appliance Datasheet. (My Oracle Support Note 1385831.1 provides the same information.)

Table 1-1. *Oracle Database Appliance V1 Specs*

Component	Specification
CPU	2x 6-core Intel Xeon X5675 3.07GHz
Memory	96GB RAM (12 x DDR3-1333 8GB DIMMs)
Network	2x 10GbE (SFP+) PCIe card 6x 1GbE PCIe card 2x 1GbE (Intel 82571) onboard integrated redundant cluster interconnect
Internal Storage	2x 500GB SATA - for operating system 1x 4GB USB internal
RAID Controller	2x LSI SAS9211-8i SAS HBA
Shared Storage	20x 600GB - 3.5" SAS 15k RPM HDD (Seagate Cheetah) - for RDBMS DATA (any slot except the top row of disks) 4x 73GB - 3.5" SAS2 SSDs - for RDBMS REDO (slot in the top row of four disks) SSD from STEC (ZeusIOPS - multilevel cell (MLC) version with SAS interface)
Operating System	Oracle Enterprise Linux 5.5 (on ODA software version 2.1), 5.8 (on ODA software version 2.2) x86_64

The ODA comes with a very powerful Intel Xeon processor, as well as enough memory and storage to accommodate a variety of Online Transaction Processing(OLTP) and some smaller data warehouse workloads. The network interconnect is built into the appliance, which removes the need for a switch for the interconnect for communication between the nodes. In terms of storage, depending on the ODA software version and redundancy layer, you can have between 4 and 6 terabytes (TB) of space.

Each ODA comes two 500GB drives per server node, which are mirrored and used for the OS, as well as software that hosts the OS, clusterware, and the Oracle Database homes (250GB is unallocated). There are twenty 600GB SAS drives per appliance and four 73GB SSDs for online redo only. The shared disks on the ODA are connected via two LSI controllers, which are connected to an onboard SAS expander. Each SAS expander, in turn, is connected to 12 of the hard disks in the ODA. Oracle uses Linux multipathing to avoid disk-path failures. Solid-state drives (SSD) have been added for redo to overcome rotating disk latency, because the controller of the rotating disk has no cache. Disk sizing on the ODA depends on many factors, including the version of the ODA software that is running on the appliance. Table 1-2 shows the various disk configurations and configuration options that are supported on the ODA.

Table 1-2. ODA Disk Configurations

Configuration Option	Disk Group	Type/Redundancy	Backup Type	Space Available (GB)	Software Version Supported
1	DATA	HIGH	External	3200	All versions
1	RECO	HIGH	External	488	All versions
1	REDO	HIGH	None	91	All versions
2	DATA	HIGH	Local	1600	All versions
2	RECO	HIGH	Local	2088	All versions
2	REDO	HIGH	None	91	All versions
3	DATA	NORMAL	External	4800	2.4 and above
3	RECO	NORMAL	External	733	2.4 and above
3	REDO	HIGH	External	91	2.4 and above
4	DATA	NORMAL	Local	2400	2.4 and above
4	RECO	NORMAL	Local	3133	2.4 and above
4	REDO	NORMAL	None	91	2.4 and above

Table 1-2 illustrates various disk configuration options supported by the ODA. As you can see, the space has approximately 4TB usable due to all disk groups being triple-mirrored (high redundancy) in configuration options 1 and 2. Depending on which configuration you chose, you will have more space in DATA or RECO disk groups.

Oracle Database Appliance 2.4 introduced the option to allow mirrored (normal redundancy) disk groups for DATA and RECO. This is highlighted in Table 1-2 as configuration options 3 and 4. This was done primarily to allow customers the choice of space based on the environment that the ODA is being deployed. Typically, the recommendation is to deploy mirroring (normal redundancy) on development/test systems.

The ODA runs Oracle Enterprise Linux OS with support only for the Unbreakable Enterprise Kernel (UEK) as of software version 2.2. The following is a snapshot of ODA software version 2.6:

```
Linux oda01 2.6.32-300.32.5.el5uek #1 SMP Wed Oct 31 22:06:21 PDT 2012 x86_64 x86_64 x86_64 GNU/Linux
Enterprise Linux Enterprise Linux Server release 5.8 (Carthage)
```

Looking at the ODA box from the outside, there are a lot of connections that need to be made. Figure 1-4 points out the various connections, which are then described in Table 1-3. Oracle also provides an easy scheme for setup. The setup poster is shown in Figure 1-5.

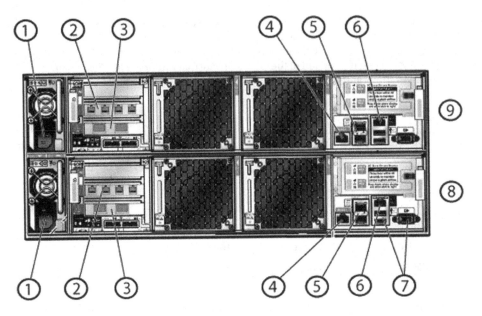

Figure 1-4. *Oracle Database Appliance V1 callouts*

Table 1-3. *Oracle Database Appliance Connector Descriptions*[2]

Callout	Label	Ethernet	Bond	Description
1				Power connectors.
2	PCIe 1	Eth 7, 6, 5, 4 (left to right)	bond1, bond2	Eth 4 and Eth 5 are configured as bond1. Eth 6 and Eth 7 are configured as bond 2. These ports are used for custom configurations or for separate backup, disaster recovery, and network management.
3	PCIe 0	Eth 8, Eth 9	xbond0	Two 10 GbE ports. In 10 GbE systems, these are connected to the public network.
4	SerMgt			Serial connector to Oracle ILOM and system console.
5	Net 0, Net 1	Eth2, Eth3	bond0	Two 1 GbE connectors. In 1 GbE systems, these are connected to the public network.
6	NetMgt			Ethernet connection for Oracle ILOM.
7	USB and Video			Used for connecting to system console.
8				Server Node 0.
9				Server Node 1.

---

[2]Part of the MOS Note 1385831.1.

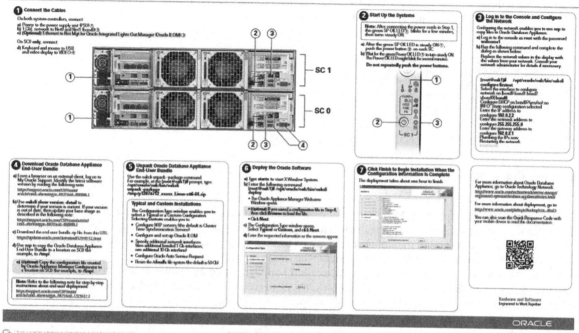

Figure 1-5. *ODA V1 setup poster*[3]

The ODA setup poster is a simple and easy-to-understand method for installing and setting up the appliance. The poster is a step-by-step guide that explains connecting the cables to deploy the software, which results in a fully functional clustered database server. Figure 1-5 shows this in detail. Oracle updates the poster with every release. The poster is available in the documentation web site for ODA at `http://docs.oracle.com/cd/E22693_01`.

The ODA comes with fully redundant hardware and includes two 10 gigabit Ethernet (GbE) interfaces that are bonded together via the Linux operating system to provide redundancy, as well as two 3×2, 1GbE interfaces that are also bonded together for purposes of redundancy. There is a connector for the ILOM, as well as USB and VGA for keyboard and external monitor connections, if needed.

The ODA is unique in the sense that it has an onboard interconnect that is used to connect the two database servers. The interconnect is 1GbE and uses an Intel 82571 board; it is not bonded. That is why there are two cluster interconnects leading to two HAIP devices seen from the clusterware. Since the private interconnects are internal to the appliance, no external cabling is required for them.

The ODA is managed by Oracle Appliance Kit (OAK), which is a proprietary piece of software that is specific to the ODA. The OAK and various ODA software features are discussed in subsequent chapters. Virtualization is added to the ODA platform as an option, and it is also discussed in subsequent chapters.

---

[3]Oracle, Oracle Database Appliance documentation, `http://docs.oracle.com/cd/E22693_01/doc.21/e40077.pdf`.

Oracle Database Appliance X3-2

The ODA X3-2 is the second generation of the ODA devices. It has a lot of new features, as well as more capacity than its predecessor. Figure 1-6 shows the appliance from the front.

Figure 1-6. *Oracle Database Appliance X3-2*

The Oracle Database Appliance X3-2 expands the capabilities found in the ODA V1 and packs a punch in terms of hardware and storage capabilities. Oracle has taken a slightly different approach in terms of hardware architecture for the X3-2. The server nodes and the storage rack are now two separate units that are connected together, and there is an option to add an expansion storage rack to double the storage capacity of the appliance.

The X3-2 is more modular in structure than the version 1 appliance and it provides flexibility. Customers are able to expand storage by adding an additional storage rack. They can create a storage rack and a server node rack in their datacenters; however, we recommend installing the components together.

The X3-2 is still a 4U rack mountable unit, but it is divided into two individual 2U units. The server units are 1U each, and the storage unit is 2U as well. The expansion rack, if selected, will add another 2U to the system. Table 1-4 lists the complete specifications for the X3-2 box, but the short story is that the box features Intel Xeon E5-2690 processors, 256GB of memory, two 10GbE external copper connections, and two 10GbE internal network interconnects. Also included are shared, serial-attached SCSI (SAS) disks. The internal disks are now 600GB, up from the previous 500GB configuration that was in V1.

Table 1-4. *Oracle Database Appliance X3-2 Specs*

Component	Specification
CPU	Two 8-core Intel® Xeon® processors E5-2690
Memory	256GB (sixteen 16GB RDIMMs at 1600 MHz)
Network	Four 100/1000/10G Base-T Ethernet ports (onboard) 1x dual-port 10GBase-T interconnect for cluster communication
Internal Storage	Two 2.5-inch 600GB 10K rpm SAS-2 HDDs (mirrored) OS
RAID Controller	1x dual-port internal SAS-2 HBA 2x dual-port external SAS-2 HBA
Shared Storage	Twenty 2.5-inch 900GB 10K rpm SAS-2 HDDs Four 2.5-inch 200GB SAS-2 SLC SSDs per shelf for database redo logs Optional storage expansion with additional storage shelf doubles storage capacity External NFS storage support
Operating System	Oracle Enterprise Linux 5.8 x86_64

ODA X3-2 provides a packed spec sheet. It is a powerful successor to the original ODA. Oracle has added a little more complexity in the install, which accommodates the flexibility of having a storage shelf that is separate from the actual server units. This allows for adding a second shelf as needed, but you will now need to ensure that the cabling is done appropriately per the setup poster that is provided with the appliance.

As with the original ODA, the setup poster for the X3-2 is enhanced to be a handy resource to help with the installation. Figure 1-7 shows the poster, which is updated with each version of the software. Currently, the setup poster has instructions on setting up the ODA as a bare metal or a virtualized environment.

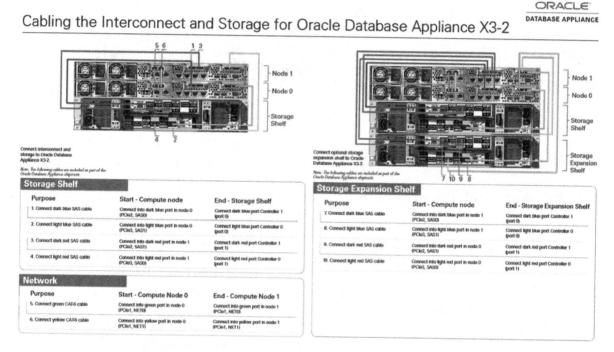

Figure 1-7. *Oracle Database Appliance X3-2 setup poster*

If you look at a poster, you'll see that it suggests a deviation from the original design, in which there is a connection and cables that need to run between the server nodes, as well as from the server nodes to the storage shelf, and optionally to an additional storage shelf as well. Figure 1-8 shows what the server node looks like. Table 1-5 describes the callouts from Figure 1-8.

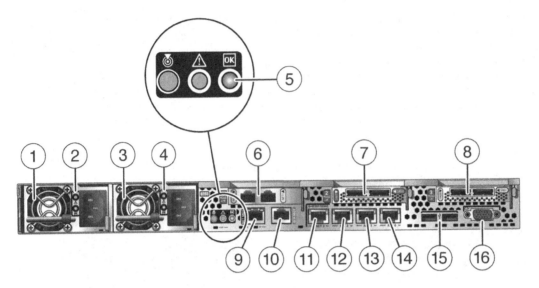

Figure 1-8. *Oracle Database X3-2 server node rear*

Table 1-5. *Callouts for the ODA Server Node Rear*

Callout	Legend	Callout	Legend
1	Power Supply (PS) 0 with fan module.	9	NetMgt port. 10/100BASE-T port used to connect to Oracle Integrated Lights Out Manager (Oracle ILOM) SP.
2	Power Supply (PS) 0 status indicators: Service Required LED: amber, AC OK LED: green.	10	Serial management (SerMgt)/RJ-45 serial port.
3	Power Supply (PS) 1 with fan module.	11	Network (NET) 100/1000/10000 Mbps Base-T EthernetRJ-45 connector: NET 3.
4	Power Supply (PS) 1 status indicators: Service Required LED: amber, AC OK LED: green.	12	Network (NET) 100/1000/10000 Mbps Base-T Ethernet port with RJ-45 connector: NET 2.
5	System status indicators: Locator LED: white, Service Required LED: amber, Power/OK LED: green.	13	Network (NET) 1100/1000/10000 Mbps Base-T Ethernet port with RJ-45 connector: NET 1.
6	PCIe card slot 1. Provides two 10GBase-T Ethernet with RJ-45 connector ports for private interconnect between server nodes.	14	Network (NET) 100/1000/10000 Mbps Base-T Ethernet port with RJ-45 connector: NET 0.
7	PCIe card slot 2. Provides two SAS-2 connectors used to connect servers to the storage shelf and storage expansion shelf.	15	USB 2.0 connectors (2).
8	PCIe card slot 3. Provides two SAS-2 connectors used to connect the servers to the storage shelf and the storage expansion shelf.		

The storage shelf is an independent component. You can see the structure and components that are part of the storage shelf in Figure 1-9. Table 1-6 describes the various callouts.

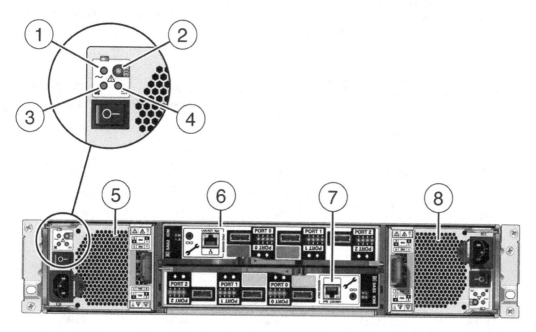

Figure 1-9. *Oracle Database Appliance X3-2 storage shelf*

Table 1-6. *Oracle Database Appliance Storage Shelf Callouts*

Callout	Legend
1	AC power fail indicator
2	Power supply status indicator
3	Fan fail indicator
4	DC power fail indicator
5	Power supply with fan module 0
6	I/O module 1
7	I/O module 0
8	Power supply with fan module 1

Due to the addition of the storage shelf and large-sized drives, Oracle Database Appliance X3-2 provides a lot more storage space than its predecessor. And its workload capability has been expanded significantly to accommodate various data mart–style workloads.

ODA X3-2 supports the same four disk configurations shown earlier in Table 1-2, but the sizing is different. Table 1-7 outlines the sizing options available on the X3-2 platform.

Table 1-7. *ODA X3-2 Disk Configurations*

Configuration Option	Disk Group	Type/Redundancy	Backup Type	Space Available (GB)	W/Expansion Shelf (GB)
1	DATA	**HIGH**	External	**4800**	**9600**
1	RECO	**HIGH**	External	**733**	**1466**
1	REDO	**HIGH**	None	**248**	**496**
2	DATA	**HIGH**	Local	**2400**	**4800**
2	RECO	**HIGH**	Local	**3133**	**6266**
2	REDO	**HIGH**	None	**248**	**496**
3	DATA	**NORMAL**	External	**7200**	**14400**
3	RECO	**NORMAL**	External	**1100**	**2200**
3	REDO	**HIGH**	External	**248**	**496**
4	DATA	**NORMAL**	Local	**3600**	**7200**
4	RECO	**NORMAL**	Local	**4700**	**9400**
4	REDO	**NORMAL**	None	**248**	**496**

Summary

This chapter looked at the Oracle Database Appliance (ODA)—both the original and the X3-2 models. Originally, the ODA was geared toward small- and medium-sized businesses, but it has gained popularity in the enterprise sector as well. The all-in-one, all-encompassing architecture that allows for capacity on demand are the features that have drawn praise. Simplicity of deployment and management allow for cost savings over traditional infrastructure deployment models. An ODA provides high availability and redundancy out of the box, and applies Oracle's best practices to the system.

CHAPTER 2

Integrated Lights Out Management

The Oracle Database Appliance (ODA) is a bundle of two server nodes that include storage and embedded cluster networking. Each server node has an Integrated Lights Out Manager (ILOM) interface that is used for management and maintenance tasks. This chapter will dive into what an ILOM is and how to use it in the context of the Database Appliance.

Introduction to ILOM

An ILOM is a service processor (SP) that is embedded into all Oracle Sun Server–based products. The aim of an ILOM is to provide support for a server in a manner such that access to the datacenter is not required for day-to-day support functions. An ILOM also provides access to a variety of diagnostic features and has integration with Oracle's Automatic Service Request (ASR) to provide call-home functionality to report hardware failures to Oracle for fast support.

The Oracle ILOM service processors provide a wide array of features, and its functional aspects improve with every release of the ILOM. The ODA V1 and X3-2 come with different ILOM versions, due to the enhancements in the service processor itself, but at its core, the ILOM allows for the following:

- Remote KVMS capabilities

- Remote boot from image

- Fault display

- Integration with a variety of authentication systems, such as LDAP (Lightweight Directory Access Protocol), SSL (Secure Sockets Layer), Radius, and Active Directory

- Remote syslog setup

- SNMP- and SMTP-based alerting

- Environmental reporting

- System serial console redirection (LAN)

- Monitoring host states remotely

- Access to various part and serial numbers

This chapter will focus on these features in the context of the ODA. The Oracle Appliance Kit (OAK), also known as the Oracle Appliance Manager, is the software that manages installation and patching, and in some cases, the gathering of diagnostic information and integration of the ILOM with ASR. However, it is still important to understand the ILOM and the basic functions it performs.

Figure 2-1 shows the starting screen that you see when you log in to an ILOM via your browser. The screen has three main components. The layout is a bit different from the ODA V1 layout in terms of design, but most common functionalities have stayed the same.

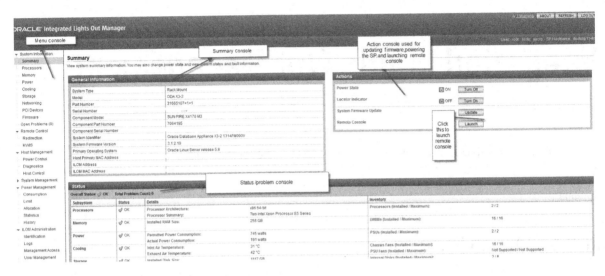

Figure 2-1. *The ILOM running on an ODA X3-2 Sun Fire X4170 M3*

The General Information section is the primary place to look at for basic system information per server node in a visually pleasing manner. Information you'll find there includes:

- System type

- Model

- Part number

- Component model

- ILOM and system MAC address

- Primary operating system

The Actions section is the place that provides easy access to various commonly used functions that an ILOM user will need to access. These include updating the firmware, powering the server on or off, and recycling the service processor by toggling various options of the power state. You can also turn on the locator beacon so that the system can be located in the datacenter (new to X3-2), and you can use the remote console to access the server nodes.

The Status section provides a real-time status on the physical state of components that are contained within a server node. The Status section looks at the following:

- Processors

- Memory

- Power

- Cooling

- Storage

- Networking

The Summary screen shown in Figure 2-1 is rich in information and allows you to get a lot of information summarized quickly. The menu section on the left allows getting more detailed information on each of the components. The menu also includes options for setup and customization of the ILOM

Figure 2-2 shows the summary screen from the original Database Appliance. As you can see, the new interface in Figure 2-1 provides a much easier way to find information, and the menu navigation is much more intuitive. As we go through the features in the sections to follow, we will point how to get to various locations from both ILOMs.

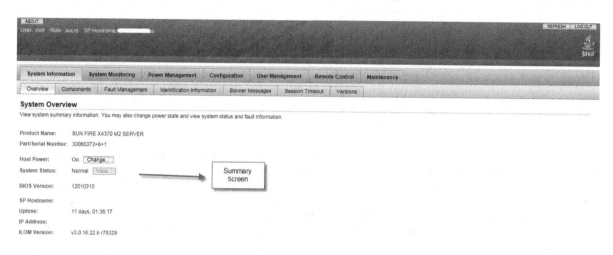

Figure 2-2. *ILOM from the original ODA (V1 X4370 M2)*

ILOM Features

The ILOM is capable of providing a vast array of services. Looking at the ILOM and all its features are beyond the scope of this book, but we will look at a few of the important features that are needed from the perspective of managing an ODA.

Remote KVMS Service

The Remote KVMS (Keyboard, Video, Mouse ,Storage is a very important part of the ILOM and is probably what you will use based on your familiarity and experience with remote access to the appliance. The Remote KVMS service allows you to remotely control a server node from a browser. The Remote KVMS uses Virtual Network Computing (VNC) to access the server nodes. Thus you should be sure to open the firewall ports shown in Table 2-1 on your workstation.

Table 2-1. *Firewall Ports Needed for RKVMS Access*

Ports	Service	Type
443	TCP	HTTPS (inbound)
5120	TCP	Remote CD (outbound)
5121	TCP	Remote keyboard and mouse
5123	TCP	Remote Floppy
6577	TCP	CURI (API) - TCP and SSL
7578	TCP	Video Data (bi-directional)
161	UDP	SNMP V3 Access (inbound)
3072	UDP	Trap Out (outbound only)

The setup of an ILOM is covered later in the chapter, but once an ILOM is setup, the Remote KVMS allows access to the server console. Remote KVMS also allows remote installation, which is needed to do a bare-metal server installation. Access to the remote control feature is a bit different between V1 and X3-2 of the ODA, but both offer the same in terms of functionality.

Figure 2-3 shows a cutout of the location of the remote control features in ODA V1 vs. ODA X3-2. The remote control feature is much more easily accessible on the ODA X3-2 via the main screen. By contrast, it takes a couple of clicks to get to the remote control feature on the ODA V1.

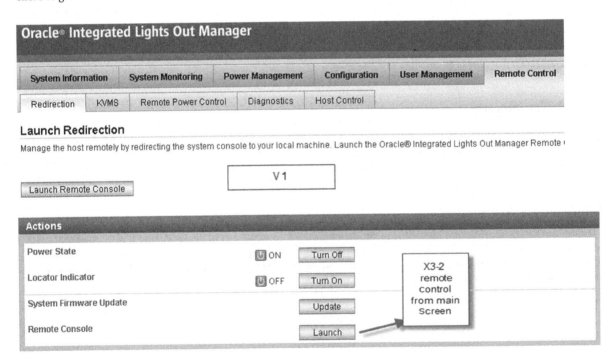

Figure 2-3. *Remote Console options in ODA V1 (top) and ODA X3-2 (bottom)*

The remote console is an easy way to get access to the server console, to configure a server, or to diagnose issues, if remote connectivity to the server itself is not available. Once the remote console is launched, you see a login prompt similar to what you see when you log in to a Unix machine. This allows you to log in to the server from the console.

The remote console provides access to the console messages and allows users to log in to the system. Each server node (SN) has its own ILOM, so in the context of an ODA, there are two ILOMs. This is very important because each physical server in the ODA has its own ILOM that has to be used for managing and maintaining that physical server.

Integrated Shell

The ILOM is also accessible via a shell that is integrated into the service processor. That shell is a convenient way to access and operate an ILOM. The ILOM shell can be accessed via various methods, as follows:

- The NET MGT port on the server node (serial connection)

- The server node using ipmitool over TCP

- TCP to SSH (Secure Shell) directly into the ILOM

- IPMITool over LAN, locally or from any device that supports ipmitool

The integrated shell is used to configure the ILOM for the first time. It can be used by the datacenter team to prepare the ODA for configuration. The integrated shell is also used to perform basic functions like ILOM password changes, checking for system faults, gaining access to the console, and so forth.

The integrated shell is accessible via the ipmitool command. It can also be accessed on the server nodes and remotely using ipmitool with the lanplus protocol. The ipmitool can be accessed via the host for which the SP manages the hardware (as root; the IPMI device in Linux only allows root access). For example:

```
# ipmitool sunoem cli
Connected. Use ^D to exit.
```

Another way to connect to the SP is via the lanplus protocol. This approach can be used on a remote machine where ipmitool is installed. Here's an example:

```
[root@mxt101 ~]# ipmitool -I lanplus -H <ilom hostname/address> -U <ilom username>
-P <ilom user's password> sunoem cli
Connected. Use ^D to exit.
->
```

The ILOM can be accessed remotely via native SSH as well. Here's how that is done:

```
$ ssh <ilom username>@<ilom hostname/address>
Password:

Oracle(R) Integrated Lights Out Manager

Version 3.0.16.10.d r74499

Copyright (c) 2012, Oracle and/or its affiliates. All rights reserved.

->
```

The ILOM integrated shell provides a pretty rich command set and allows you to perform a variety of tasks directly from the interface itself. Table 2-2 lists some of the key commands and how they can be accessed.

Table 2-2. *Common ILOM CLI Commands*

ILOM CLI Command	Description
`show /SYS power_state fault_state`	Shows the `power_state` (On or Off) for the host, and the fault state. OK means nothing faulted. If the ILOM/SP detects failure, the fault state will not be OK.
`stop /SYS`	Stops the host in a graceful way. If the host doesn't respond or doesn't go down, you can force the host to stop by adding `-f`. For example: `stop -f /SYS`
`start /SYS`	Starts a host.
`show faulty`	Lists all detected failures, if any.
`start /SP/console`	Starts text-based console access.
`set /SP/users/root password=welcome1`	Sets a new password for the ILOM.

`set /SP/network`
`pendingipdiscovery=static`
`pendingipaddress=10.0.0.1`
`pendingipnetmask=255.255.255.0`
`pendingipgateway=10.0.0.255`
`commitpending=true`
	Configures the network for the ILOM.

`reset /SP`	Resets the SP, which means the host as well as the SP will be rebooted.
`Show /SP/version`	Displays the current SP version.

In order to access and execute these commands remotely, it is very important to ensure that that the ILOM integrated shell is accessible and available. We discussed the ports needed for Remote KVMS in Table 2-1. You should also consider the ports listed in Table 2-3. Ports are based on standard Oracle defaults and can be configured based on requirements.

Table 2-3. *Ports Used for ILOM Access*

Port	Type	Description
22	SSH over TCP	SSH - Secure Shell (inbound)
69	TFTP over UDP	TFTP (outbound)
80	HTTP over TCP	Web (user-configurable; inbound)
123	NTP over UDP	NTP - Network Time Protocol (outbound)
161	SNMP over UDP	SNMP - (user-configurable; inbound)
162	IPMI over UDP	IPMI - Platform Event Trap (PET) (outbound)
389	LDAP over UDP/TCP	LDAP (user-configurable; outbound)
443	HTTPS over TCP	(user-configurable; inbound)
514	Syslog over UDP	Syslog - (outbound)
623	IPMI over UDP	IPMI (bidirectional)
546	DHCP over UDP	DHCP (bidirectonal)
1812	RADIUS over UDP	RADIUS (outbound)

Security Management

The ILOM allows account management and integration with a variety of popular authentication protocols. Discussing them all in detail would be out of the scope of this book. We will look at Active Directory integration as part of this section and also discuss how to manage users locally.

Local Account Management

The ILOM provides a secure way to authenticate and perform day-to-day functions via locally authenticated accounts. This is the default authentication method to get access to an ILOM. ILOM Account management allows an administrator to provision accounts for a variety of functions. Table 2-4 lists all the roles that are available to users.

Table 2-4. *Roles Available for ILOM Authentication*

Role	Description
a (Admin)	Complete admin privileges
u (User)	Provides access to allow creation and deletion of users and to configure authentication services
c (Console)	Access to console functions that allow for BIOS updates
r (Reset)	Allow for control of the host power, as well as power cycle the SP
o (Read Only)	Allows for read-only access to logs and environmental information

Based on the role selected (Administrator, Operator, Advanced Roles), various privileges are given to the user. Users can be created via the ILOM GUI or via the command line.

Figure 2-4 and the preceding command-line example shows some of the various means that can be used to add a user to the ILOM for local authentication. The roles and privilege assignment, as well as user deletion, can also be done via the GUI or the command line, depending on your comfort level.

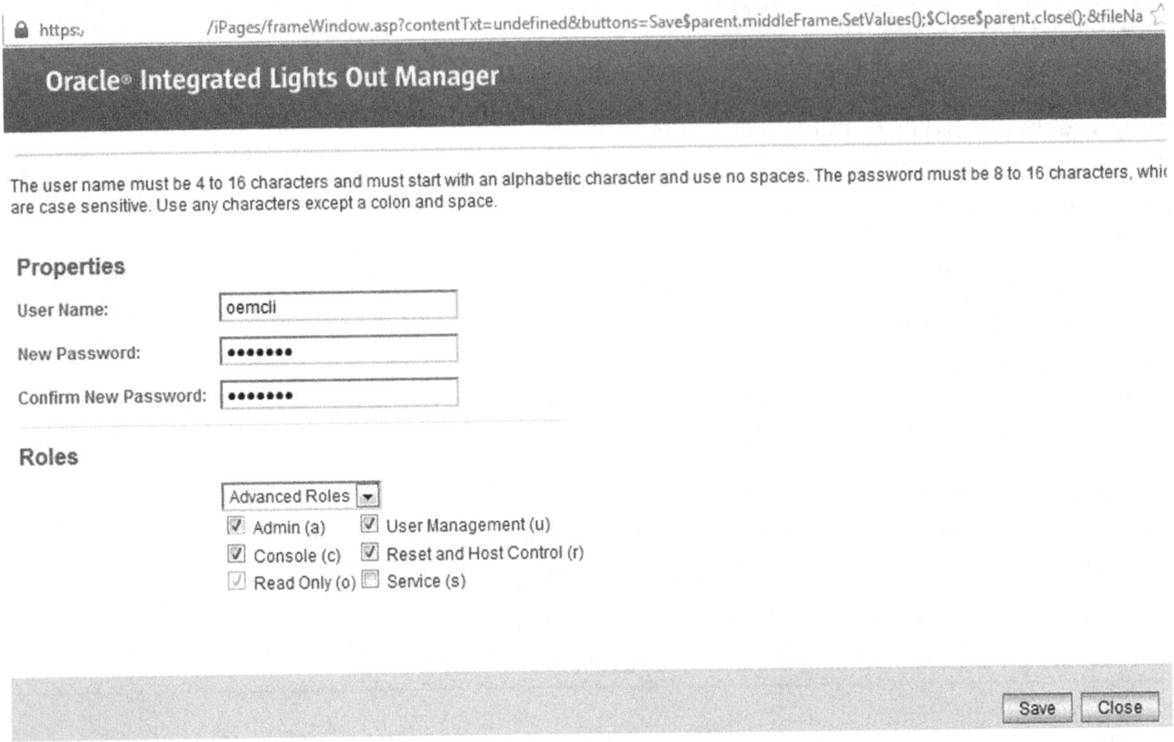

🔒 https:,   /iPages/frameWindow.asp?contentTxt=undefined&buttons=Save$parent.middleFrame.SetValues();$Close$parent.close();&fileNa

Oracle® Integrated Lights Out Manager

The user name must be 4 to 16 characters and must start with an alphabetic character and use no spaces. The password must be 8 to 16 characters, whic are case sensitive. Use any characters except a colon and space.

Properties

User Name: [oemcli]

New Password: [•••••••]

Confirm New Password: [•••••••]

Roles

[Advanced Roles ▼]
☑ Admin (a)   ☑ User Management (u)
☑ Console (c)   ☑ Reset and Host Control (r)
☑ Read Only (o) ☐ Service (s)

[Save] [Close]

Figure 2-4. *Add User screen*

The following is an example of a command to create a new user named rick:

```
create /SP/users/rick password=my_secret role=administrator
```

Having created the user, you can modify the user's role as follows:

```
set /SP/users/rick role=operator
```

You can also delete the user:

```
delete /SP/users/rick
```

It is very important to understand the roles and privileges available, and to assign them appropriately to secure your environment. Also take care to change the default ILOM root password immediately after deployment.

Alerting and Syslog Setup

Logging is a very important way of understanding and debugging issues. The Oracle ILOM provides various ways of disseminating logging information. Syslog is disabled by default, but it is the preferred way to centralize logging. SNMP traps can also be set to allow for alerting to remote systems.

Syslog is an ILOM service that needs to be enabled and configured. The process to enable syslog on the ILOM is to add the IP address of the syslog server. Figure 2-5 and Figure 2-6 show the syslog configuration screen that is available in ODA V1 and ODA X3-2, respectively. That screen can be used to configure the ILOM to send data to an external syslog server.

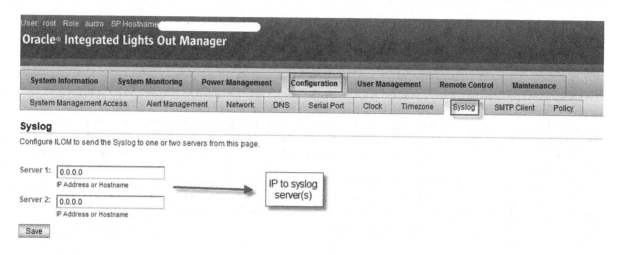

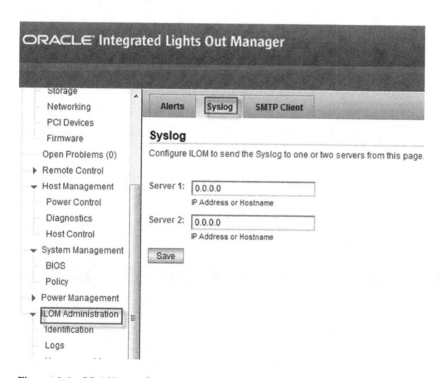

Figure 2-5. *ODA V1 syslog setup*

Figure. 2-6. *ODA X3-2 syslog setup*

Setting up logging to the syslog server is similar for both versions, via command line. Just execute the following command:

```
set /SP|CMM/clients/syslog destination_ip=syslog_server_
```

SNMP alerts can also be set up in a similar fashion. The SNMP service is enabled by default and is configured dependent on the target SNMP trap receiving system. The ILOM supports SNMP protocols v1, v2c, and v3. SNMP protocols v1 and v2c use communities as the authentication method. A default read-only community named public and a read/write community named private are pre-created on the ILOM. A customized string can be used to send SNMP traps, if needed, depending on the environmental setup. SNMP protocol v3 requires username/password–based authentication.

SNMP is set up in a similar fashion in both ODA V1 and X3-2. On X3-2, the settings are accessible under the following menu option: ILOM Administration ➤ Management Access ➤ SNMP. On V1, go to Configuration Management ➤ System Management Access ➤ SNMP. Figure 2-7 shows the settings screen that you are taken to.

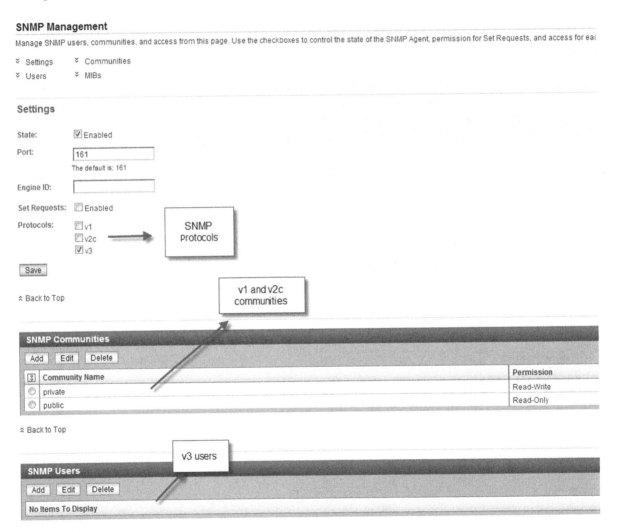

Figure 2-7. SNMP settings screen

So far, we've looked at various ILOM features and setup tasks. The ILOM also provides a wealth of logging information that can be tapped for a variety of purposes. Table 2-5 describes the types of logs that the ILOM provides.

Table 2-5. *ILOM Logging*

Log Type	Description
Syslog	Syslog produces output that can be used by logging services like Manage Engine, Splunk and syslogd to name a few. These services run on remote systems. They aggregate logs to provide a unified view for all the events that happen across multiple ILOMs.
Event	An ILOM event tracks various types of messages that are generated. These can be messages about errors and warnings, or they can be informational items. Event logs also track the addition and removal of components along with the status of various components that the ILOM Is responsible for.
Audit	Audit events are related to privileged calls, and are recorded to ensure the appropriate level of access is being granted. SNMP calls are also audited.

Oracle Database Appliance and the ILOM

The Oracle ILOM is a fully integrated service processor providing complete monitoring and remote access capabilities. It is very important to understand the ILOM and the important role it plays in the context of the ODA.

Oracle Database Appliance Setup via Serial Connection

When the ODA is first setup in the rack at the datacenter, there are steps that need to be followed to allow access to the ODA. These steps are outlined in the Setup Poster.[1] After the cabling, the first step is to provide both ODA server nodes with an IP address. This can be done by either accessing the ODA in the datacenter via a serial cable, or by using a KVM (keyboard, video, mouse) device like Avocent to remotely access the serial port of the device.

The ODA ILOM can be accessed via a serial management (SER MGT) port. MOS Note ID 1395445.1 explains the process of connecting to the ODA to configure the ILOM. The process requires direct physical access to the serial port, which means that this process needs to be executed in the same physical place at which the ODA is located.

Each ODA ships with an RJ-45 serial convertor like the one pictured in Figure 2-8.

---

[1]The Oracle Setup Poster is available at http://docs.oracle.com/cd/E22693_01/.

Figure 2-8. *RJ-45 serial converter*

Using an RJ-45 cable, you can connect the cable to the serial port on your laptop or datacenter terminal cart, and connect to access the ILOM using a terminal emulator such as PuTTY or ITerm2. If you lack a serial port, then you can buy one of the many USB-to-serial converter cables that are on the market. Once the connection cable is connected to the laptop and the ODA serial port (and assuming that you are using Windows), check the device manager to see which COM port the USB device is connected to. Then specify that COM port in your PuTTY connection, as shown in Figure 2-9. (If running Linux, then see MOS Note ID 1395445.1 for instructions). Once the port is determined, you can open a terminal and connect to the ODA over the serial line.

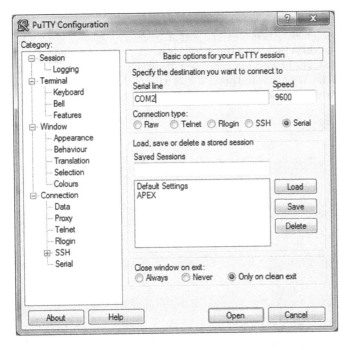

Figure 2-9. *PuTTY screen for making a serial connection*

Once the connection is made, you will see a login prompt to the ILOM. You need to use the root account and the default root password (changeme) to connect to the ILOM.

An initial configuration of the ILOM should have no IP configuration. You can validate that this is the case by issuing the following command:

```
# show /SP/network
```

The Oracle Appliance Kit deployment can set IP networking details of the ILOM, but it is always faster to configure the ILOM IP addresses using the method we describe next. It allows a faster deployment by using the ILOM to deploy the ODA. You need the following information to be able to set the IP configuration for the ILOM for both ODA servers:

- Public IP address

- Netmask

- Gateway address

Depending on your requirements, a static IP or a dynamic IP (DHCP) address can be assigned to the ILOM. The following is an example of assigning a static IP address:

```
# set /SP/network pendingipdiscovery=static pendingipaddress=1.2.2.65 pendingipnetmask=255.255.255.0
pendingipgateway=1.2.2.254 commitpending=true
```

Each ODA has two server nodes, and thus also has two ILOMs. The network configuration has to be performed twice, once for every ILOM. After the IP configuration has been established, SSH access via a browser should be available. Navigating to the IP address of the ILOM via a browser should result in a screen like that shown in Figure 2-10.

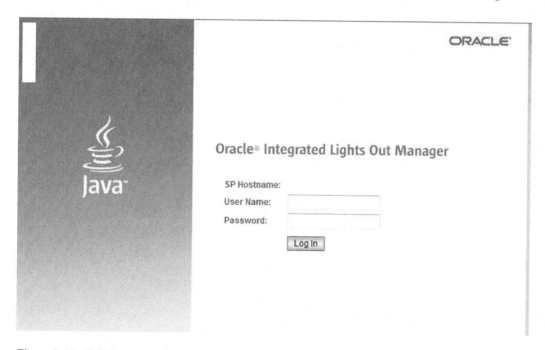

Figure 2-10. *ILOM screen via browser*

The screen shown in Figure 2-10 is the ILOM console; seeing it confirms the successful configuration of the ILOM. Now that the ILOM is successfully configured, you can move on to configure the ODA database nodes.

The ILOM is always turned on as soon as the Database Appliance is cabled and powered on, but the server nodes need to be manually powered on. Execute the following command from an ILOM-integrated shell session to power on a server node. Be sure to execute the command for both nodes.

```
# start /SYS
```

The server node can also be powered on via the ILOM GUI accessible through a browser. ODA V1 and ODA X3-2 have slightly different screens from which to perform various server power–related activities. Figure 2-11 and Figure 2-12 show the screens for V1 and X3-2, respectively.

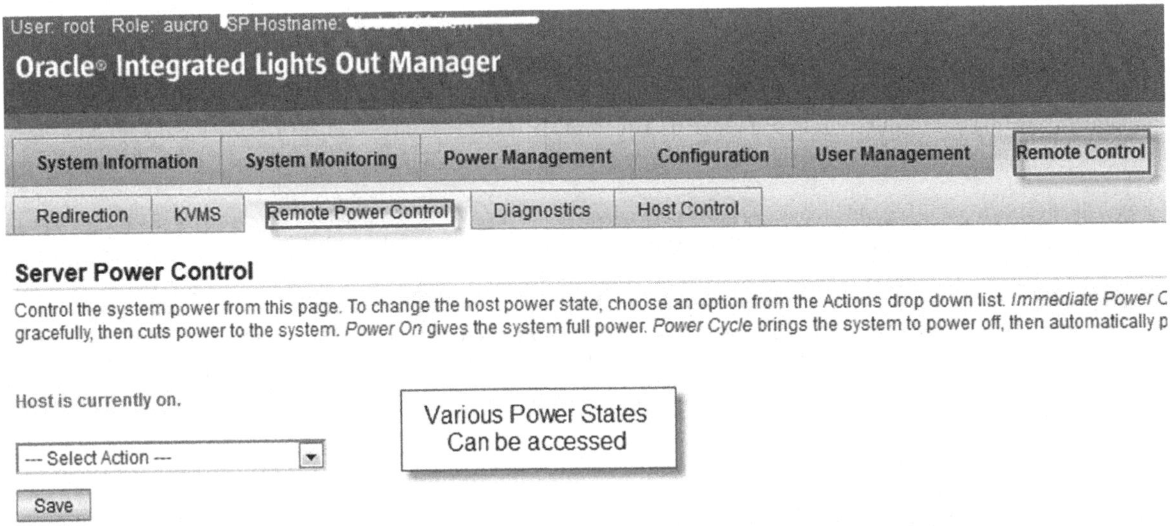

Figure 2-11. *ODA V1 server power control*

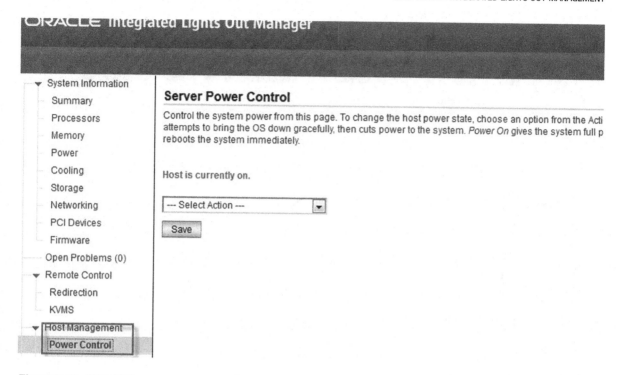

Figure 2-12. *ODA X3-2 server power control*

Bare-Metal Oracle Database Appliance

The Oracle Database Appliance comes preinstalled with base software, but there are circumstances when the ODA servers have to be reimaged. The need to reimage could be due to corruption, or to get the software to the latest version in a fast manner.

The procedure requires downloading the ISO image for the software that needs to be imaged onto the Database Appliance. The latest ISO image is available by following the instructions in MOS Note 888888.1. Download the ISO and unzip it on a laptop or desktop. Go to the Remote Control ➤ Redirection menu, and select Launch Remote Console. Doing so will open the screen that provides console messages and access to the server node. Perform this process on both server nodes.

Once the remote console screen is available, click the Devices menu and select CD ROM Image. You will get a dialog asking you to locate the ISO image.

Once the ISO image has been selected, ensure that the ISO image is mounted. Messages will be displayed on screen to confirm mount of the image. A message indicating a virtual CD-ROM image has been attached will be displayed on screen.

Go to the ILOM. Select the next boot device as CDROM, as shown in Figure 2-13. Then cycle the server node's power, as shown in Figure 2-14.

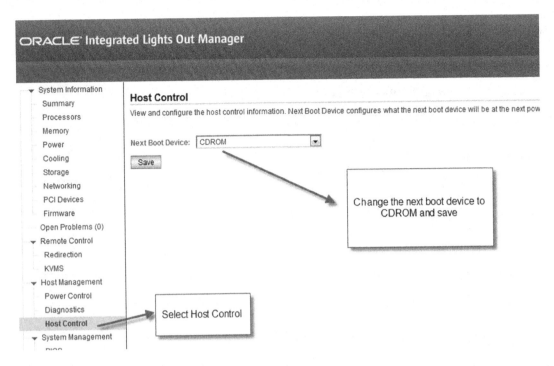

Figure 2-13. *Next boot selection*

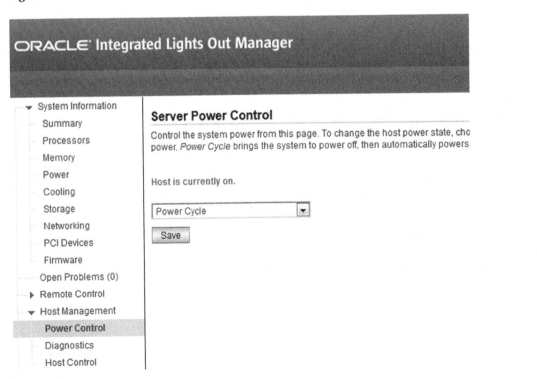

Figure 2-14. *Power cycle a server node*

After the power cycle, the redirection screen will show console messages while the system reboots. After the messages, the bare-metal imaging process will begin. Figure 2-15 shows the start of that process.

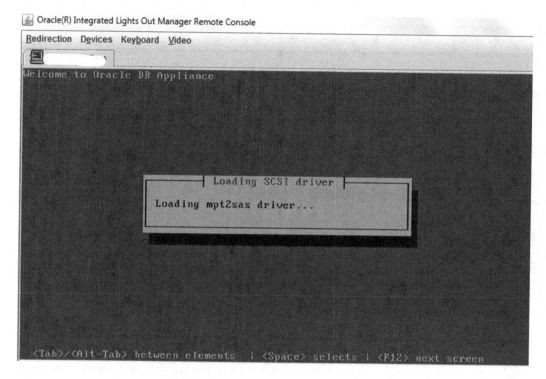

Figure 2-15. Start of Oracle Database Appliance imaging

The post-install process can take a long time. You have to ensure that you have consistent connectivity to the server during the entire process. Figure 2-16 shows the post-install screen.

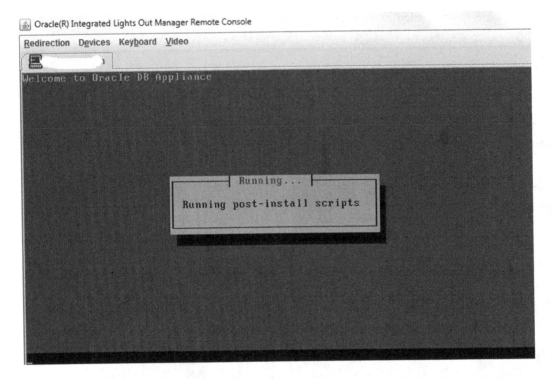

Figure 2-16. Post-install screen for ODA imaging

The complete imaging process can take from one to two hours, and can be run in parallel on both server nodes to speed up access to the appliance. It is very important to keep in mind that a reimage is a very destructive process that will wipe out all information on an appliance. It is important to back up any information that you have stored in the ODA prior to the image.

Summary

The ILOM is a service processor that is embedded into the ODA. It is the brain of the hardware. The ILOM provides many capabilities from the management and the monitoring perspective. Remote KVMS or shell access allows access to the server nodes remotely to perform "like you are there" functions.

The ILOM can be accessed via a GUI using a modern browser running Java, and also via an integrated shell. Both methods can be used to perform setup and management, as well as to monitor tasks. The ILOM can be integrated with most common authentication mechanisms, like LDAP and Active Directory. The ILOM also provides a comprehensive logging mechanism and allows logging data to be replicated via remote syslog servers or SNMP traps.

The ILOM provides the functionality to set up the Database Appliance via serial access, as well as provide server power control features. When needed, the ILOM is the console to allow reimaging of the appliance server nodes via CD-ROM images that are available from the Oracle Support web site.

CHAPTER 3

■ ■ ■

Installation

You already covered the basic tasks to perform a bare-metal restore on the Oracle Database Appliance. Now you need to prepare the Oracle Database Appliance for installation of a Real Application Cluster (RAC) database. With the automation built into the Oracle Database Appliance, this is a straightforward task and can be completed within a few hours. Before starting, you need to finalize some of the prerequisites.

Network and Power Connections

The ODA comes preconfigured for high-availability network access for the primary and secondary networks. These network bonds are preconfigured in the installation image, making installation quick and simple. There are two versions of the Oracle Database Appliance: the original model and the X3-2. They are slightly different from a network aspect. The original Oracle Database Appliance had 12 1000BASE-T Ethernet ports, and the availability of 10G Ethernet using four SPF fiber connections. The X3-2 model simply comes with 8 10GBaseT ports, supporting connection speeds up to 10GBit.

Original ODA

The first-generation Oracle Database Appliance contains two compute nodes integrated into the chassis. Each of these servers has four sets of bonded Ethernet ports. By default, bond0 is used for public traffic, with bond1, bond2, and xbond0 used for auxiliary access, which is covered in more detail later in Chapter 6. Prior to installing the Oracle Database Appliance, connect two cables to the eth2 and eth3 ports. Normally these will be connected into separate switches in the datacenter for fault tolerance. The default configuration of the bond will load balance traffic between the two ports, which means the bond will automatically recover from a single network path failure. In Figure 3-1 and Table 3-1, you are provided a detailed diagram of the Oracle Database Appliance, along with explanations of the numbered callouts on the diagram.

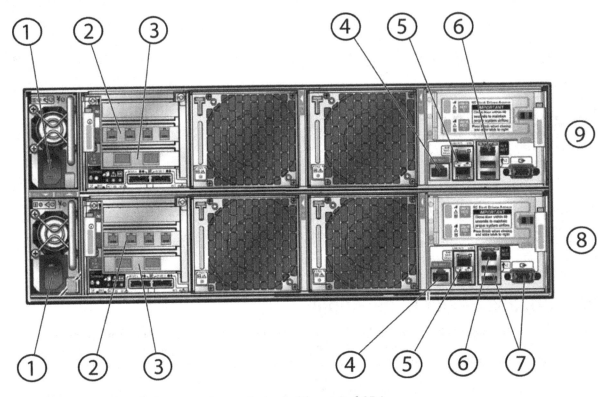

Figure 3-1. Network and other connections on the back of the original ODA

Table 3-1. Descriptions of the Connections Highlighted in Figure 3-1

Callout	Description
1	C13 Power Connectors, shared power bus for both nodes
2	eth4, eth5, eth6, and eth7 from right to left for Node 0; eth4 and eth5 are bond1 and eth6 and eth7 are bond2
3	10BaseT SFP ports for eth8 and eth9 for Node 0, configured as xbond0
4	ILOM Serial Port for Node 0
5	eth2 and eth3, bond0 for public network access
6	ILOM 10/100 BaseT port
7	USB and VGA ports
8	Node 0
9	Node 1

ODA X3-2

The second-generation Oracle Database Appliance uses two X3 servers for the compute nodes. Each of these servers has two sets of bonded Ethernet ports. By default, bond0 is used for public traffic, and bond1 is used for auxiliary access, which is covered in detail in Chapter 6. Prior to installing the Oracle Database Appliance, connect two cables to the eth2 and eth3 ports. Typically, these will be connected into separate switches in the datacenter for fault tolerance. The default configuration of the bond will load balance traffic between the two ports, automatically recovering from a single network path failure. Figure 3-2 and Table 3-2 illustrate and provide details on the connections on the rear of an X3-2 Oracle Database Appliance.

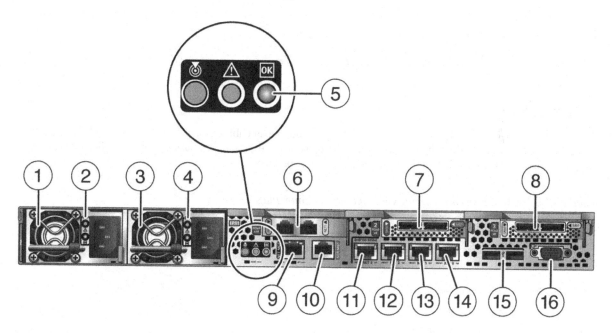

Figure 3-2. *Network and other connections on the back of the X3-2 ODA*

Table 3-2. *Descriptions of the Connections Highlighted in Figure 3-2*

Callout	Description
1	Power Supply 0 Fan
2	Power Supply 0
3	Power Supply 1 Fan
4	Power Supply 1
5	System indicator and locator lights
6	Cluster Interconnect, eth0 and eth1
7	SAS Card 0
8	SAS Card 1
9	ILOM Port, 10/100BASE-T

(continued)

Table 3-2. (*continued*)

Callout	Description
10	ILOM Serial Port
11	10GBASE-T, eth2 bind0
12	10GBASET, eth3 bind0
13	10GBASET, eth4 b0nd1
14	10GBASET, eth5 bond1
15	USB Ports
16	VGA Port

Power Cables

Nothing is worse than racking a new system and finding that the power cables are not the ones you need. Connector names such as C13 and C14 don't mean a lot to many end users of the Oracle Database Appliance. Table 3-3 lists the common plugs used with North American Oracle Database Appliances.

Table 3-3. *North American Oracle Database Appliance Common Plugs*

Connector Name	Use	Diagram
C13	This is the connector that goes into the Oracle Database Appliance.	
C14	Often used in racks. 110V or 220V.	
C14RA	Right-angle version of the C14. The cord enters on the right side.	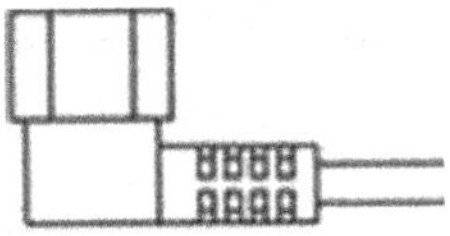
5-15P	Standard plug for 110V applications.	

(*continued*)

Table 3-3. (*continued*)

Connector Name	Use	Diagram
6–15P	200V version of the 5–15P.	
L6-20P	Locking 200V plug, usually use DIN high-amp draws.	

Oracle Database Appliance Initial Deployment

Once the bare-metal installation of the Oracle Linux operating system is complete, you need to log onto the console on one of the nodes and do the initial configuration of the Oracle Database Appliance network using the command firstnet. That command allows you to establish the network interfaces for the Oracle Database Appliance upon first usage.

■ **Note** Before you can run firstnet, you should allocate the required Internet protocol (IP) addresses and verify that their entries in the Domain Naming Service (DNS) have been completed. If you need help in gathering or assigning IP addresses, contact your local systems administrator.

ILOM Network

The Oracle Integrated Lights Out Manager (ILOM) runs on the service processor (SP) and is used for hardware installation, maintenance, and troubleshooting. Each node on the Oracle Database Appliance has a dedicated SP, with a dedicated 10/100BaseT port.

Network Information

Each Oracle Database Appliance node requires access for the external network; there are multiple Ethernet ports on the rear of the Oracle Database Appliance to establish these connections. The bond supporting public network access is redundantly connected via cables connected on ports net0 and net1 on each Oracle Database Appliance. The examples in this chapter will be based on an Oracle Database Appliance named "ejb". Table 3-4 provides an idea of what needs to be established for bond0 on both nodes of the Oracle Database Appliance.

Table 3-4. Internet Protocol Information for node0

Node	Bond name	IP Address	Network Mask	DNS Entry
0	bond0	172.30.0.20	255.255.255.0	ejb1.m57.local
1	bond0	172.30.0.21	255.255.255.0	ejb2.m57.local

■ **Note**   Notice that you only need to be concerned about the bond0 interface on both nodes. The bond0 interface is configured when using the `firstnet` utility.

The Oracle Database Appliance also uses the normal network resources like DNS, Gateways, and Network Time Protocol (NTP). Configured examples of these resources are shown in Table 3-5.

Table 3-5. Additional Resources for Oracle Database Appliance

Resource	Entry
DNS Servers	172.16.11.215
DNS Suffix	m57.local
DNS Search Order	m57.local
NTP Servers	172.30.0.1
Default Gateway	172.30.0.1
SMTP Relay	172.30.0.1

Real Application Cluster (RAC) Network

Oracle Real Application Cluster 11g Release 2 (RAC) comes preinstalled on the Oracle Database Appliance. This version of RAC introduces the concept of a Single Client Access Name (SCAN) addressing. A SCAN address provides the cluster with an alias for the database by providing two or more IP addresses. This alias-like approach allows remote clients to connect without the need to change connection information related to the environment.

■ **Note**   SCAN requires either a corporate DNS or the Oracle Global Naming Service to work. For the Oracle Database Appliance, the approach is to use your corporate DNS. More information on SCAN can be found at www.oracle.com/technetwork/products/clustering/overview/scan-129069.pdf.

SCAN addressing uses DNS in a round-robin approach. This approach ensures that network traffic is load balanced across multiple IP addresses. This approach ensures that remote hosts can configure local naming without needing to change connection information if changes in the environment occur. Table 3-6 provides an example of how to configure entries in your corporate DNS server.

Table 3-6. *Domain Name Service (DNS) Settings*

DNS Name	IP Address(es)
ejb-vip1.m57.local	172.30.0.22
ejb-vip2.m57.local	172.30.0.23
ejb-scan.m57.local	172.30.0.24, 172.30.0.25, 172.30.0.26

▦ **Note**   DNS entries for SCAN should have no less than three IP addresses associated with it.

At this point, you should have a basic understanding of the components that are needed to configure the network on an Oracle Database Appliance. Next you need to configure all these network-related items by connecting to the ILOM.

Network Configuration

With all Oracle Database Appliances, once you have the basic network configuration done, you will be able to connect to the Oracle Database Appliance using secure shell (SSH). Using SSH, you need to connect to the console and start the ILOM console using the command start /SP/console. Listing 3-1 provides an example of what the interaction should look like.

With all Oracle Database Appliances, once you have the network resources set up (DNS, IP addresses) and the ILOM networking configuration done, you are able to connect to the ILOM using the SSH protocol. Once connected to the ILOM, you can connect to system's console to get the Linux console terminal. The system's console can be accessed using the ILOM command start /SP/console. Listing 3-1 provides an example of what the interaction should look like.

Listing 3-1. Starting the ILOM Console

```
oak1 login: -> start /SP/console
Are you sure you want to start /SP/console (y/n)? y

Serial console started.  To stop, type ESC (

Oracle Linux Server release 5.9
Kernel 2.6.39-400.111.1.el5uek on an x86_64

login: root
Password:
Last login: Sun Sep  8 13:43:28 on tty1
[root@oak1 ~]#
```

Now that you are connected to the console, you need to configure the initial IP address for the node you are connected to. As discussed earlier in the chapter, this is done by issuing the firstnet command. Listing 3-2 illustrates how this command is used to configure the networks on the first node.

Listing 3-2. Issuing firstnet

```
[root@oak1 ~]# /opt/oracle/oak/bin/oakcli configure firstnet
INFO: Non VM environment detected
Select the interface to configure network on (bond0 bond1 bond2 xbond0) [bond0]:
Configure DHCP on bond0 (yes/no) [no]:
INFO: Static configuration selected
Enter the IP address to configure:172.30.0.20
Enter the netmask address to configure:255.255.255.0
Enter the gateway address to configure[172.30.0.1]:172.30.0.1
INFO: Plumbing the IPs now
INFO: Restarting the network
Shutting down interface bond0:  bonding: bond0: Warning: the permanent HWaddr of eth2 -
00:21:28:e7:c1:e8 - is still in use by bond0. Set the HWaddr of eth2 to a different address to avoid
conflicts.
bond0: mixed no checksumming and other settings.
[  OK  ]
Shutting down interface bond1:  bonding: bond1: Warning: the permanent HWaddr of eth4 -
00:1b:21:c5:c4:21 - is still in use by bond1. Set the HWaddr of eth4 to a different address to avoid
conflicts.
bond1: mixed no checksumming and other settings.
[  OK  ]
Shutting down interface bond2:  bonding: bond2: Warning: the permanent HWaddr of eth6 -
00:1b:21:c5:c4:23 - is still in use by bond2. Set the HWaddr of eth6 to a different address to avoid
conflicts.
bond2: mixed no checksumming and other settings.
[  OK  ]
Shutting down interface eth0:  [  OK  ]
Shutting down interface eth1:  [  OK  ]
Shutting down interface eth8:  bonding: xbond0: Warning: the permanent HWaddr of eth8 -
00:1b:21:c2:20:f0 - is still in use by xbond0. Set the HWaddr of eth8 to a different address to
avoid conflicts.
[  OK  ]
Shutting down interface eth9:  xbond0: mixed no checksumming and other settings.
[  OK  ]
Shutting down interface xbond0:  bonding: xbond0: Error: cannot release eth8.
bonding: xbond0: Error: cannot release eth9.
[  OK  ]
Shutting down loopback interface: [  OK  ]
Bringing up loopback interface: [  OK  ]
Bringing up interface bond0: [  OK  ]
Bringing up interface bond1: [  OK  ]
Bringing up interface bond2: [  OK  ]
Bringing up interface eth0: [  OK  ]
Bringing up interface eth1: [  OK  ]
Bringing up interface xbond0: [  OK  ]
```

Once the network interfaces have been configured, you need to test them by using the ping command on the node. Additionally, you can test the network by pinging the configured node from your remote client. Listing 3-3 shows ping results from pinging the default gateway on the node that was configured.

Listing 3-3. Ping Results from Default Gateway

```
[root@oak1 ~]# ping 172.30.0.1
PING 172.30.0.1 (172.30.0.1) 56(84) bytes of data.
64 bytes from 172.30.0.1: icmp_seq=1 ttl=64 time=1.31 ms
64 bytes from 172.30.0.1: icmp_seq=2 ttl=64 time=0.245 ms
64 bytes from 172.30.0.1: icmp_seq=3 ttl=64 time=0.255 ms

--- 172.30.0.1 ping statistics ---
3 packets transmitted, 3 received, 0% packet loss, time 2001ms
rtt min/avg/max/mdev = 0.245/0.606/1.319/0.504 ms
```

Since the network interfaces for the first node came up, copy the End User Bundle, which was discussed and downloaded earlier to the temp directory (/tmp) on the first node. Depending on the network connection between your client machine and the first node of the ODA, the copy may take several minutes (see Figure 3-3). Once the End User Bundle is transferring, you can continue with configuration.

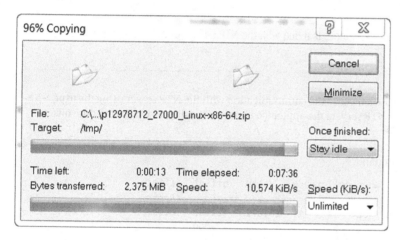

Figure 3-3. *Copying the End User Bundle to the Oracle Database Appliance*

Network Time Protocol (NTP) Configuration

Before deploying the database, it is very important to verify that the time between both nodes is accurate and within a few seconds of each other. The default configuration file (/etc/ntp.conf) that is deployed with the Oracle Database Appliance is actually valid. The appliance is initially configured to use the public RedHat NTP pool of servers; for systems access to the Internet, this should keep the time in the Oracle Database Appliance in sync. Listing 3-4 provides the server portion of the NTP configuration file, which has the Oracle Database Appliance pointing to the RedHat NTP pool.

Listing 3-4. RedHat NTP Pool

```
# Use public servers from the pool.ntp.org project.
# Please consider joining the pool (http://www.pool.ntp.org/join.html).
server 0.rhel.pool.ntp.org
server 1.rhel.pool.ntp.org
server 2.rhel.pool.ntp.org
```

For some installations this is fine, but many data centers have their own NTP infrastructure. In that case, the "server" lines pointing to the pool should be commented out (placing a hash ("#") symbol at the start of a line), and lines that point to the local NTP servers should be added. Listing 3-5 shows how to add your own local NTP server.

Listing 3-5. Configure Local NTP Server

```
# Use public servers from the pool.ntp.org project.
# Please consider joining the pool (http://www.pool.ntp.org/join.html).
#server 0.rhel.pool.ntp.org
#server 1.rhel.pool.ntp.org
#server 2.rhel.pool.ntp.org
server 172.30.0.1
```

Once the /etc/ntp.conf file is changed, the NTP daemon (ntpd) needs to be restarted using the service ntpd restart command. This will stop the daemon, synchronizing the clock to the NTP source, and will then restart the daemon.

■ **Note** In Oracle Database Appliance Release 2.2, there is a bug with the NTP being out of sync. Refer to Note 1489263.1 for solutions to resolve.

Once the ntpd process has restarted, you can verify the communication with the NTP server using the ntpq -p command. This command will show all the NTP servers the appliance is currently using, as well as the time offset experienced by each server (see Listing 3-6).

Listing 3-6. Output from the ntpdq -p Command

```
     remote           refid      st t when poll reach   delay   offset  jitter
==============================================================================
 205-196-146-72.  209.51.161.238   2 u   62   64    1   26.872   -2.682   0.001
 name1.glorb.com  128.174.38.133   2 u   61   64    1   17.005   -2.099   0.001
 ntp1.rescomp.be  169.229.128.214  3 u   60   64    1   77.270    3.740   0.001
 LOCAL(0)         .LOCL.          10 l   59   64    1    0.000    0.000   0.001
```

Reviewing Listing 3-6, we see that three external servers and the system clock are in use. The system clock offset is approximately –2 to 3 seconds off. The NTP daemon (ntpd) will now drift the time to get the system clock within one hundred to two hundred milliseconds of real time.

Grid Infrastructure and Database Installation

At the end of Chapter 2, you were left with an Oracle Database Appliance that was "bare metal" installed. What this means is that you should now have a clean Oracle Database Appliance running Oracle Enterprise Linux. At this point, you need to install the Oracle Grid Infrastructure and the Oracle Database software on an Oracle Database Appliance. How do you do this? Well, since the Oracle Database Appliance is an engineered system, you cannot just download and install these Oracle products. Oracle provides packages for the installation of these products.

As you begin to look around for the packages to install the Oracle products, you may want to visit My Oracle Support and download the latest End User Bundle for the Oracle Database Appliance. The End User Bundle provides an updated version of the Grid Infrastructure and Oracle Database for a "factory shipped" or reimaged Oracle Database Appliance. Keep in mind, when you begin the download for the End User Bundle, it is a fairly large download and may take a bit of time to retrieve before you can begin installation.

■ **Note**   To download the End User Bundle or any other major patches needed for the Oracle Database Appliance, you might want to follow the instructions in Note ID 888888.1.

Database Installation

Once you have the End User Bundle copied over to the Oracle Database Appliance, you need to install it on the Appliance by unpacking it. Unpacking consists of using the oakcli unpack command. Listing 3-7 shows the End User Bundle for release 2.7 being unzipped in the temp directory.

Listing 3-7. Using oakcli unpack

```
[root@oak1 tmp]# /opt/oracle/oak/bin/oakcli unpack -package /tmp/p12978712_27000_Linux-x86-64.zip
Unpacking takes a while, pls wait....
```

Once the End User Bundle is unzipped into the temporary directory, you need to install the Oracle products using a GUI interface. In order to do this, you need to start a Virtual Network Computing (VNC) server to interact with the Oracle Database Appliance.

VNC Configuration and Connection

VNC is a graphical desktop-sharing technology that allows you to use an X11 desktop and execute programs locally on the server, while only the screen output is sent to the VNC client on your PC or MAC. Before you can install the End User Bundle, you need to configure the VNC server with an initial password. To set the initial VNC password, run the vncserver command and set your password. The command will also give you your VNC session number. Listing 3-8 provides an example of what you should see when setting the password for the VNC server.

Listing 3-8. Setting the VNC Server Password and Port

```
[root@oak1 tmp]# vncserver

You will require a password to access your desktops.

Password:
Verify:
xauth:  creating new authority file /root/.Xauthority
xauth: (stdin):1:  bad display name "oak1:1" in "add" command

New 'oak1:1 (root)' desktop is oak1:1

Creating default startup script /root/.vnc/xstartup
Starting applications specified in /root/.vnc/xstartup
Log file is /root/.vnc/oak1:1.log
```

Once the password is set and the session number identified, you can connect to the system using the VNC client. For the remote host, you use the IP address and the session identified when starting the VNC server. Figure 3-4 illustrates connecting to the Oracle Database Appliance using a VNC client.

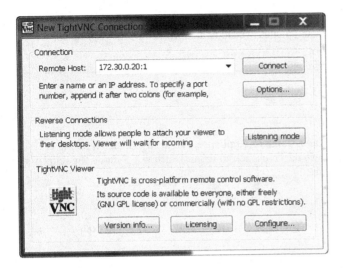

Figure 3-4. VNC client connecting to the Oracle Database Appliance

If you are using the correct session ID with the IP address, you should now be prompted for a password. Enter the password you provided when you configured the VNC server (see Figure 3-5).

Figure 3-5. Password prompt from VNC server on client

If your password was accepted, you should now see an X11 desktop. In the command window that is present, you can start the deployment of the Oracle Database Appliance. To start the deployment, the oakcli deploy command must be used. This will start the Oracle Appliance Manager (OAM). Once the Oracle Appliance Manager starts, you will be able to configure the Oracle Grid Infrastructure plus Automatic Storage Management (ASM) storage and the Oracle Database. Listing 3-9 shows you how to start the deployment process with oakcli deploy.

Listing 3-9. Deployment with oakcli

```
[root@oak1 ~]# /opt/oracle/oak/bin/oakcli deploy
Log messages in /tmp/oak_1378687999949.log
Running Oracle Appliance Manager
```

Now that you have kicked off the deployment on the Oracle Database Appliance, you need to become familiar with the Oracle Appliance Manager. In the next section, you will take a look at the Oracle Appliance Manager and the options that should be chosen for a base configuration.

Oracle Appliance Manager and Deployment

By running the `oakcli deploy` command, you initiate the GUI installation wizard for the Oracle Appliance Manager. The Oracle Appliance Manager is much like other Oracle installation wizards. It will walk you through the various steps needed for configuration of your Oracle Database Appliance. Figure 3-6 shows the Oracle Appliance Manager welcome screen.

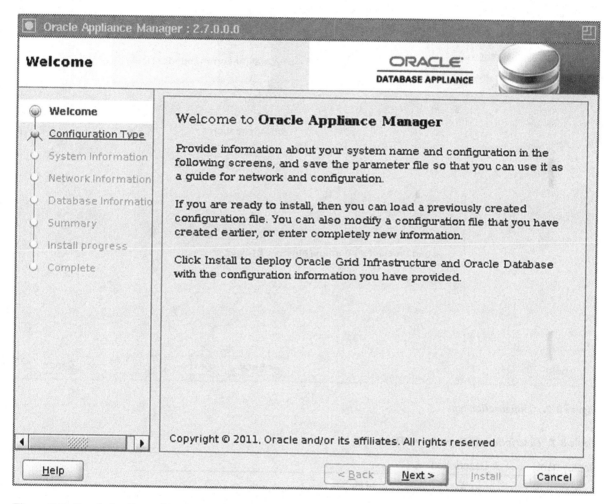

Figure 3-6. *Oracle Appliance Manager welcome screen*

Just like many other Oracle wizards, Oracle provides a menu (on the left-hand side) to help you navigate the wizard as you click the Next button to progress through the wizard. In the next screen in the wizard, you can select the type of deployment you would like to perform on the Oracle Database Appliance. In Figure 3-7, the options are presented for you to choose from. Table 3-7 provides a quick description of what these options are. After you made your selection for the deployment, you can progress through the wizard by clicking the Next button.

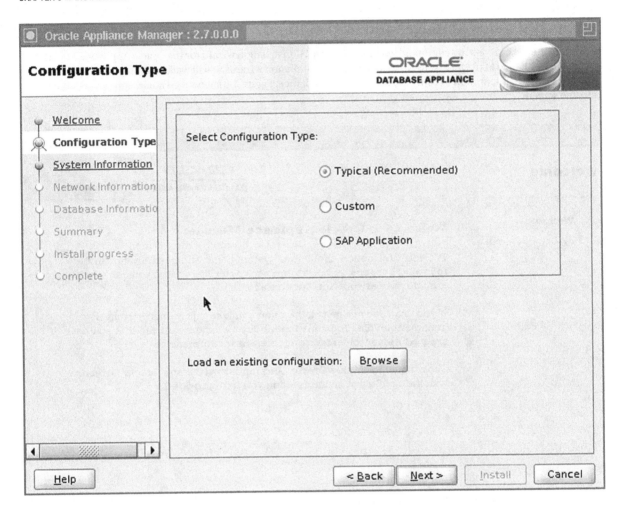

Figure 3-7. *Configuration type*

Table 3-7. *Descriptions of Deployment Types*

Deployment	Description
Typical	The default setting for all Oracle Database Appliances
Custom	Allows you to override default setting; that is, disk mirror settings ASM
SAP Application	Used only for appliances that will be running SAP

In the next step on the wizard, you need to set the System Information for the Oracle Database Appliance. Figure 3-8 illustrates what the wizard should look like. You need to select or input the desired information.

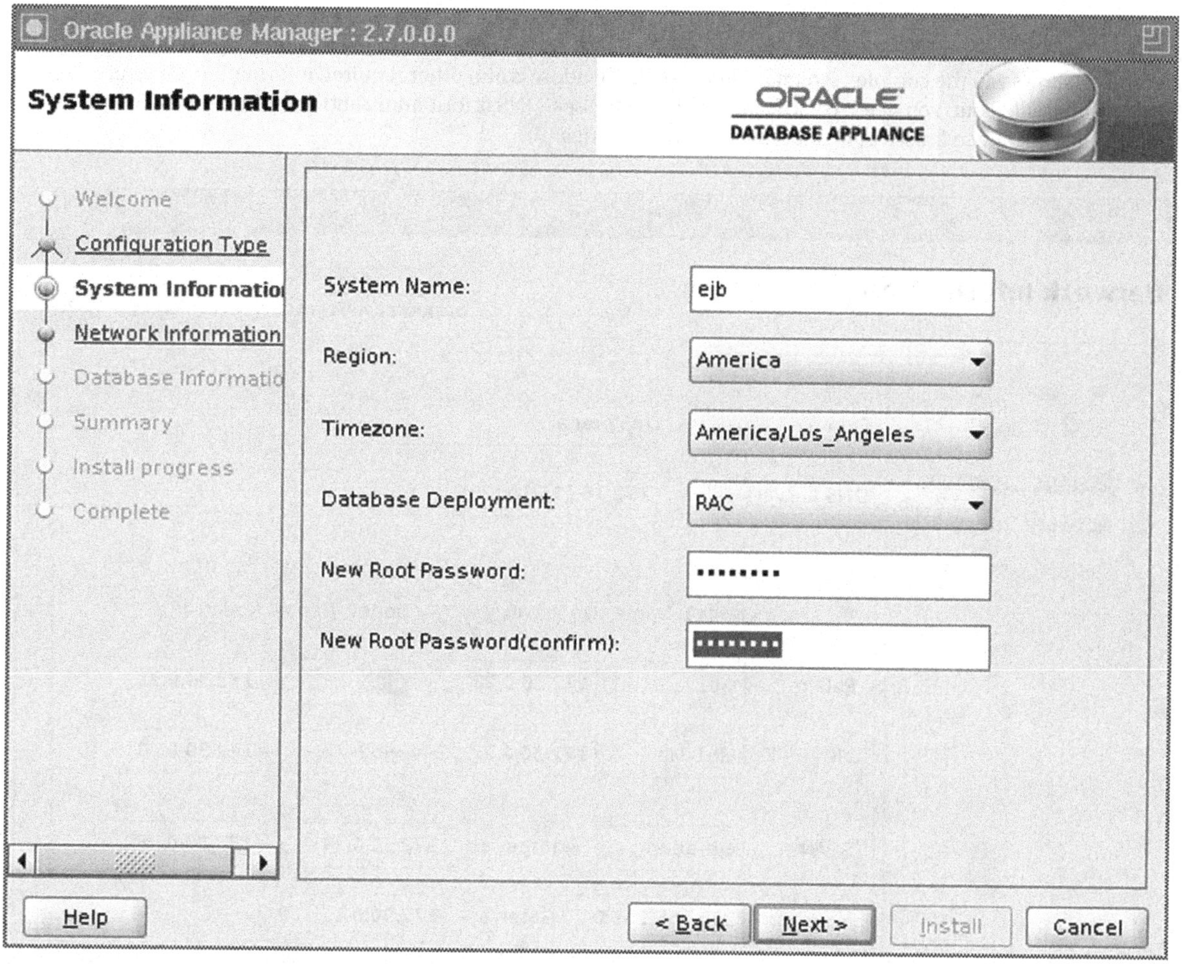

Figure 3-8. *System information for the Oracle Database Appliance*

In the System Information step, there are a few things to keep in mind. First, the system name is used for the deployment and each node in the Oracle Database Appliance, and will automatically have a one or two appended to the system name as hostname on each node. Once the deployment is complete, hostnames of the nodes should look something like ejb1 or ejb2.

The next system information needed is the region that the Oracle Database Appliance resides in. This is a drop-down list where you select the region of the world where the Oracle Database Appliance runs. In Figure 3-8, the region selected is America.

Next is the time zone drop-down menu, which provides a list to select the time zone where the Oracle Database Appliance resides. Figure 3-8 shows the Pacific time zone selected (America/Los_Angeles).

The Database Deployment drop-down menu provides a list of options for deploying a database on the Oracle Database Appliance. You can select either to deploy a Real Application Cluster (RAC), Real Application Cluster (RAC) One Node, or an Enterprise Edition database. In Figure 3-8, the option Real Application Cluster (RAC) is chosen.

The final piece of information needed for the System Information is the root password. By default, the root password is set to welcome1. After you provide a root password for the deployment, the password will be changed on both nodes in the Oracle Database Appliance. At this point, if you are happy with all the items provided on the System Information screen, you can click Next to continue progressing through the wizard.

As you progress through the wizard, you enter the Network Information screen. Here you need to provide the required IP addresses and DNS information. Along with the IP addresses, you also need to provide a domain name. Figure 3-9, shows you the complex screen for filling in the IP address and other required information. Once all information is filled out, you need to verify that all the addresses, DNS information, and other items are correct. Most deployments fail due to incorrect IP addresses and DNS entries.

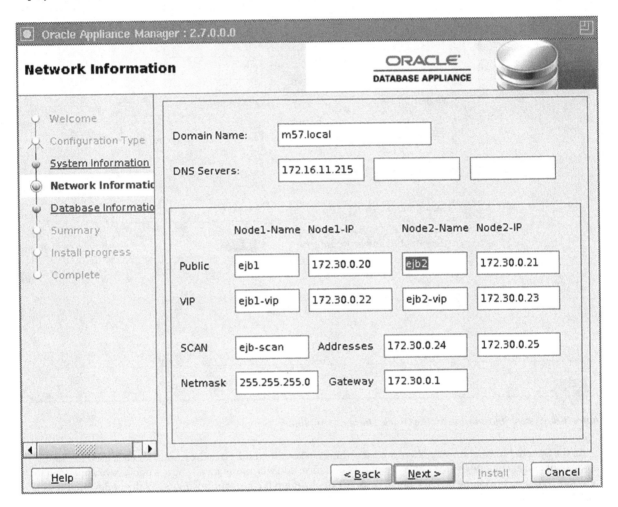

Figure 3-9. *Network Information screen*

The next step in the deployment wizard is to set up the database-specific options. In Figure 3-10, you are presented with three options: Database Name, Database Class, and Database Language. All three of these items need to be either filled in or selected. Once these items are filled in, the installer will know what to name the database that is created, what the database size should be, and the national language that should be used.

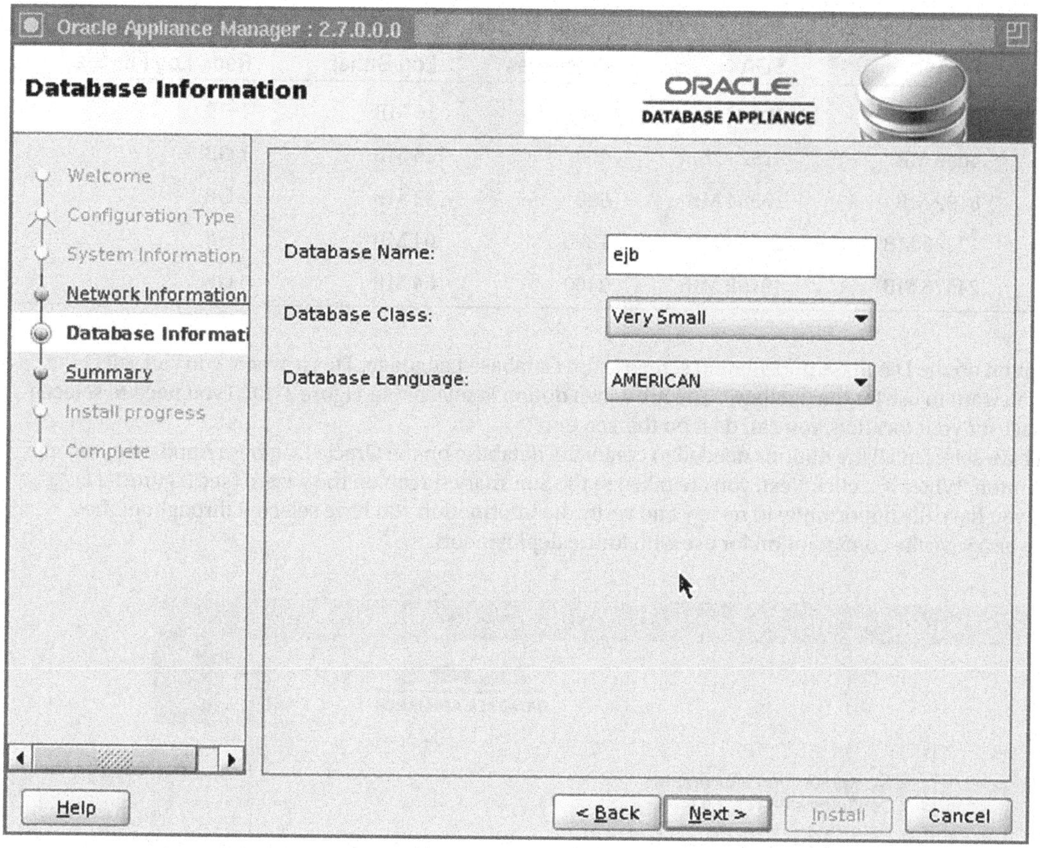

Figure 3-10. *Database Information screen*

The database class depends on the Database Deployment you selected on the System Information screen. Part of the Oracle Database Appliance software includes preconfigured templates for the database size selected. This approach to the deployment of databases optimized the database along with the associated performance for the selected database size. The templates also incorporate Oracle best practices and are slightly different, depending on the model of Oracle Database Appliance used. Table 3-8 and Table 3-9 provide the breakdown of Database Class that is selected.

Table 3-8. *Database Templates for the X2-2 Oracle Database Appliance*

Class	PGA	SGA	Processes	Log Buffer	Redo Log File Size
Very Small	2048 MB	4096 MB	200	16 MB	1 GB
Small	4096 MB	8192 MB	400	16 MB	1 GB
Medium	8192 MB	16384 MB	800	32 MB	2 GB
Large	12288 MB	24576 MB	1200	64 MB	4 GB
Extra Large	24576 MB	49152 MB	2400	64 MB	4 GB

Table 3-9. *Database Templates for the X3-2 Oracle Database Appliance*

Class	PGA	SGA	Processes	Log Buffer	Redo Log File Size
Very Small	2048 MB	4096 MB	200	16 MB	1 GB
Small	4096 MB	8192 MB	400	16 MB	1 GB
Medium	8192 MB	16384 MB	800	32 MB	2 GB
Large	12288 MB	24576 MB	1200	64 MB	4 GB
Extra Large	24576 MB	49152 MB	2400	64 MB	4 GB

The last option on the Database Information screen is the Database Language. This is where you can select the language that you want to use for the database. The American option is selected in Figure 3-10. If you need to select a different language for your location, you can do it on this screen.

Once you have selected all the options needed to create the database on the Oracle Database Appliance, you can click the Next button. When you click Next, you are taken to the Summary screen on the wizard (see Figure 3-11). On this screen, you have the opportunity to review and verify the information you have selected throughout the wizard. You can also save the configuration for use with future deployments.

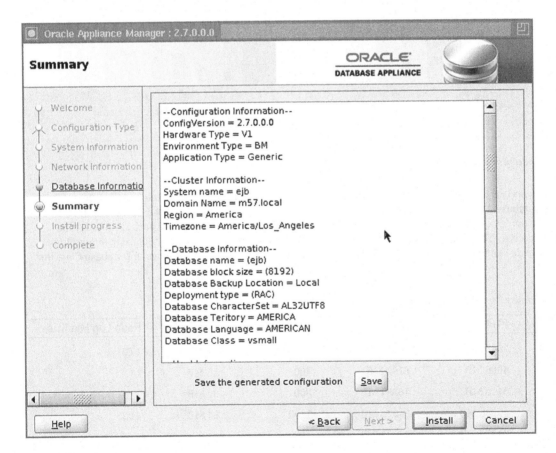

Figure 3-11. *Summary screen*

The Summary screen in the deployment wizard provides a scroll bar (on the right-hand side) to review all the information in the window. Listing 3-10 provides a more detailed view of the information contained in the Summary screen.

Listing 3-10. Summary Screen—Detailed Information

```
--Configuration Information--
ConfigVersion = 2.7.0.0.0
Hardware Type = V1
Environment Type = BM
Application Type = Generic

--Cluster Information--
System name = ejb
Domain Name = m57.local
Region = America
Timezone = America/Los_Angeles

--Database Information--
Database name = (ejb)
Database block size = (8192)
Database Backup Location = Local
Deployment type = (RAC)
Database CharacterSet = AL32UTF8
Database Teritory = AMERICA
Database Language = AMERICAN
Database Class = vsmall

--Host Information--
Host VIP Names = (ejb1-vip ejb2-vip)

--SCAN Information--
Scan Name = ejb-scan
Scan Name = (172.30.0.24 172.30.0.25)
Is DNS Server used = true
DNS Servers = (172.16.11.215   )
VIP IP = (172.30.0.22 172.30.0.23)

--Network Information--
Public IP = (172.30.0.20 172.30.0.21)
Public Network Mask = 255.255.255.0
Public Network Gateway = 172.30.0.1
Public Network interface = bond0
Public Network Hostname = (ejb1 ejb2)
NET1 Interface = bond1
NET2 Interface = bond2
NET3 Interface = xbond0
Disk Group Redundancy = ( HIGH HIGH HIGH )
```

```
--CloudF FileSystem Info--
Configure Cloud FileSystem = True
Cloud FileSystem Mount point = /cloudfs
Cloud Filesystem size(GB) = 50

--Automatic Service Request--
Configure ASR = False
Configure External ASR = False
ASR proxy server port = 80
```

After reviewing the Summary of items you have selected, you need to click the Install button to begin the deployment. At this point, the Oracle Appliance Manager will start to configure both nodes of the Oracle Database Appliance. This deployment process can take several hours, depending on your Oracle Database Appliance and the selected database size.

Once the installation begins, there are 25 steps that run during the deployment. Figure 3-12 provides a view of these steps during the deployment. Notice that on the installation screen, there is a Show Details button. This button can be used to look at the details of the step being performed during the deployment.

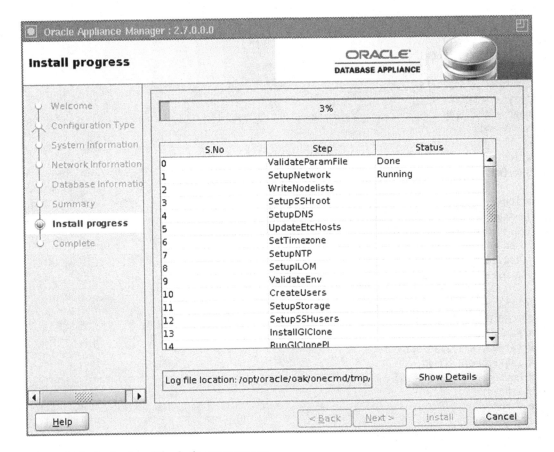

Figure 3-12. *Beginning of the deployment process*

Additionally, it is important to verify the location of the deployment log file. If the installation should fail, you will need to access the deployment log to understand why it failed. By default, the deployment log is located at /opt/oracle/oak/onecmd/tmp/.

Once the deployment is complete, the Oracle Appliance Manager will change to the Complete Screen (see Figure 3-13). At this point, you can click the Close button to exit the Oracle Appliance Manager.

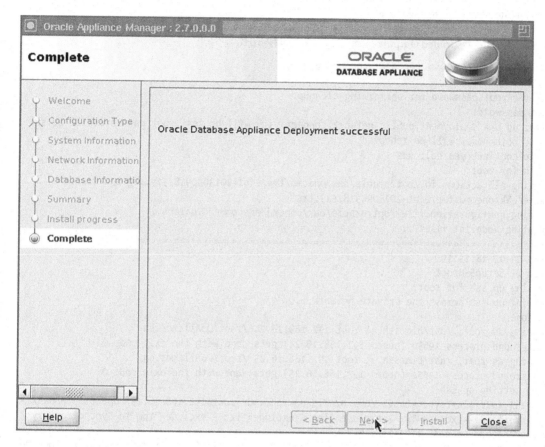

Figure 3-13. *Complete screen*

▪ **Note** Sometimes items are missed and the deployment does not work. The most common items that are missing are DNS entries or duplicate IP address. When the deployment runs, each step reports on its status. If a step fails, look at the log file in /opt/oracle/oak/onecmd/tmp/.

Oracle Database Appliance Redeploy

Sometimes you need to redeploy the base image to the Oracle Database Appliance. Redeploying will wipe out your all your databases and the ASM configuration associated with the Oracle Database Appliance. To perform a redeploy for the Oracle Database Appliance is a very simple task and is executed with the cleanupDeploy.pl script (see Listing 3-11).

Listing 3-11. The cleanupDeploy.pl script

```
/opt/oracle/oak/onecmd/cleanupDeploy.pl
```

Once this cleanupDeploy.pl script completes, you can rerun the deployment process using the Oracle Appliance Manager utility discussed earlier. To execute the cleanupDeploy.pl and review the associated output, Listing 3-12 gives some insight into what you are looking at.

Listing 3-12. Execute and Associated Output of cleanupDeploy.pl (Partial)

```
[root@oak1 ~]# /opt/oracle/oak/onecmd/cleanupDeploy.pl

Please enter the root password for performing cleanup:
Re-enter root password:
About to clear up OAK deployment,public network connectivity will be lost,root password will be set
to default and both nodes will be rebooted
Do you want to continue(yes/no): yes
Setting up ssh for root
INFO   : Logging all actions in /opt/oracle/oak/onecmd/tmp/ejb1-20130909181519.log and traces
in /opt/oracle/oak/onecmd/tmp/ejb1-20130909181519.trc
INFO   : Loading configuration file /opt/oracle/oak/onecmd/onecommand.params...
INFO   : Creating nodelist files...
=============================================================================
INFO   : 2013-09-09 18:15:19
INFO   : Step 1  SetupSSHroot
INFO   : Setting up ssh for root...
INFO   : Setting up ssh across the private network...
............done
INFO   : Running as root: /usr/bin/ssh -l root 192.168.16.24 /root/DoAllcmds.sh
INFO   : Background process 19630 (node: 192.168.16.24) gets done with the exit code 0
INFO   : Running as root: /usr/bin/ssh -l root 192.168.16.25 /root/DoAllcmds.sh
INFO   : Background process 19654 (node: 192.168.16.25) gets done with the exit code 0
INFO   : Done setting up ssh
INFO   : Running /usr/bin/rsync -tarvz /opt/oracle/oak/onecmd/ root@192.168.16.25:/opt/oracle/oak/
onecmd --exclude=*zip --exclude=*gz --exclude=*log --exclude=*trc --exclude=*rpm to sync directory</
opt/oracle/oak/onecmd> on node <192.168.16.25>
SUCCESS: Ran /usr/bin/rsync -tarvz /opt/oracle/oak/onecmd/ root@192.168.16.25:/opt/oracle/oak/onecmd
--exclude=*zip --exclude=*gz --exclude=*log --exclude=*trc --exclude=*rpm and it returned: RC=0
sending incremental file list
.
.
.
.
=============================================================================
INFO   : 2013-09-09 18:19:49
INFO   : Step 11  resetpasswd
INFO   : Resetting root password
...
INFO   : Running as root: /usr/bin/ssh -l root 192.168.16.24 /opt/oracle/oak/onecmd/tmp/secuser.sh
...
INFO   : Running as root: /usr/bin/ssh -l root 192.168.16.25 /opt/oracle/oak/onecmd/tmp/secuser.sh
INFO   : Running as root: /usr/bin/ssh -l root 192.168.16.24 /opt/oracle/oak/onecmd/tmp/
```

```
DoAllcmds-20130909181950.sh
INFO    : Background process 3206 (node: 192.168.16.24) gets done with the exit code 0
INFO    : Running as root: /usr/bin/ssh -l root 192.168.16.25 /opt/oracle/oak/onecmd/tmp/
DoAllcmds-20130909181950.sh
INFO    : Background process 3229 (node: 192.168.16.25) gets done with the exit code 0
INFO    : Time spent in step 11 resetpasswd is 1 seconds.
================================================================================
INFO    : Log file is /opt/oracle/oak/onecmd/tmp/ejb1-20130909181949.log...
Exiting...
Resetting dns, ntp and Rebooting
INFO    : Logging all actions in /opt/oracle/oak/onecmd/tmp/ejb1-20130909181950.log and traces
in /opt/oracle/oak/onecmd/tmp/ejb1-20130909181950.trc
INFO    : Loading configuration file /opt/oracle/oak/onecmd/onecommand.params...
INFO    : Creating nodelist files...
================================================================================
INFO    : 2013-09-09 18:19:51
INFO    : Step 12   reboot
INFO    : Running as root: /usr/bin/ssh -l root 192.168.16.24 /opt/oracle/oak/onecmd/tmp/reboot.sh
INFO    : Running as root: /usr/bin/ssh -l root 192.168.16.25 /opt/oracle/oak/onecmd/tmp/reboot.sh
```

Preparing for a ZFS Array As External Storage

While you can add an additional storage tray to the X3-2, you also have the option of growing storage from an NFS share, like Oracle ZFS Array. Growing from a ZFS Array allows you to introduce technologies like Hybrid Columnar Compression (HCC) and Storage Tiering. HCC allows you to store your user data in significantly less space and retrieve data with less I/O. Utilizing HCC warehouse compression, you see 5x to 10x in storage savings, and with HCC archive compression you can have 10x to 50x of storage savings. These savings are strongly dependent on actual data. The increased storage savings may cause data load-times to increase modestly. Storage Tiering allows you to leverage partitioning to keep your active data on the Oracle Database Appliance internal disks, and inactive data on the ZFS Array. This allows significantly more data to be accessible to the database without affecting the performance of active data.

When using NFS-based storage, it is recommended to enable a technology called Direct NFS. Oracle looks for the mount settings in $ORACLE_HOME/dbs/oranfstab, which specifies the Direct NFS Client settings for a single database. Next, Oracle looks for settings in /etc/oranfstab, which specifies the NFS mounts available to all Oracle databases on that host. Finally, Oracle reads the mount tab file (/etc/mtab on Linux) to identify available NFS mounts. If there are duplicate entries in the configuration files, the Direct NFS Client will use the first entry it finds. Listing 3-13 provides an example of the Direct NFS settings in the oranfstab file.

Listing 3-13. Example of oranfstab

```
[orahost1]# cat $ORACLE_HOME/dbs/oranfstab
server: zfs.m57.local
path: 172.30.0.90
export:/oranfsdata  mount:/oranfsdata
export:/oranfsarch  mount:/oranfsarch
```

■ **Note**   The IP address used in the path line is the virtual IP (VIP) address of the node that the NFS mount will connect to.

Before Direct NFS can be used with the database, it needs to be enabled. In Oracle Database 11g Release 2, this is easily done by recompiling binaries with the make command. Listing 3-14 shows you have to execute the make command and enable Direct NFS within the Oracle Database.

Listing 3-14. Recompile with make

```
cd $ORACLE_HOME/rdbms/lib
make -f ins_rdbms.mk dnfs_on
```

Before recompiling, all databases need to be shut down, and then recompiling of the binaries can be done using make. After the recompile is complete, additional databases can be brought back online. After starting the instances, the database instance alert.log will show that Direct NFS is enabled (see Listing 3-15).

Listing 3-15. Entry in the alert.log

```
Oracle instance running with ODM: Oracle Direct NFS ODM Library Version 3.0
```

Once Direct NFS is configured for the database and verified in the alert log, you can create tablespaces on the now accessible NFS storage. Listing 3-16 illustrates how to create a new tablespace and show the status of the file on a Direct NFS mount.

Listing 3-16. Create Tables on Direct NFS

```
SQL> create tablespace archive_data datafile
'/oranfsarch/archive_data01.dbf' SIZE 40960M;
Tablespace created.
SQL> select file#, name, status from v$datafile;
 FILE# NAME STATUS
------ ------------------------------------------------ -------
 1 +DATA/pbrb/datafile/system.272.781351553 SYSTEM
 2 +DATA/pbrb/datafile/sysaux.273.781351557 ONLINE
 3 +DATA/pbrb/datafile/undotbs1.274.781351561 ONLINE
 4 +DATA/pbrb/datafile/undotbs2.276.781351569 ONLINE
 5 +DATA/pbrb/datafile/users.277.781351571 ONLINE
 6 +DATA/pbrb/datafile/users.bigfile ONLINE
 7 /oranfsarch/nfs/archive_data01.dbf ONLINE
```

With the ability to add additional storage space by Direct NFS on the Oracle Database Appliance, you now have a powerful and expandable environment to run your Oracle Database.

Summary

With a little planning and preparation, the Oracle Appliance Manager (OAM) allows you to quickly deploy a new system in a few hours. Full RAC deployments can be online and ready in a fraction of the time it takes to build a system using the traditional methods from in the past. The OAM can be accessed via a VNC session, allowing you to deploy from most platforms without the need for installing the X-window system. This saves time, while still allowing you to rapidly deploy the system.

CHAPTER 4

Database Configuration

Up until now, this book has given the big picture of the Oracle Database Appliance and Integrated Lights Out Management (ILOM), and has shown how to install the Oracle Database Appliance from the hardware and software perspectives. What has not been covered until now is creating and configuring the Oracle database for the Oracle Database Appliance. In this chapter, we will focus on the `oakcli` command and the options associated with creating and deleting various types of database configurations.

The oakcli Command

The `oakcli` command provides the command-line interface to managing the appliance. It is the command you'll use to create and delete databases, and those are the uses we'll focus on in this chapter.

Command Options

Listing 4-1 shows the help output from the `oakcli` command. You will be focusing on the last two options of the `oakcli` command: `create` and `delete`. These options provide a single non-GUI interface to creating an Oracle database on the Oracle Database Appliance. By using the `oakcli` command-line tool, we can easily and quickly create databases.

Listing 4-1. The Help Output from oakcli

```
[oracle@patty bin]$ ./oakcli -h
Usage:  oakcli show      - show disk, diskgroup, expander, controller, storage, version, dbhomes,
        databases, db_config_params, core_config_key, env_hw
        oakcli apply      - applies the core_config_key
        oakcli locate     - locates a disk
        oakcli deploy     - deploys the Database Appliance
        oakcli update     - updates the Database Appliance
        oakcli validate   - validates the Database Appliance
        oakcli manage     - manages the oak repository, diagcollect e.t.c
        oakcli unpack     - unpack the given package to oak repository
        oakcli copy       - copies the deployment config file
        oakcli upgrade    - upgrades database
        oakcli stordiag   - run storage diagnostic tool on both node
        oakcli test       - test asr
        oakcli odachk     - performs configuration settings check on ODA
        oakcli configure  - configures the network or asr
        oakcli create     - create database, dbhome, db_config_params file
        oakcli delete     - deletes database, dbhome, db_config_params file
```

Now that you have an overview of what can be done with the `oakcli` command, let's take a look at how to create databases, and then delete them, using `oakcli`.

Executing the Command

Let's take a look at the `oakcli create` command. By using the help (`-h`) flag, we can get a description of what the command does. Listing 4-2 shows the output from issuing the help flag.

Listing 4-2. oakcli Create Help Output

```
[oracle@patty bin]$ ./oakcli create -h
Usage:
oakcli create {database | dbhome | db_config_params } [<options>]
where:
        database              - creates the database
        dbhome                - creates the database home
        db_config_params      - creates the database config parameter file
```

Each one of these options can be drilled down into as well by using the same help (`-h`) flag. Listing 4-3 through Listing 4-5 shows help output for some common `oakcli` operations.

Listing 4-3. The Help Output for Creating a Database

```
[oracle@patty bin]$ ./oakcli create database -h
Usage:
        oakcli create database  -db <db_name> [[-oh <home>] | [-version <version>]]  [-params <params_file>]
        where:
          db_name       - Name of the database to be created.
          home          - Existing oracle home for creating the database. By default we create a new
database home.
          version       - Database Version information for creating the database home. [ex. 11.2.0.2.7]
If not provided create the database home from latest available bits.
          params_file  - Name of the db_config_parameter file [This file can be created using using
'oakcli create db_config_param'].  If not provided, create the database using  default configuration file
```

Listing 4-4. The Help Output for Creating a Database Home

```
[oracle@patty bin]$ ./oakcli create dbhome -h
Usage:
        oakcli create dbhome  [-version <version>]

        where:
          version  - Version information for creating the database home. If not provided create the
database home from latest available bits.
```

Listing 4-5. The Help Output for Creating a Parameter File

```
[oracle@patty bin]$ ./oakcli create db_config_params -h
Usage:
        oakcli create db_config_params -conf <filename>  - Generates the database configuration parameter file.
        where:
        filename  -  configuration file name (path should NOT be there in the filename)
```

Now, that you have an understanding of the create command, let's put the command to use by creating a few of the database types that were discussed earlier. Let's start with a Real Application Cluster (RAC) database, and then you'll take a look at a RAC-One database and end with a simple standalone database.

ENTERPRISE EDITION

All databases that are created on the appliance are done so using the Enterprise Edition of the Oracle Database management system. The Enterprise Edition gives you many more features and allows for scalability as you begin growing your database environments.

The use of Enterprise Edition also allows you to expand on the number of cores that the database can use. The Standard Edition of the database is limited to a total of four cores on a two-node Real Application Cluster (RAC) system. With the Enterprise Edition, the Oracle Database Appliance can be scaled up to a total of 32 cores. This ability to expand the number of cores is much more valuable with the Oracle Database Appliance when configured and scaled for your environment.

With the Oracle Database Appliance becoming a centerpiece for consolidation for small- to medium-sized businesses, the scalability and flexibility that this appliance provides enables businesses to achieve more with less. The sheer scalability factor enables much of the need for the Enterprise Edition database.

Database Configuration Types

With the Oracle Database Appliance, there are three different configurations that can be configured and used within the appliance framework. The most obvious is the Real Application Cluster. Outside of the RAC configuration, the Oracle Database Appliance can have databases that are configured either as Real Application Cluster One (RAC One) databases, or as standalone databases. Let's take a look these different configuration types.

Real Application Cluster

The Real Application Cluster option is the primary option for use with the Oracle Database Appliance. RAC databases provide a level of high availability for a database, and allow for application scalability through the use of services. In order to configure the Oracle Database Appliance with a Real Application Cluster database, you need to use the oakcli command.

Let's configure a Real Application Cluster Database using oakcli:

```
[oracle@patty bin]$su -
[root@patty bin]$cd /opt/oracle/oak/bin
[root@patty bin]$ ./oakcli create database -db bcodatst
```

You will notice that I'm using a very simple create statement to create a database named *bcodatst*. There are other options that allow you to make a more customized database installation. These other options are the ones outlined earlier in Listings 4-4 and 4-5.

■ **Note** If you try to create a database as the `oracle` user, you will get told you do not have the privilege to do so. This is due to the `root` user owning the `oakcli` command, and it is why the preceding code example begins with a `su` to `root`. The following error is what will be presented if you forget and execute the command as the `oracle` user:

`ERROR: 2013-11-11 21:19:13: Insufficient privileges to create the database`

Once you kick off the `oakcli create database -db` command, you will be asked a series of questions to help configure the database on the Oracle Database Appliance. These questions range from asking about user passwords to what type of database you want to configure. Let's get started.

```
[root@patty bin]# ./oakcli create database -db bcodatst
INFO: 2013-11-11 21:20:59: Database parameter file is not provided. Will be using default parameters
for DB creation
```

Notice that we didn't provide a parameter file? The `oakcli` command picks up on this and makes the decision to use a default one. You are then asked to provide some passwords.

```
Please enter the 'root' user password:
Please re-enter the 'root' user password:
Please enter the 'oracle' user password:
Please re-enter the 'oracle' user password:
Please enter the 'SYSASM' user password: (During deployment we set the SYSASM password to
'welcome1'):
Please re-enter the 'SYSASM' user password:
INFO: 2013-11-11 21:25:24: Installing a new home: OraDb11203_home3 at
/u01/app/oracle/product/11.2.0.3/dbhome_3
```

After providing all the passwords that are needed to interact with the hardware of the Oracle Database Appliance, the `oakcli` command wants to know what type of database deployment you want to perform. Since you are creating a Real Application Cluster (RAC) database, you need to select option three.

```
Please select one of the following for Database Deployment  [1 .. 3]:
1    => EE : Enterprise Edition
2    => RACONE
3    => RAC
Selected value is: RAC
```

With a RAC installation, the installer next wants to know what size database you want to create. There are five different types of size classes to choose from. For demo purposes, we are going to go with a middle of the road database. Select option three to continue with the installation of the database.

```
Please select one of the following for Database Class  [1 .. 5]:
1    => Very Small
2    => Small
3    => Medium
4    => Large
5    => Extra Large
Selected value is: Medium
```

Because you are the administrator, you or your group needs to manage the database. As part of the installation, you will be prompted if you want to create a database console, also known as Database Control. Here's the prompt: n

```
Do you want to set up the EM Dbconsole for this database: [ Y | N ]? Y
```

Note In Chapter 6, you will review how to set up a database control maually. You will also see how to install a management agent for Oracle Enterprise Manager 12c.

Next, you will be asked to provide a password for the ASMSNMP user. This user is used to interact with Automatic Storage Management (ASM) on the appliance. Provide the password that you configured for this user.

```
Please enter the 'ASMSNMP' user password: (During deployment we set the ASMSNMP password to
'welcome1'):
Please re-enter the 'ASMSNMP' user password:
```

Once all the passwords have be provided and stored, the installer begins to install the Oracle Database in a Real Application Cluster configuration. This type of installation can run for a few minutes, depending on the size of the database that was requested to be created. Eventually, you'll receive a message stating that the database was created successfully, and that message will include a date and timestamp of the completion. For example:

```
SUCCESS: 2013-11-11 21:50:56: Successfully created the database bcodatst
```

When the database is created, entries in the Cluster Ready Services (CRS) stack will be available for review (see Listing 4-6). Use the command `crsctl` from the Oracle Grid home to review the status of the database that has been created. A complete listing of the `crsctl` output is in Listing 4-6. The lines in bold correspond to the database just created.

Listing 4-6. Cluster Ready Services (CRS) Output

```
[grid@patty bin]$ ./crsctl status res -t
--------------------------------------------------------------------------------
NAME           TARGET  STATE      SERVER               STATE_DETAILS
--------------------------------------------------------------------------------
Local Resources
--------------------------------------------------------------------------------
ora.DATA.dg
               ONLINE  ONLINE     patty
               ONLINE  ONLINE     selma
ora.LISTENER.lsnr
               ONLINE  ONLINE     patty
               ONLINE  ONLINE     selma
ora.RECO.dg
               ONLINE  ONLINE     patty
               ONLINE  ONLINE     selma
ora.REDO.dg
               ONLINE  ONLINE     patty
               ONLINE  ONLINE     selma
```

```
ora.asm
                ONLINE   ONLINE    patty                   Started
                ONLINE   ONLINE    selma                   Started
ora.gsd
                OFFLINE  OFFLINE   patty
                OFFLINE  OFFLINE   selma
ora.net1.network
                ONLINE   ONLINE    patty
                ONLINE   ONLINE    selma
ora.ons
                ONLINE   ONLINE    patty
                ONLINE   ONLINE    selma
ora.reco.acfsvol.acfs
                ONLINE   ONLINE    patty                   mounted on /cloudfs
                ONLINE   ONLINE    selma                   mounted on /cloudfs
ora.registry.acfs
                ONLINE   ONLINE    patty
                ONLINE   ONLINE    selma
--------------------------------------------------------------------------------
Cluster Resources
--------------------------------------------------------------------------------
ora.LISTENER_SCAN1.lsnr
        1       ONLINE   ONLINE    patty
ora.LISTENER_SCAN2.lsnr
        1       ONLINE   ONLINE    selma
ora.bcodatst.db
        1       ONLINE   ONLINE    patty                   Open
        2       ONLINE   ONLINE    selma                   Open
ora.cvu
        1       ONLINE   ONLINE    selma
ora.dboda.db
        1       ONLINE   ONLINE    patty                   Open
        2       ONLINE   ONLINE    selma                   Open
ora.oc4j
        1       ONLINE   ONLINE    selma
ora.patty.vip
        1       ONLINE   ONLINE    patty
ora.scan1.vip
        1       ONLINE   ONLINE    patty
ora.scan2.vip
        1       ONLINE   ONLINE    selma
ora.selma.vip
        1       ONLINE   ONLINE    selma
ora.slob.db
        1       ONLINE   ONLINE    patty                   Open
```

As you can see, by looking at the ora.bcodatst.db entry, the oakcli command did all the work for you and created a RAC database with no issues. The database has a status of open as well, which indicates the database is ready to use.

Real Application Cluster One

There are times when your organization wants only to have a single instance that can fail over between two nodes. To allow for this, Oracle has enabled a feature called RAC One. RAC One is a real application cluster that runs on a single node, and then fails over to the second when needed or desired.

Configuring a RAC One database is much the same as configuring a RAC database on the Oracle Database Appliance. You need to use the oakcli command and then provide the input required to tell Oracle what to configure. Let's take a look at configuring a RAC One cluster now.

Just as before, you need to start the oakcli command from the root user. Notice this time that we changed the database name to *bcrac1tst*.

```
[oracle@patty bin]$su -
[root@patty bin]$cd /opt/oracle/oak/bin
root@patty bin]$ ./oakcli create database -db bcrac1tst
```

If you try to use a name that is longer than eight characters, the oakcli command provides a warning and some information about the warning. Then it asks you to provide another name for the database. For example:

```
WARNING: 2013-11-12 07:18:22: bcrac1tst is not a valid database name
INFO: 2013-11-12 07:18:22: Only alphanumeric characters are allowed in the database name, and the
database name must start with an alphabetical character
INFO: 2013-11-12 07:18:22: Database name should not be more than 8 chars
```

As indicated, we have been told that the database name cannot be more than eight characters long. At the prompt, provide a new database name that is eight characters or less.

```
Please enter a different name for the Database: bcrac1
```

Just as with a RAC database, the oakcli installer will prompt us for various user passwords. Enter the passwords as expected and the installer continues. Once all the passwords have been provided, the installer will provide you the location where the new Oracle Home will be located by means of an INFO message.

```
Please enter the 'root' user password:
Please re-enter the 'root' user password:
Please enter the 'oracle' user password:
Please re-enter the 'oracle' user password:
Please enter the 'SYSASM' user password: (During deployment we set the SYSASM password to
'welcome1'):
Please re-enter the 'SYSASM' user password:
INFO: 2013-11-12 07:23:49: Installing a new home: OraDb11203_home4 at
/u01/app/oracle/product/11.2.0.3/dbhome_4
```

As with creating a RAC database, you will be asked what type of database you want to create. To create a RAC One database, you need to select option two (2), which indicates the RACONE database option. After selecting the option for RAC One, the installer asks what size you would like to make this database. Select the size that is desired for your organization.

```
Please select one of the following for Database Deployment  [1 .. 3]:
1    => EE : Enterprise Edition
2    => RACONE
3    => RAC
Selected value is: RACONE
Please select one of the following for Database Class  [1 .. 5]:
1    => Very Small
2    => Small
3    => Medium
4    => Large
5    => Extra Large
```

The last question to be asked while installing an Oracle RAC One database is about configuring the database console. Just as with the RAC configuration, you can say yes or no.

```
Do you want to set up the EM Dbconsole for this database: [ Y | N ]?
```

As with the RAC installation, once the oakcli command has completed, you will be able to see the newly created database in the Cluster Ready Services (CRS) stack. Listing 4-7 shows the stack for the database just created.

Listing 4-7. Cluster Ready Services (CRS) Output

```
[grid@patty bin]$ ./crsctl status res -t
--------------------------------------------------------------------------------
NAME            TARGET  STATE     SERVER             STATE_DETAILS
--------------------------------------------------------------------------------
Cluster Resources
--------------------------------------------------------------------------------
ora.bcrac1.bcrac1_racone.svc
      1         ONLINE  ONLINE    selma
ora.bcrac1.db
      1         ONLINE  ONLINE    selma                          Open
```

The example of the crsctl output in Listing 4-7 shows that the RAC One database was created and is located on the Selma server. Additionally, the database is open and accessible to end users.

Single Instance (EE Option)

Setting up a single instance database on the Oracle Database Appliance is just as simple as the options you've seen so far. To create a single instance database, you start off the same way as you did for the RAC and RAC One configurations. For example:

```
[oracle@patty bin]$su -
[root@patty bin]$cd /opt/oracle/oak/bin
[root@patty bin]$ ./oakcli create database -db bcsingle
```

Your database name needs to be different as well. In the preceding example, the name *bcsingle* is used. When executed, you will be prompted about the type of database you want to be created. After selecting the type of database to create, you are asked which node you would like to have the database created on. Listing 4-8 provides an example of the question about what node to install the database. Then the installer will ask you the normal questions, like configuring a RAC or RAC One database. As with the previous runs of the oakcli command for the other database types, you will be prompted to select the installation type and size, and asked whether the database console should be created.

Listing 4-8. Select a Node for Installing an EE Database

```
Please select one of the following for Node Number  [1 .. 2]:
1    => patty
2    => Selma
```

Once the single instance database installation is done, the database status can be viewed from the CRS stack using the `crsctl` command. Listing 4-9 shows a sample of a CRS stack with a single instance.

Listing 4-9. Cluster Ready Services (CRS) Status for an EE Database

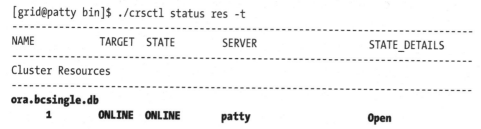

```
[grid@patty bin]$ ./crsctl status res -t
--------------------------------------------------------------------------------
NAME            TARGET  STATE     SERVER               STATE_DETAILS
--------------------------------------------------------------------------------
Cluster Resources
--------------------------------------------------------------------------------
ora.bcsingle.db
     1          ONLINE  ONLINE    patty                Open
```

Database Deletion

We've just taken a look at how to create three different types of databases by using the `oakcli` command. What if you want to remove a database from the Oracle Database Appliance? The `oakcli` command provides an option to do this as well. As you reviewed at the beginning of the chapter, the `oakcli` command has a delete option.

The delete option of the `oakcli` command has the same command-line options as the create option. Listing 4-10 shows the available options.

Listing 4-10. oakcli Delete Options

```
[root@patty bin]# ./oakcli delete -h
Usage:
oakcli delete {database | dbhome | db_config_params}  [<options>]
where:
        database             - deletes the database
        dbhome               - deletes the database home
        db_config_params     - deletes the database config parameter file
```

Now that you understand what the delete option can do, let's take a look at removing one of the databases that we created earlier. To delete a database from the Oracle Database Appliance, issue the following:

```
[root@patty bin]# ./oakcli delete database -db bcodatst
```

When the delete option is invoked, you will be asked to provide the password for the `root` and `oracle` users. The `oakcli` utility will then log in as those users, and connect by a secure shell (SSH) connection between the nodes so that the database can be deleted. Listing 4-11 shows the complete output for removing a RAC database from the Oracle Database Appliance.

Listing 4-11. Prompts for root and oracle Users (Passwords Not Typed)

```
Please enter the 'root' user password:
Please re-enter the 'root' user password:
Please enter the 'oracle' user password:
Please re-enter the 'oracle' user password:

INFO: 2013-11-12 18:18:44: Setting up ssh
...........done
SUCCESS: Ran /usr/bin/rsync -tarvz /opt/oracle/oak/onecmd/ root@192.168.16.25:/opt/oracle/oak/onecmd
--exclude=*zip --exclude=*gz --exclude=*log --exclude=*trc --exclude=*rpm and it returned: RC=0
sending incremental file list
./
T4DBTemplate.dbt
delete_database.params
tmp/
tmp/DoAllcmds-20131112175008.sh
tmp/DoAllcmds.sh
tmp/all_nodes
tmp/bcsingleDBTemplate.dbt
tmp/db_nodes
tmp/dbca-bcsingle.sh
tmp/dbupdates-bcsingle.lst
tmp/dbupdates-bcsingle.sh
tmp/priv_ip_group
tmp/racclonepl.sh
tmp/u01apporacleproduct11.2.0.3dbhome_5-optoracleoakpkgreposorapkgsDB11.2.0.3.7Basedb112.tar.gz.out
tmp/vip_node
 sent 8774 bytes  received 8945 bytes  35438.00 bytes/sec
 total size is 17857762  speedup is 1007.83
.........done
.........done
...
SUCCESS: All nodes in /opt/oracle/oak/onecmd/tmp/db_nodes are pingable and alive.
INFO: 2013-11-12 18:19:51: Successfully setup the ssh
INFO: 2013-11-12 18:19:52: Deleting the database bcodatst. It will take few minutes. Please wait...
...
...
SUCCESS: 2013-11-12 18:23:54: Successfully deleted the database bcodatst
```

Database Configuration Assistant

As you can see, Oracle has implemented very simple ways for creating and deleting an Oracle database from the Oracle Database Appliance. This simplicity is driven by many of the Oracle utilities that are available from the Oracle Home directories. However, while the command line is nice and simple, you also have a GUI option available in the form of the Database Configuration Assistant. It's abbreviated as DBCA, and you'll most often here it referred to in that way.

Creating a Database

The oakcli command-line tool invokes the Database Configuration Assistant (DBCA) in silent mode. You are not limited to silent mode, and can invoke DBCA in GUI mode to create a RAC, RAC One, or single-instance database.

To invoke the DBCA on the Oracle Database Appliance, you need to go to the Oracle Home and invoke it from under the bin directory. Listing 4-12 gives an example of how to invoke the DBCA.

Listing 4-12. Invoke the Database Configuration Assistant (DBCA)

```
[oracle@patty ~]$ cd $ORACLE_HOME/bin
[oracle@patty bin]$ ./dbca
```

Figure 4-1 shows the start screen for the DBCA once invoked from the Oracle Home.

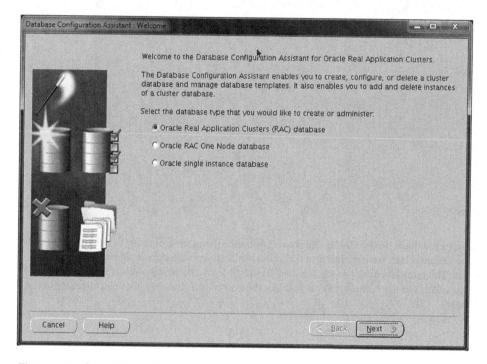

Figure 4-1. *The DBCA start screen*

Once the DBCA is invoked and started, you can perform all the normal functions of creating or managing a database as you would in normal everyday management. Figure 4-2 provides five different options that either create or manage a database. These options are ones that many database administrators are used to seeing when creating or managing databases with the DBCA.

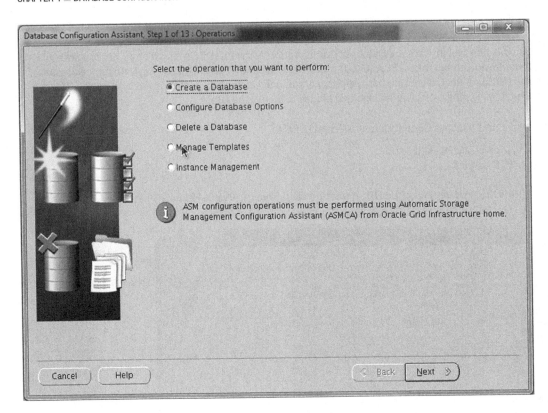

Figure 4-2. DBCA Operations

Let's take a look at creating a database on the Oracle Database Appliance using the Database Configuration Assistant tool. By selecting the Create A Database option and then clicking Next, you are presented with the template options for creating a database. The template options (see Figure 4-3) match up to the sizing options that you are presented when you invoke the oakcli at the command line. Just like the command-line options, select the size of the database you would like to create.

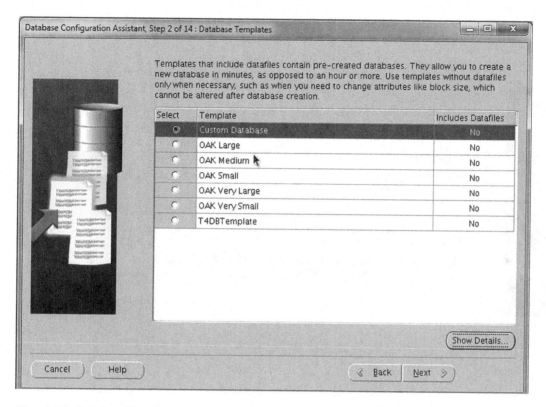

Figure 4-3. Database Templates

Once you click Next, the DBCA will ask you for naming information associated with the database (see Figure 4-4). What you will also notice on the DBCA screen are two options: Admin-Managed and Policy-Managed. These two options determine how the database will be managed by the clusterware within the Oracle Database Appliance.

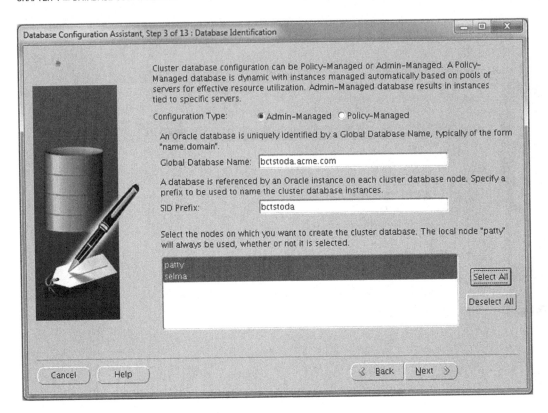

Figure 4-4. *Database Identification*

■ **Note** *Admin-Managed* means that the database will be tied to specific servers. *Policy-Managed* means the instances are dynamic and automatically based on pools of servers for effective resource utilization.

Additionally, you will notice that the two node names associated with the cluster are listed. By selecting one or both of these nodes, the databases will be created on all nodes selected. By default, the node from where you are running DBCA will be highlighted and required. If a node is not selected, then it will not be included in the configuration of your database.

By using DBCA to create a database on the Oracle Database Appliance, you will get the option to attach the database to an Oracle Enterprise Manager (see Figure 4-5) if you wish to monitor the databases on the appliance from a central point. The option to configure the database console is still available as well, if desired. This is a flexibility that is provided without using the `oakcli` command-line option.

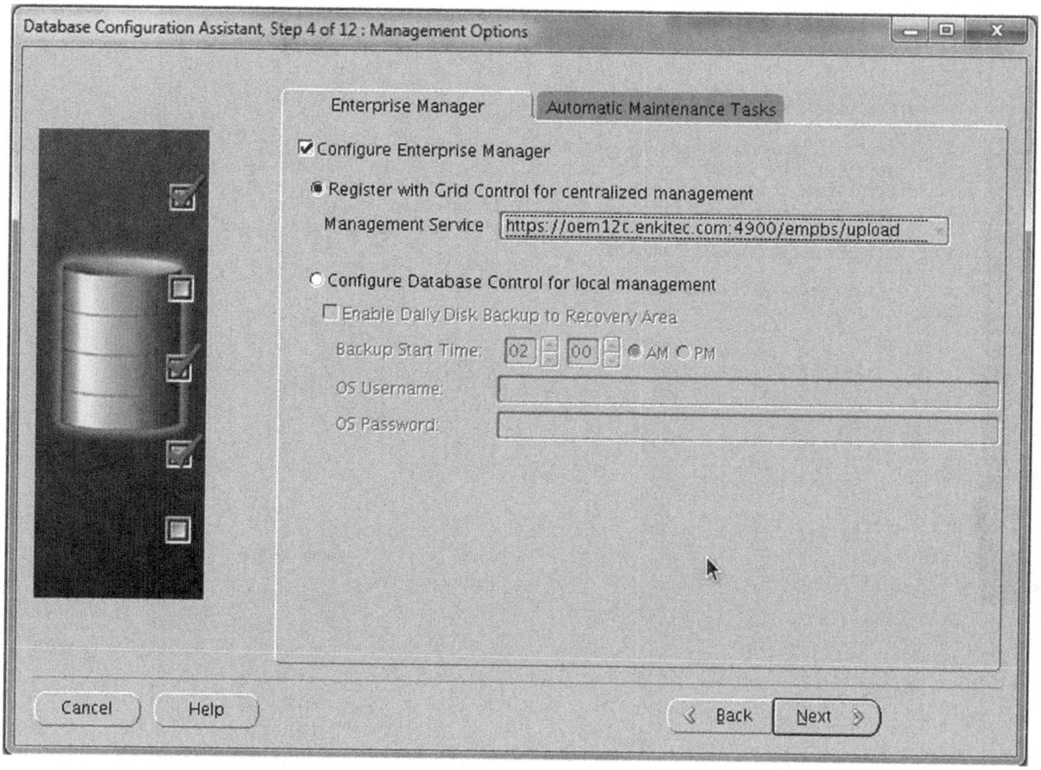

Figure 4-5. *Configure monitoring*

On the same screen, you see a tab titled Automatic Maintenance Tasks (see Figure 4-6). Enabling automatic tasks can help you manage a range of administrative functions. On this tab, you can enable or disable this automation of tasks by either checking or unchecking the associated check box.

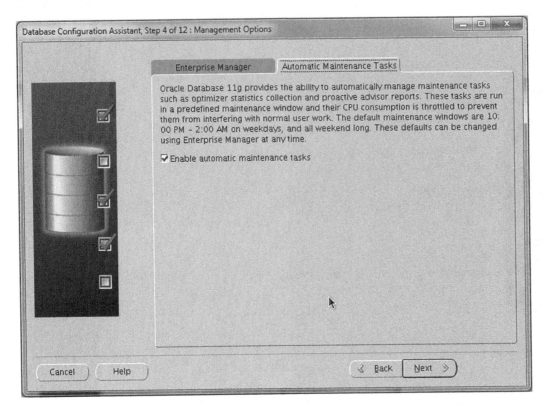

Figure 4-6. Enable/disable automatic maintenance tasks

Depending on your security requirements, the database can be configured with the same password for every account, or different passwords for different accounts (see Figure 4-7). This is a standard DBCA approach to securing the database. Using the DBCA here allows you to set the passwords for the SYS and SYSTEM accounts; whereas with the oakcli command-line option, these passwords are handled by a default password until they are changed after creation.

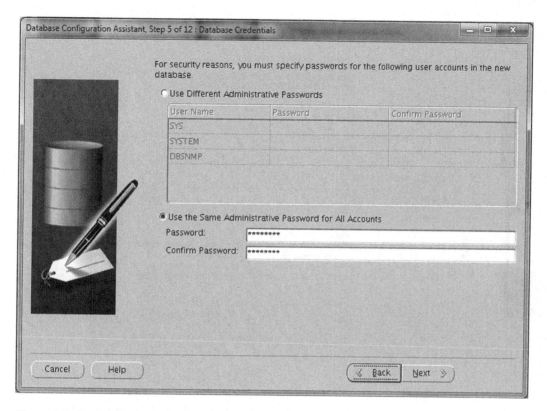

Figure 4-7. *Setting database credentials*

After you provide the passwords for the accounts, the DBCA asks where you would like to place the database-specific items, such as data files, log files, and control files. The Oracle Database Appliance has everything built-in and Automatic Storage Management (ASM) configured, and the default is to store these items on ASM. However, you can see in Figure 4-8 that you can choose between Cluster File System (CFS) and ASM as storage locations.

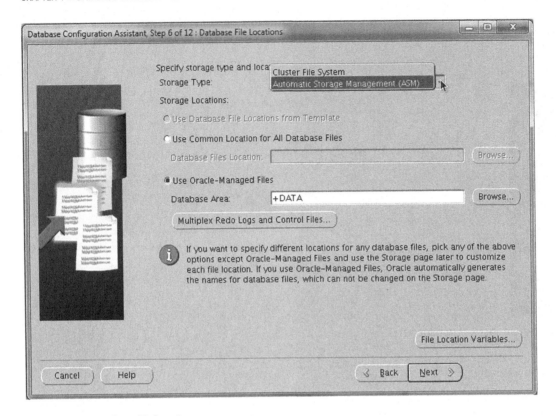

Figure 4-8. *Database file locations*

When configuring the database from oakcli, you are automatically configured on ASM. By using the DBCA to manage a database, you can have greater control over where the database files are installed and configured.

Another major difference between using the oakcli and the DBCA is when you specifically want to configure archivelog mode and the Fast Recovery Area (FRA). Using the oakcli, these options are not readily available from the command line. With DBCA, you can specify the location, size, and whether the archive log should be enabled. Figure 4-9 highlights the items that can be configured within the DBCA utility.

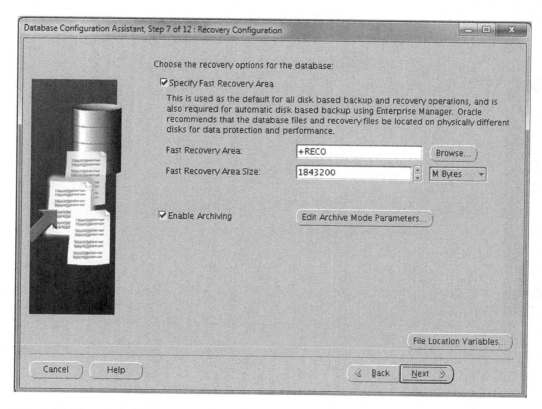

Figure 4-9. *Recovery information configuration*

Up to this point, when using the Database Configuration Assistant (DBCA) on the Oracle Database Appliance, you have been able to select and change settings that you could not touch from the oakcli utility. Part of the flexibility of using the DBCA to create a database is that, although you selected a template for database sizing, you can adjust the SGA and PGA as desired. The dialog in Figure 4-10 allows you to make these adjustments as you would do with any normal database being created with the DBCA. When compared to the oakcli command, you see the DBCA again provides a level of flexibility that the command line does not provide.

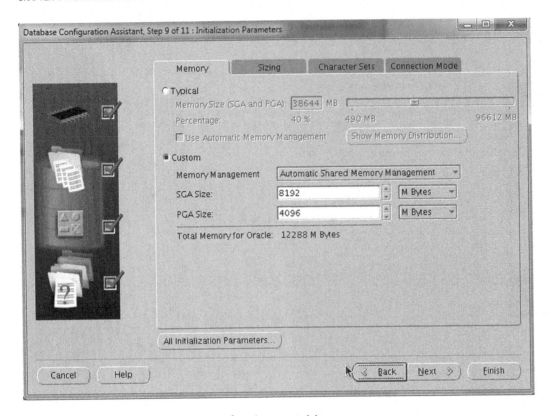

Figure 4-10. Initialization parameters and environment sizing

Although the memory settings can be configured, you also can configure the size, character set, and connection modes of the database. However, keep in mind that the information on the size, character set, and connection mode tabs are configured by the ODA template that you selected on an earlier screen. Although many of these items can be changed, they are also dependent on the template that was selected when the DBCA was initially started.

When you finally reach the last step of the DBCA (see Figure 4-11), you have the option to save the configuration as a template and generate scripts that can be used for future database deployments or on other Oracle Database Appliances.

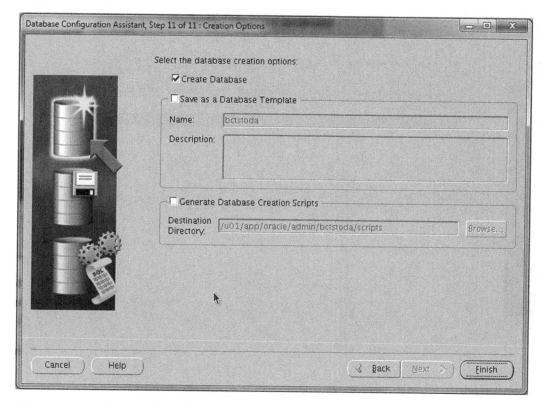

Figure 4-11. *Creation Options*

As you can tell, using the Database Configuration Assistant (DBCA) requires more time to configure a database than it took with the oakcli command. With both tools, databases can be created; which tool is better for the job is up to you. Oracle has done a very good job at providing a way to quickly create a database in a short amount of time using the oakcli option. On the other hand, Oracle has also given the DBA a great deal of flexibility when it comes to creating databases with the configuration assistant.

Deleting a Database

As with creating a database with the Database Configuration Assistant (DBCA), a database can be deleted from the Oracle Database Appliance with the DBCA. Earlier in the chapter, we took a look at the oakcli command-line approach to deleting a database. The oakcli approach is much simpler and quicker. However, the DBCA provides the same functionality. In fact, the DBCA is actually called silently by the oakcli command.

When you take a look at Figure 4-2 (earlier in the chapter), you see that there is an option to delete a database. If you select this option and continue with the wizard, you will be asked what database you would like to remove (see Figure 4-12).

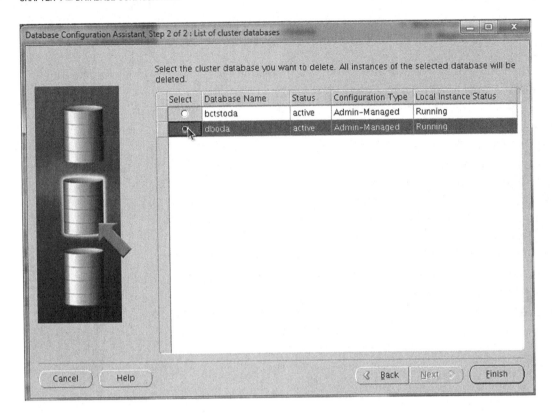

Figure 4-12. *Select database to delete*

Notice that the DBCA in Figure 4-12 tells you the current status of the database, which configuration type it uses, and whether it is running or not. These are all indicators to help you make the decision whether or not you want to remove the database. Once you click Finish, the database that has been highlighted will be removed from the Oracle Database Appliance.

The first portion of this chapter has been about how to add or delete a database from the Oracle Database Appliance. You have taken a look at how this can be done from the command line using the oakcli commands for creating and deleting a database. Also, you have taken a look at how to do these same tasks using the Database Configuration Assistant. Both approaches provide benefit and pitfalls, depending on your approach to creating a database within this type of an engineered environment. One topic that we have not covered in this chapter is Automatic Storage Management. We touched on it earlier while talking about the Database Configuration Assistance; however, what tools are available to help you manage ASM on the appliance?

Automatic Storage Management (ASM)

Since Oracle released Database 10g over a decade ago, the concept of Automatic Storage Management has either been confusing, intriguing, or both for many DBAs and storage administrators. The base concept around ASM was to provide a central point of storage for Oracle databases, while minimizing overhead of management. For these reasons, ASM was used with Oracle Real Application Clusters and has quickly become a stable storage option for configuring RAC clusters. At this point, let's take a look at how ASM is configured on the Oracle Database Appliance and what tool is available to help you manage the ASM that is configured.

Automatic Storage Management Configuration Assistant

The Automatic Storage Management Configuration Assistant (ASMCA) is the central tool for interacting with Automatic Storage Management (ASM) in a GUI environment. Figure 4-13 shows you the interface that is used when working with ASM from a GUI interface.

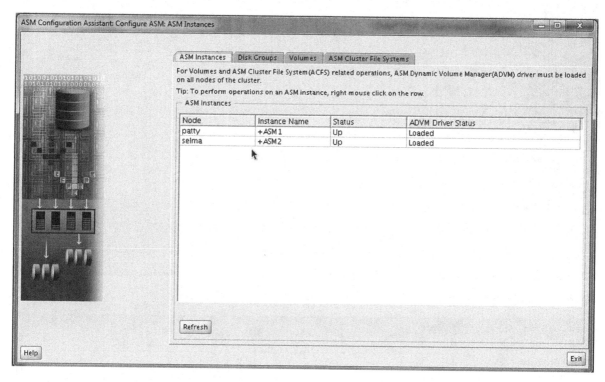

Figure 4-13. *Automatic Storage Management Configuration Assistant*

By using the ASMCA tool, you can get a sense of how the Oracle Database Appliance has been configured at the storage level. There are tabs to help identify which ASM instances are currently running on the Oracle Database Appliance, which disk groups have been allocated within the ASM, which mount points have been formatted as volumes, and which ASM Cluster File Systems have been defined on the appliance.

Given that most Oracle Database Appliances have all their storage provisioned by default when initially installed, the ASMCA tool is mostly used for reconfiguring or adding additional storage. The initial size of an ASM disk group can be identified from the Disk Groups table of the ASMCA. From this tab (see Figure 4-14), the Create button would be used if you wanted to add additional disks or create a new disk group; the tab also brings up the interface to add additional disks (see Figure 4-15).

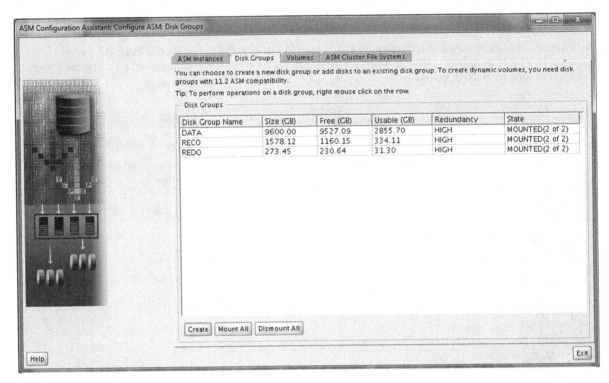

Figure 4-14. *ASM Disk Groups*

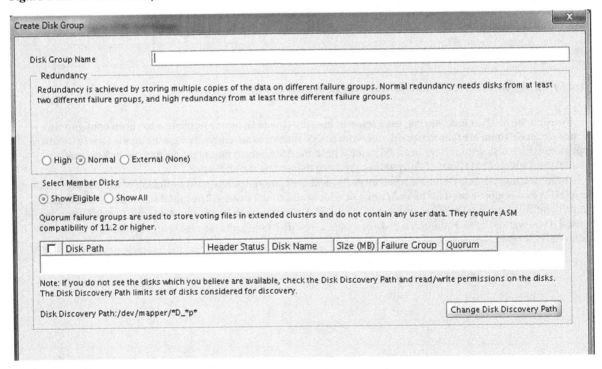

Figure 4-15. *Adding disk groups*

It is recommended that you review the details of ASM and the associated SAN on the Oracle Database Appliance before making any major changes.

Now let's dive into more about the Automatic Storage Management and how it is configured.

Automatic Storage Management Command Line

Another way to interact with ASM is from the command line; a user can access ASM from the command line by using the asmcmd command-line tool. In order to access ASM from the command line, a user needs to be signed into the operating systems as the owner of the Grid Infrastructure software. This is typically the grid user. Listing 4-13 illustrates how to get to the asmcmd prompt after logging in as the grid user.

Listing 4-13. Access the ASM from Command Line

```
[root@patty bin]# su - grid
[grid@patty ~]$ . oraenv
ORACLE_SID = [grid] ? +ASM1
The Oracle base has been set to /u01/app/grid
[grid@patty ~]$ asmcmd -p
ASMCMD [+] >
```

One thing to notice is that the -p option was used. This option places the [+] at the end of the ASMCMD prompt and will change every time you change directories. Accessing ASM in this manner allows you to view the files associated with the database and identify any issues that there may be within ASM. All commands that are used with ASM, on both windows and UNIX, are UNIX-style commands.

Summary

In this chapter, you looked at how to create and delete databases on the Oracle Database Appliance. We took a quick look at how to interact with Oracle's Automatic Storage Management. As outlined, the Oracle Database Appliance is simply a two-node Real Application Cluster that can be configured with many different styles of databases, and it is flexible enough to enable a business to build and scale using minimal resources.

CHAPTER 5

Networking

Understanding network deployment is important for anyone considering ODAs as a solution for their company. You need to understand the networks provided by an ODA to determine how they mesh with your requirements and data center standards. Security requirements may need to be considered during your network planning. The deployment of engineered systems often involves blending or broadening job roles, because tasks that used to be handled by multiple teams are now packaged into the engineered system solution. When deploying new solutions at your company, you can seldom just pass the documentation on to your networking and data center teams and ask them to develop the network requirements. You may need to become directly involved in preparing the network specifications for deploying your ODAs, or at least understand the options to answer questions that come from other teams. This chapter will help you understand your ODA network deployment options.

ODA Models

Oracle has released two ODA models. The networking aspects of these models differ noticeably. The next two subsections describe the networking available on each of the two models.

Oracle Database Appliance V1

The first ODA model is called the Oracle Database Appliance. It is often referenced as ODA V1. The ODA V1 is a single unit appliance that houses two standard Sun Fire X4370 M2 servers and 24 disk drives, 20 of which are used for shared storage. The V1 has the same 4u rack space footprint as the current modular model, the X3-2.

The ODA V1 server nodes differ from those in the current X3-2 model in that they include a fiber network card that support 10G fiber cabling. The new X3-2 model currently only supports copper cabling. The ODA V1 10G fiber network can be deployed for either the public network or as a private backup network. Since only one 10G network is supported, it has to be used for either the public or backup networks, but not for both.

In addition to the 10G network, the ODA V1 supports a bonded pair of 1G interfaces for the public network, and four additional 1G network interfaces that can be deployed as two bonded networks for other purposes. The ODA V1 can potentially be deployed with one 10G bonded network and three additional 1G bonded networks, in addition to the ILOM and serial connections.

The 10G fiber network requires a 10G small form-factor pluggable (SFP) transceiver on both ends of the fiber cable connections. This includes the connection to the PCIe0 network port on the appliance, and the connection to the fiber cable connection to the switch or network fabric extender. As an example, a bonded 10G backup network requires four fiber cables, or two per server node. A total of 8 SFP adapters are thus required, at two per fiber network cable. The SFP adapters are a little pricey, so their cost needs to be accounted for. They resemble a typical USB flash drive in size and appearance.

The ODA network interfaces are typically bonded. This means that two network interfaces are combined together as a single logical unit, managed by the OS networking software components. This provides network redundancy. The network cables for each bonded pair can be routed to different switches or network fabric extenders. In this manner, if a switch, cable connection, or server network interface fails, the network traffic will failover to the surviving interface to avoid a network outage.

The networks deployed for the original Oracle Database Appliance V1 model are listed in Table 5-1. Please note that the ODA V1 appliance has two server nodes, and each node will contain these network interfaces.

Table 5-1. *Networks Deployed on the Original ODA Model*

Network	Bond / Ports	Usage
10G Fiber	Bond: Xbond0 - Ports: eth8, eth9 (labeled as PCIe0)	Two 10G fiber ports that can be used for either the public network or a backup network, but not both.
1G Copper	Bond: bond0 - Ports: eth2, eth3 (labeled as net0, net1)	Two bonded ports that if used, have to be used for the public network.
1G Copper	Bond: bond1 - Ports: eth4, eth5 (labeled as PCIe1)	An additional 1G network that could be used as a backup network if the 10G network is used for the public network, or as an additional network for other purposes, such as mounting NFS storage.
1G Copper	Bond: bond2 - Ports: eth6, eth7 (also labeled as PCIe1)	An additional 1G network that can be deployed as needed.
Management	NetMgt	This is the 10/100 Mbps RJ45 network connection for the ILOM connection. This is a single, unbonded connection.
Serial connection	SerMgt	This connection is used to support either a serial connection from an external KVM (keyboard, video, mouse) appliance or device, or from your laptop to deploy the ODA.

The original ODA V1 model also comes with a USB connection and video port.

The details on the physical appliance network connections are documented in the ODA Owner's Guide. The chapter name is currently titled as "Attaching Cables and Power Cords". Keep in mind that Oracle updates their manuals quarterly for each new release. The structure of Oracle's documentation can change.

You have to be careful when reviewing the Owner's Guide for reference information. The Owner's Guide is currently split into two sections. Part One covers the original Oracle Database Appliance Model. Part Two covers the successor model and is labeled "Oracle Database Appliance X3-2."

We're not going to include a lot of information on the original Oracle Database Appliance model in this Networking chapter. Oracle stopped selling this model in April 2013. Anyone who purchased this model will have already deployed it. In addition, the model is covered in the Oracle manuals. Oracle has retained information in the manuals for the models that are no longer sold for two simple reasons: (1) the information doesn't change and (2) the new ODA software releases are backward compatible to the older models. For example, when the ODA 2.8 release was issued, it was tested on the original V1 model. The documentation includes any special instructions for new release deployments on the older models. A bare-metal deployment can still be done on the older models, and Oracle has updated the Oracle Appliance Manager Configurator utility with the hardware models to account for the differences in networks between the models.

Oracle Database Appliance X3-2

The next release of the ODA resulted in some major networking changes. The X3-2 model no longer includes a fiber network card. This change caught quite a few ODA customers—and even a few people inside Oracle, as well as its partners—by surprise, since some customers only support fiber for their 10G networks.

In the end, some customers settled on a solution of bridging 10G copper from an ODA to a network fabric extender or switch. From the switch, 10G fiber could be deployed to their data center fiber network. Oracle even started selling switches for this purpose. This workaround to 10G fiber support can be a little pricey, so you will need to account for the costs.

Oracle can change the supported networks as new models are released, so it's possible that 10G fiber support may come back in the future. You need to check the Oracle manuals for every new release to review any changes to the number or types of networks included.

The X3-2 ODA model migrated from a single encapsulated box with two server nodes and a set of disk drives to a modular design with two servers from the general Oracle X3-2 server line, with one or two separate storage units. The new, modular X3-2 ODA comes with support for four external network interfaces. The networks can be 100M, 1G, or 10G. The connections are copper only, and the network speeds are autonegotiated.

Oracle's release of multiple products with the X3-2 name was a little confusing at first. You could order an X3-2 server as a standalone ASR server or as an Exadata Platinum Support Gateway, and you could order an X3-2 Oracle Database Appliance and also an X3-2 Exadata machine.

The networks available for the X3-2 ODA model are listed in Table 5-2. The X3-2 ODA has two server nodes, and each server will contain the network interfaces listed in the table.

Table 5-2. *Networks Deployed on the Second-Generation ODA Model*

Network	Bond / Ports	Usage
100M/1G/10G Copper	Bond: bond0 - Ports: eth2, eth3 (labeled as net0, net1)	Two 100/1000/10000 copper ports that can be used for the public network. The ODA deployment process will target bond0 as the public network.
100M/1G/10G Copper	Bond: bond1 - Ports: eth4, eth5 (labeled as net2, net3)	Two 100/1000/10000 copper ports that are typically used for the backup or other network of your choice.
Management	NetMgt	This is the 10/100 Mbps RJ45 network connection for the ILOM connection. This is a single, unbonded connection.
Serial connection	SerMgt	This connection is used to support either a serial connection from an external KVM (keyboard, video, mouse) appliance or device, or from your laptop to deploy the ODA.

The Oracle Appliance Manager Configurator utility used to deploy an ODA will assume that the network connections are bonded. However it is possible to deploy networks as standalone nonredundant connections by skipping the bonding. In order to do this, some manual work is involved and the process is not included in the standard ODA documentation. You'll probably need to ask an experienced sysadmin to give you a hand if you decide to deploy the networks outside the process that comes out-of-the-box with an ODA.

The X3-2 ODA network details are covered in Part Two of the Oracle Database Appliance Owner's Guide in the chapter titled "Attaching Cables and Power Cords, and Powering On Oracle Database Appliance X3-2." This chapter is mainly focused on the implementing the cabling shipped with an ODA to connect all of the ODA components together. You have to read the chapter closely to find the details on the external network connections. Additional reference information can be found in Chapter 1 and Appendix A of the ODA Getting Started Guide.

ODA Network Deployment Process

ODA networks can be deployed using the process outlined in the subsections to follow. Most of these steps are necessary, but are fairly simple in nature. The steps are listed roughly in the order in which they should occur. Of course, each company has their own standards and methods for getting a server deployed in their data center and on their network. The key steps are as follows:

1. Plan which ODA networks will be deployed.

2. Define network security considerations.

3. Complete work that can be accomplished before the ODA arrives.

4. Spec and order the ODA network cabling.

5. Request IP addresses.

6. Build the offline configuration file.

7. Rack the ODA.

8. Cable the ODA, including internal cabling.

9. Apply the ILOM IP addresses and configure the ODA public network.

10. Run the ODA deployment process to configure the remaining networks.

Plan the ODA Networks to Be Deployed

The X3-2 ODA model supports two bonded networks. One of them will certainly be used for the public network. The second network is generally used as the backup network. It is possible to unbond one or both networks to take advantage of all four external network connections at the cost of network redundancy. An example would be deploying a bonded public network and a single connection for a backup network and an additional network to support an NFS storage mount. While it is also possible to mount NFS storage over the public network, performance issues can arise when large volumes of data are streamed between the server and NFS storage. The need for external storage mounts has somewhat diminished due to the very large amount of internal storage supplied with an ODA.

▪ **Note** The key point in this section is that the first network deployment step is to plan out what networks are required for your solution, and matching those requirements to the ODA network options. Understanding the workloads that need to be supported can also be an important consideration in planning ODA networks.

ODAs can now store a great deal of data. If the databases deployed have tight RTO (recovery time objective) requirements, and they are large in size, using a 10G backup network can help drive better backup and recovery performance. This would be in addition to deploying the standard RMAN tuning steps. If you are connected to a backup network through an NFS mount, DNFS (Direct NFS) can be implemented to speed up the backup and recovery throughput. There is an old adage followed by many long-term Oracle DBAs and architects: "It is better to focus on architecting for recovery than to architect for backups." If you want to make sure that you have all of your recovery bases covered, your network planning plays a key role.

If your company only uses 10G fiber or other fiber network infrastructure, then additional planning, and potentially costs, may be needed to bridge the ODA copper cabling to your fiber network. As mentioned previously, this is subject to change when new models are released.

Define Network Security Considerations

The nature of your data and the associated security risk considerations may require that your ODA be placed on specific IP ranges, on VLANs, or behind specific firewalls. It is best to plan out the network security requirements with your security and networking people as early as possible to avoid delaying your project. Every company has its process and standards for network security, as well as its choice as to whether encryption needs to be deployed at the network layer. This work can start before you order your ODA so that the network requirements don't become a bottleneck that will slow down your ODA deployment.

In today's rush to DBaaS (Database as a Service) and cloud deployments, it isn't unusual to predeploy infrastructure according to application and security tiering. The more that security or other network requirements are worked out in advance, the better your chances are for realizing the fast deployment benefits of the ODA. There are financial benefits for deploying infrastructure "Just-In-Time," instead of "way too early" or "way too late."

Complete Work That Can Be Accomplished Before the ODA Arrives

Identify when you can complete work in advance or do things in parallel so that when an ODA arrives, it can be immediately cabled and deployed using the "one button" deployment automation feature. Some of the tasks that can be done before the ODA arrives include a number of the implementation steps outlined in this chapter, including:

- Plan your networks.

- Finalize security considerations.

- Request IP addresses.

- Submit cabling requests and order any necessary cables.

- Submit DNS and firewall requests.

- Identify the rack locations.

- Build the deployment configuration files using the Oracle Appliance Manager Configurator utility in offline mode.

This author has personally witnessed multiple ODAs land on the dock, only to be running as fully deployed RAC clusters within 48 hours. Shipping time is not time to be wasting. Use that time to your advantage to prepare and be ready when your ODA units arrive.

Now that it is possible to deploy applications in addition to databases on an ODA, your network planning may need to extend to the application tier. Oracle supports deploying applications on an ODA to have a complete application solution running very quickly. Oracle includes information in the Getting Started Guide to detail the process for installing and supporting virtualization on an ODA.

Application requirements can impact your network planning. In addition to the need for more IP addresses, applications may need to reside on different networks than your database servers. This can be due to security considerations, for example.

When ODAs were first released, there were a number of partners and consultants that produced videos or blogs detailing how fast it is to deploy ODAs. In one case, the network cables were run to the dock to deploy the ODA while it was still on the shipping pallet. You can still find some of these videos on YouTube. Live ODA builds were highlighted at several Oracle user conferences.

While it has been proven many times that an ODA can be deployed quickly, it is always important to make sure to deploy them correctly. Planning can help accomplish this. It's always possible to change the networks after an ODA has been deployed. Options for making some of these changes will be discussed in an upcoming section. If worse comes to worst, you can always bare metal an ODA to start over. But if you follow the old carpenters rule to "measure twice, cut once," costly reworks can be eliminated.

Spec and Order the ODA Network Cabling

The good news about deploying ODAs on your network is that once you deploy an ODA model the first time, all of the additional ODAs released for that model are identical. You only have to work out the cabling diagrams for a model once. It's a good idea to formally prepare network and cabling specs for each ODA deployment using a standard template. Unless you are working for a very small IT shop, don't assume that your networking and data center teams will remember what they did to deploy the last ODA.

A couple of other good rules of thumb include understanding the lead times in your data center for requesting cabling, and to "make friends with your networking and data center people." The lead times may vary according to cabling type; for example, are you bridging copper to fiber? The point regarding making friends speaks for itself.

Request IP Addresses

The IP addresses needed to deploy an ODA are documented in the ODA Getting Started Guide chapter titled "About Oracle Database Appliance." The requirements to deploy an ODA are common to both the original Oracle Database Appliance and second-generation X3-2 models. The IP address range requirements for a physical ODA deployment, also known as a bare-metal install, are listed in Table 5-3.

Table 5-3. *Oracle Database Appliance IP requirements for a Bare-Metal (Nonvirtualized) Install*

IP Type	Number of IPs	Comment
Public	2	Two IP addresses are required for the two ODA server nodes. Each server requires an IP address for the physical host name.
Scan IPs	2	Two IP addresses to support the scan listener. ODAs run 2 scan listeners. The scan IP addresses need to be configured in DNS to be returned in round-robin order.
RAC VIP IPs	2	Typical RAC VIP address needed for each server node.
ILOM IPs	2	One ILOM or management network IP address per server node.
Additional networks	2	Two IP addresses per additional network, or one per server node; for example, a PBN or private backup network to support backups or NFS file system mounts.

The six public (host, scan, VIP) IP addresses need to be on the same network subnet, and they should be sequential. The minimum number of IP addresses needed to deploy an ODA is eight. This includes six public and two ILOM IPs. The Getting Started Guide lists the ILOM as required. ILOM connections can be made through the serial port, in addition to creating a permanent connection through the NetMgt interface. It should be noted that the configuration utility does not require ILOM IPs for the deployment.

In addition to the external networks, an ODA assigns four additional IPs to support the RAC interconnect and the deployment of two internal RAC networks to support HAIP (Highly Available IP) redundancy and failover. The RAC interconnect IP addresses are internally assigned, so they do not need to be requested from your network team.

The additional IP addresses required for a virtualized ODA deployment are listed in Table 5-4.

Table 5-4. Additional Oracle Database Appliance IP Requirements for a Virtualized Install

IP Type	Number of IPs	Comment
Dom0	2	Two IP addresses that are fixed by Oracle at 192.168.16.24, and 192.168.16.25.
Virtual machines	1	One additional IP address is required for each virtual machine that is deployed.

A virtualized ODA deployment only assigns two IPs to the RAC interconnect.

If possible, the IPs should be requested and assigned as soon as possible, or at least as soon as the security considerations are decided. Assigning the IP addresses in advance is a key step to support the implementation of DNS and firewall rules, as well as building the deployment configuration files. When these dependencies have been completed, the ODA deployment process can begin as soon as the ODA is racked and the network cabling is complete.

Build the Offline Configuration File

ODA deployment files are built using the Oracle Appliance Manager Configurator utility. The Appliance Manager can serve as an offline configurator to build the deployment files in advance. The Oracle Appliance Manager Configurator can currently be downloaded from Oracle using the following link:

www.oracle.com/technetwork/server-storage/engineered-systems/database-appliance/index.html

The Getting Started Guide details the process for using the Oracle Appliance Manager Configurator utility. The configuration utility can be run on the ODA in real-time mode to build the ODA interactively.

The ODA configuration utility can be run on your laptop or on the ODA. If you are running the ODA configuration utility from your laptop or desktop, make sure that you are running the version that matches the ODA software release you intend to install.

Figures 5-1 through 5-4 show a number of IP addresses. Those addresses were pulled from the ODA Getting Started Guide examples (or were otherwise manufactured) to avoid the use of real IP addresses. The following lists what the screenshots in the figures show:

- **Figure 5-1.** Select the hardware model and deployment type (physical or virtual).

- **Figure 5-2.** Configure the public and ILOM networks.

- **Figure 5-3.** Configure an additional network for backups or other purposes.

- **Figure 5-4.** Run the optional network validation step.

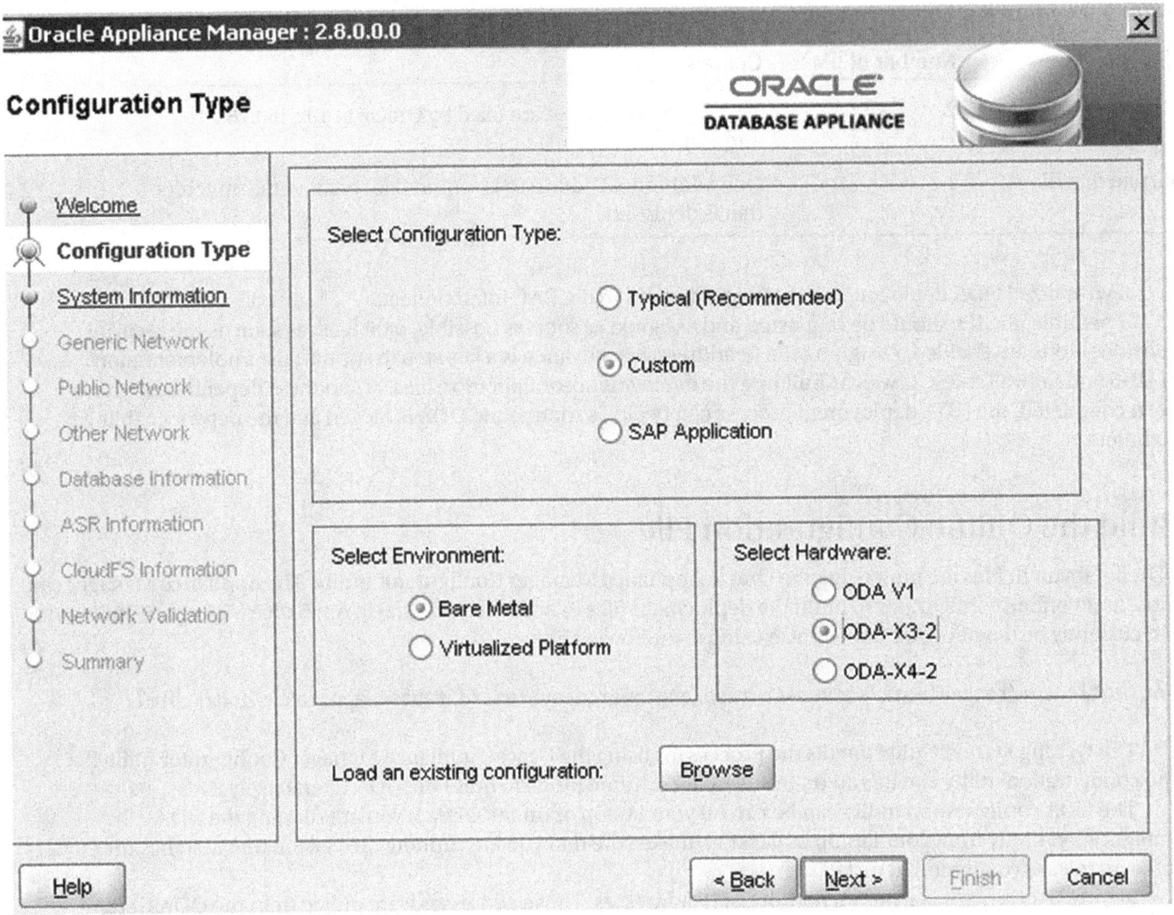

Figure 5-1. *Select the hardware model and deployment type (physical or virtual)*

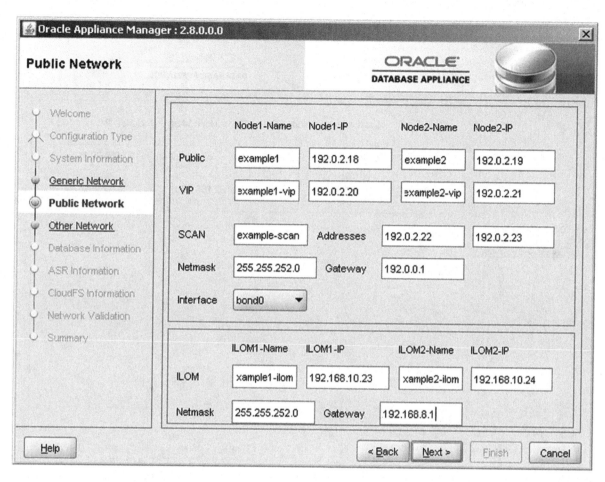

Figure 5-2. *Configure the public and ILOM networks*

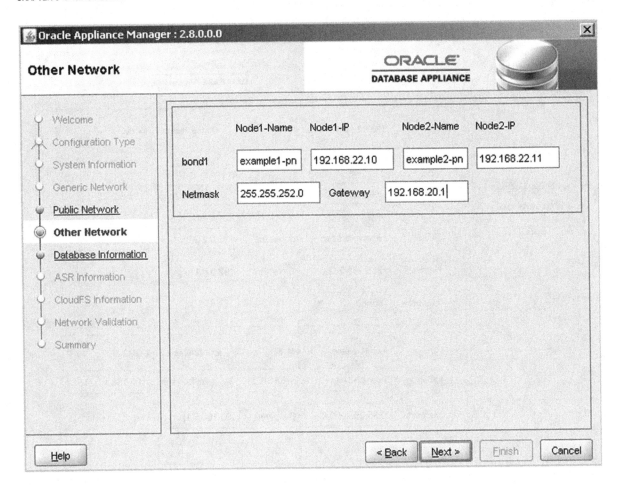

Figure 5-3. *Configure an additional network for backups or other purposes*

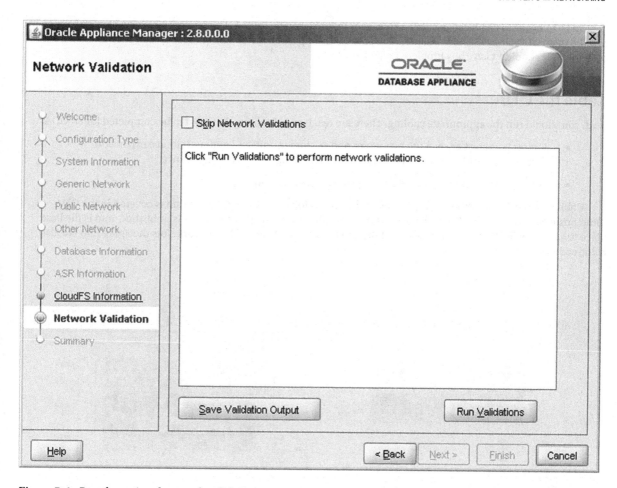

Figure 5-4. *Run the optional network validation step*

The network validation checks performed ensure that the following are true:

- The IP addresses about to be deployed are not already in use. The IP addresses should not be pingable.

- The network gateways should already be available. These IP addresses need to be pingable.

- All of the IP addresses and host names need to be resolvable in DNS, both in forward (host name to IP) and reverse (IP address to host name) lookup mode.

Rack the ODA

The ODA is a 4u rack mount unit, including the storage unit. Thus, it follows that you should put the unit into a rack in your data center. The ODA ships with a rack mount kit for that purpose.

■ **Note**   With a second storage unit, the rack footprint grows by another 2u to 6u.

An ODA needs to be placed in a data center rack before it can be cabled. The process for racking an ODA is covered in an ODA Owner's Guide chapter. The process is simple and the documentation is easy to follow. Your data center people shouldn't have any problem racking the ODA.

Cable the ODA

Next, you should run the appropriate cabling. There are two types of cabling that need to be completed for an ODA:

- Internal cabling between the two server nodes, storage unit, and optional storage expansion unit. Use the cabling supplied by Oracle, which is shipped with your appliance.

- Cabling to the external network. Here you must use your own cables.

Cabling together the server nodes, storage unit, and optional storage expansion unit is covered in the ODA setup poster shown in Figure 5-5. The poster represents the simplest explanation that is published, and is the best place to start. The first thing you notice is that the cables are color-coded. The network slots they plug into are also color-coded.

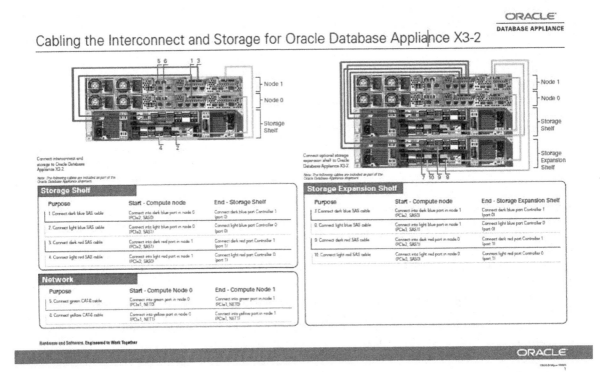

Figure 5-5. *The Oracle Database Appliance X3-2 setup poster shipped with each ODA*

■ **Note** The setup posters are shipped with each ODA and are also available in the Oracle manuals at http://docs.oracle.com.

The process outlined in the setup poster seems simple enough. And it is, almost. Some of the colors are very close to each other, so you have to pay attention to the shades. I've seen a few issues where data center people have made some mistakes with the connections, and sometimes it is the coloring that has thrown them off. This is an area where you can have someone on the team specialize in making these connections, rather than spreading this work around.

A more expanded set of documentation covering the connections between the server nodes and storage units is included in both the ODA Getting Started Guide and the ODA Owner's Guide. The manuals include additional charts that provide more details and can be easier to read than the setup poster.

To help validate the internal connections, Oracle recommends that you run `oakcli` to validate the cabling before starting the configuration of the public networks. This step is documented in the Getting Started Guide in both the "Deployment" and "Troubleshooting" chapters. The following is the command to validate the cabling:

```
# /opt/oracle/oak/bin/oakcli validate -c storagetopology
```

In addition to the cabling needed to connect the ODA components together, the external cabling needs to be completed. The external cabling includes the connections between the ODA and the network in your data center, as outlined in Table 5-2. This includes the cabling for your public network, private network, and ILOM connections. If the connections are bonded, each server node will have two public cable connections, two private network connections, and one ILOM connection—for a total of ten network cables for the two ODA server nodes. Of course, the connections can be reconfigured to not be bonded to deploy additional networks, if necessary. The procedures for modifying the network interfaces are covered in several Oracle support MOS notes, including 1422563.1, 1436335.1, and 1442113.1, as well as the Oracle Linux Administration manuals.

Apply the ILOM IP Addresses and Configure the ODA Public Network

There are a number of options for applying IP addresses to the ODA's network interfaces. These options are covered in the Oracle deployment documentation starting with the setup poster, Getting Started Guide, MOS note 1373617.1 for bare-metal deployments, or MOS note 1520579.1 for virtual deployments.

One area where the documentation could be a little clearer is the process for applying IP addresses to an ODA. All of the documentation points to logging into each of the ODA nodes as root using the default password, and then running the `firstnet` script on each server node to configure the public network for each host. There are also some references in the manuals on setting up the ILOM first, but the information isn't very clear. Accordingly, we'll try to clear things up.

First, setting up the ILOM to begin the process of adding IP addresses is the same on an ODA as it is on an Oracle Solaris server or any other piece of Oracle Linux hardware. If you have an experienced sysadmin working with you to deploy the ODA, he or she will already know what to. Starting the deployment of the ODA by applying the ILOM IPs first is a very efficient way to start the deployment.

If you are on your own to deploy the ODA, don't worry—getting started by adding the IP addresses to the ILOMs on each server is not hard. However, first you have to decide how you are going to connect to the ILOM device. There are at least two options:

- Connect to the ODA serial port using a laptop and a serial connection cable.

- Connect to the ODA using a serial console device such as a data center KVM cart or a data center KVM (keyboard, video, and mouse) appliance.

Connecting to the ODA ILOM through an ODA server serial port using your laptop with a serial cable is documented by Oracle in MOS note 1395445.1. Again, if you have people used to deploying Oracle hardware, they have already done this many times and know what to do. Regardless, the process is straightforward. Just follow the procedure outlined in the MOS note.

The key steps of the process are as follows:

1. Connect to the serial port on each node, starting with node 0 (the bottom unit).

2. Log in using the root account; use the ILOM default password "changeme".

3. Apply the ILOM IP address

The ILOM IPs are applied to each server using the following command syntax:

```
set /SP/network pendingipdiscovery=static
set /SP/network pendingipaddress=<IP Address>
set /SP/network pendingipgateway=<gateway-IPaddr>
set /SP/network pendingipnetmask=<netmask>
set /SP/network commitpending=true
```

Here is what the commands look like using non-real IP addresses:

```
set /SP/network pendingipdiscovery=static
set /SP/network pendingipaddress=10.0.0.3
set /SP/network pendingipgateway=10.0.0.1
set /SP/network pendingipnetmask=255.255.255.0
set /SP/network commitpending=true
```

The commands can also be chained together, as follows:

```
set /SP/network pendingipdiscovery=static pendingipaddress=10.0.0.3 pendingipgateway=10.0.0.1
pendingipnetmask=255.255.255.0 commitpending=true
```

You can validate the IP address by running the following command to display the ILOM IP addresses that have been configured:

```
-> show /SP/network
```

Most data centers will have a rolling KVM cart that can be used to start the deployment process. Some data centers will also have a KVM appliance with a web interface that can launch a console session for an ODA. The KVM appliances have multiple ports with serial cables that can be run to a data center rack and then connected to ODAs as needed. Using a KVM appliance avoids the need to go onsite to the data center to deploy the ODA.

Once the ILOM IP addresses have been applied, the public network IP addresses can be applied to the ODA. Oracle recommends that the cabling connections be validated first:

```
# /opt/oracle/oak/bin/oakcli validate -c storagetopology
```

If any issues are reported, you'll need to check the cabling on the system and then rerun the checks.

Once the ILOM IP addresses are in place and the cabling connections have been validated, you can connect from the ILOM to each server node to run the "firstnet" script to configure the public network for each host. The following public network configuration script is run on each node using the root account with the default root password "welcome1", starting with node 0 (the bottom unit):

```
# /opt/oracle/oak/bin/oakcli configure firstnet
```

Configure the Remaining Networks

Once you have applied the ILOM and host public network IP addresses, you are ready to continue with the deployment, which will apply the remaining IP addresses to your system. Run the ODA deployment process to configure the remaining networks.

If you used the Oracle Appliance Manager Configurator offline to build your deployment configuration file, which includes the IP addresses that have been assigned, you need to prepare the configuration file by running the oakcil copy command. If you're not using a configuration file, you can run the Appliance Manager Configurator interactively.

Prepare the previously created ODA configuration file by running oakcli with the full path and file name, where the file was copied to the ODA. The command syntax for this step is documented in the oakcli command reference in the appendix of the ODA Getting Started Guide.

```
# ./oakcli copy -conf /path/file_name.param
```

Deploy the ODA using the previously prepared configuration file:

```
# ./oakcli deploy -conf /path/file_name.param
```

Alternatively, you can deploy the ODA interactively (without a previously prepared configuration file):

```
# ./oakcli deploy
```

If you plan on using the interactive approach, be sure to run the command using a GUI interface through the ODA startx command or through the VNC Server that ships with ODAs.

Please be sure to read the complete set of documentation detailing all of the tasks required to deploy an ODA. Since this chapter only concerns ODA networking, I have limited the deployment steps to those related to the deployment of the ODA networks.

Post Deployment Options for Making Network Changes

There are a number of options for making network changes after the ODA has been deployed. One option is to start all over again by "bare metaling" your machine and starting over with your deployment. The procedures for doing this are outlined in MOS note 1373599.1. Depending on the status of your deployment, this may or may not be a practical option.

If you have an experienced Oracle hardware and OS sysadmin working with you, he or she will already be ready familiar with setting up the hardware and making network changes.

Oracle has published a number of MOS notes for making the following types of network changes:

- Implementing network bonding after the deployment has already been completed (MOS 1422563.1)

- Changing the ILOM Network IPs (MOS 1442113.1)

- Changing the DNS servers (MOS 1600317.1)

These notes are worth reading even if you don't need to change the IP addresses on any of your ODAs, because they highlight one of the automation features of an ODA: the GridInst.pl script.

The GridInst.pl script is documented in MOS note 1409835.1 and can be found in the following directory:

```
/opt/oracle/oak/onecmd/GridInst.pl
```

Here are some of the additional things that you can learn from reviewing these notes:

- The network configuration files are stored in /etc/sysconfig/networking and /etc/sysconfig/network-scripts.

- The DNS server entries are stored in the /etc/resolve.conf file.

- The ifconfig command can be used to display your ODA network settings.

- Your ODA deployment settings are stored in /opt/oracle/oak/onecmd/onecommand.params. After updating your ODA, you may need to generate new files or changes to files using the Oracle Appliance Manager configuration utility. The appliance manager version has to match the ODA version of the machine. This file is only readable by the root account.

- You can use the GridInst.pl script, which is run by the deployment process, to modify the existing ODA configurations, including changing the networks.

- Running the GridInst.pl script with the -l option—as in GridInst.pl -l—displays a current list of the individual deployment steps run by the script. The -l option is used to make sure you rerun the correct step when making changes to an ODA configuration.

- The ipmitool command can change the ILOM IPs by providing a wrapper to generate /SP/ Network commands.

Finally, if you have any questions regarding what version of the ODA software you are running on, you can run the following command as root: /opt/oracle/oak/bin/oakcli show version.

Virtualization Considerations

If you are virtualizing your ODA, you need an additional IP address for each virtual machine that will be created on the ODA. Support for multiple VLANs on an ODA was released in version 2.8, which was a week old at the time this chapter was written. Currently, all of the documentation for ODA virtualization support is published in the Getting Started Guide. Currently, this documentation details the following:

- How to create a VLAN

- How to delete a VLAN

- How to list the VLANs deployed on an ODA

Since multiple VLAN support on a virtualized ODA was just released, it will take some time for the documentation to cover all of the details needed to fully understand multiple VLAN support. Until the ODA virtualization documentation catches up, there are a couple of ways to try to fill the gap. First, you have to start with understanding why you might want to use multiple VLANs on a virtualized ODA. Second, you have to understand the background of virtualization on an ODA. VLANs, or virtualized local area networks, segment a physical network into multiple logical networks. This can be done to create multiple networks to share a single physical network, which will increase the number of available networks on an ODA. VLANs can also be created to provide multiple networks on an ODA to support network segmentation for security reasons, or to create VMs on specific networks to match the networks deployed for other components of the application. VLANs can be configured to control which network segment traffic can be routed between addresses to enhance network security.

Examples of virtualized networks that may be deployed on an ODA include a database network, multiple application networks, the management (ILOM) network, and backup or other special purpose networks. ODAs have a lot of capacity, and customers might only license part of the database cores on the appliance for database processing. This leaves capacity for other purposes, including running applications on ODAs.

Virtualization on an ODA was introduced in March 2013 under release 2.5 on the ODA V1, and 2.5.5 on the X3-2 model. Oracle virtualization has been around for a while, but the implementation is customized and simplified on an ODA. Instead of a separate virtual manager with a GUI console for managing VMs, their server pools, and networks, all of the deployment and management steps have been built into the command-line oak appliance kit (oakcli) utility. Accordingly Oracle, VM functionality has to be ported to ODAs, which means there is a development cycle with functionality delivered according to a roadmap and timelines.

The ODA virtualization functionality may lag behind the mainstream Oracle VM product. Regardless, Oracle is porting VM templates to ODAs. To keep up with the release cycle for supporting application templates, you can search "Oracle Database Appliance Solution in a Box" to learn about the new ODA application solutions being deployed by Oracle and its partners.

You have to remember that ODA virtualization implements VLANs created by your network team. They are not created by the ODA. Configuration work has to be performed at the network switches connected to the ODA to enable the virtual networks.

The key points to remember are that ODAs can implement virtual networks to support both the databases and applications deployed on a virtualized ODA appliance. Design and planning are required to properly create the networks for virtualized ODA solutions.

Summary

This chapter outlined the requirements for implementing the networks needed to support an ODA deployment. It provided a list of available networks, IP addresses, and cabling requirements, and detailed the process for deploying ODA networks.

The process for changing network information on an ODA after it has been deployed was outlined. Finally, some of the considerations that have to be made in a virtualized ODA environment were discussed.

ODAs offer a "keep it simple" model for deploying the appliances, including the configuration and setup of the networks. ODAs support the standard key Oracle Linux and hardware utilities for managing the appliance. As a result, the management of the appliance is flexible, while offering additional options, such as the GridInst.pl script for automating post deployment network changes.

CHAPTER 6

■ ■ ■

Monitoring the Oracle Database Appliance

The Oracle Database Appliance can be viewed as a single box or as two separate boxes, depending on how you want to monitor it. In reality, the Oracle Database Appliance is a machine that solves problems for businesses by shrinking the physical hardware footprint, yet increases overall usability. The Oracle Database Appliance can be used to help organizations be scalable with their architecture. When scaling out architectures with new hardware, especially with an engineered system like the Oracle Database Appliance, monitoring becomes a concern. How does one monitor the Oracle Database Appliance?

Monitoring the Oracle Database Appliance is quite the same as monitoring any other database environment; the difference is that you have two physical servers collocated in a single box. As discussed in previous chapters, the Oracle Database Appliance can have an associated database configured in Stand Alone (Enterprise Edition), Oracle RAC One, or Oracle Real Application Clusters (RAC) modes. All three configurations can be monitored in a few different ways. In this chapter, we will look at how to configure, verify, reconfigure, start, stop, and deconfigure a utility called Database Control for an Oracle 11g Release 2 database on the Oracle Database Appliance. This is the utility by which you control the appliance. Then later we will take a look at how to deploy Oracle Enterprise Manager Agents against the appliance.

■ **Note**   Oracle Database 12c has not been certified with the Oracle Database Appliance. The use of Enterprise Manager (EM) Express with the Oracle Database 12c on the Oracle Database Appliance has not been verified.

Configuring Database Control

Database Control is the lightweight version of the Oracle Enterprise Manager for Oracle Database 11g. The functionality provided by Database Control helps database administrators and developers identify and resolve performance and administrative issues that may be related to current and ongoing processing in the database.

There are three ways to configure Database Control: during installation, from Database Configuration Assistant (DBCA), and from the command line using the Enterprise Manager Configuration Assistant (EMCA). For the purpose of this chapter, let's focus on configuring the Database Control with the EMCA tool.

Using the Enterprise Manager Configuration Assistant (EMCA)

As with anything a DBA does from the command line, you need to set your Oracle Home for the database that is to be configured. On the Oracle Database Appliance, this is as simple as running the oraenv command to set the environment. Listing 6-1 gives an example of how to set the environment and how to check the environment once set.

Listing 6-1. Setting the Oracle Environment and Checking It

```
$ . oraenv
ORACLE_SID = [oracle] ? dboda
The Oracle base has been set to /u01/app/oracle

$ env | grep ORA
ORACLE_SID=dboda
ORACLE_BASE=/u01/app/oracle
ORACLE_HOME=/u01/app/oracle/product/11.2.0.3/dbhome_1
```

Now that the Oracle environment is set, you can run the emca utility from either the bin directory under the Oracle Home or from where you currently are. Listing 6-2 illustrates running the emca utility from the Oracle Home bin directory.

Listing 6-2. Execute EMCA from bin

```
$ cd $ORACLE_HOME/bin
$ ./emca
```

When running the emca command, there are optional parameters that can be passed on the command line to help configure the Database Control. Table 6-1 will help you understand what these parameters are. The Enterprise Manager Configuration Assistant (EMCA) command follows a simple form, as outlined in Listing 6-3.

Listing 6-3. EMCA Command Pattern

```
./emca [operation] [mode] [flags] [parameters]
```

Table 6-1. *EMCA Command-Line Parameters*

Parameter	Description
-respFile	Specifies the path of an input file listing parameters for EMCA to use while performing its configuration operation. For more information, see "Using an Input File for EMCA Parameters."
-SID	Database system identifier.
-PORT	Port number for the listener servicing the database.
-ORACLE_HOME	Database Oracle Home, as an absolute path.
-ORACLE_HOSTNAME	Local database hostname.
-LISTENER_OH	Oracle home from which the listener is running. If the listener is running from an Oracle Home other than the one on which the database is running, the parameter LISTENER_OH must be specified.

(continued)

Table 6-1. (*continued*)

Parameter	Description
-HOST_USER	Host system user name (for automatic backup).
-HOST_USER_PWD	Host system user password (for automatic backup).
-BACKUP_SCHEDULE	Schedule in the form of "HH:MM" for daily automatic backups.
-EMAIL_ADDRESS	E-mail address for notifications.
-MAIL_SERVER_NAME	Outgoing Mail (SMTP) server for notifications.
-ASM_OH	Oracle ASM Oracle Home.
-ASM_SID	System identifier for Oracle ASM instance.
-ASM_PORT	Port number for the listener servicing the Oracle ASM instance.
-ASM_USER_ROLE	User role for connecting to the Oracle ASM instance.
-ASM_USER_NAME	User name for connecting to the Oracle ASM instance.
-ASM_USER_PWD	Password for connecting to the Oracle ASM instance.
-DBSNMP_PWD	Password for the DBSNMP user.
-SYSMAN_PWD	Password for the SYSMAN user.
-SYS_PWD	Password for the SYS user.
-SRC_OH	Oracle Home of the database with Enterprise Manager configuration to be upgraded or restored.
-DBCONTROL_HTTP_PORT	Use this parameter to specify the port that you use to display the Database Control Console in your web browser. For more information, see "Specifying the Ports Used by Database Control."
-AGENT_PORT	Use this parameter to specify the Management Agent port for Database Control. For more information, see "Specifying the Ports Used by Database Control."
-RMI_PORT	Use this parameter to specify the RMI port for Database Control. For more information, see "Specifying the Ports Used by Database Control."
-JMS_PORT	Use this parameter to specify the JMS port for Database Control. For more information, see "Specifying the Ports Used by Database Control."
-CLUSTER_NAME	Cluster name (for cluster databases).
-DB_UNIQUE_NAME	Database unique name (for cluster databases).
-SERVICE_NAME	Database service name (for cluster databases).
-EM_NODE	Node from which Database Control console is to be run (for cluster databases). For more information, see "Using EMCA With Oracle RAC."
-EM_NODE_LIST	Comma-delimited list of NODEs for agent-only configurations, uploading data to -EM_NODE. For more information, see "Using EMCA With Oracle RAC."
-EM_SWLIB_STAGE_LOC	Software library location.
-PORTS_FILE	Path to a static file specifying the ports to use. The default value is :${ORACLE_HOME}/install/staticports.ini.

To provide additional information, the -help option can be used to list all parameters associated with the emca utility. Listing 6-4 provides the syntax required to bring up the help options.

Listing 6-4. EMCA Help Option

```
$ ./emca -help
```

Now that you have a basic understanding of the emca utility, you are going to configure Database Control on the Oracle Database Appliance. In many cases, you will be configuring Database Control against a Real Application Cluster. Before you can configure Database Control, you will need to change the job_queue_processes for the database that you are working with. Listing 6-5 shows you the alter system command that is required to change the job_queue_processes parameter. In order to do that, you need to specify a few extra parameters on the command line. The example in Listing 6-5 increases the allowed number of job queue processes to a number greater than zero. Doing that helps later with the configuration of Database Control.

Listing 6-5. Change the job_queue_processes for the Database

```
SQL> alter system set job_queue_processes = 10 scope=both sid='*';
```

To configure Database Control for a cluster database on the Oracle Database Appliance, the command is as simple as the example listed in Listing 6-6. Again, notice that Listing 6-6 is showing you how to run the emca utility from the Oracle Home bin directory.

Listing 6-6. Configuring Database Control for a RAC database

```
$ cd $ORACLE_HOME/bin
$ ./emca -config dbcontrol db -repos create -cluster
```

When the configuration is started, emca will ask you for a series of inputs. Provide the inputs required. The parameters that emca is looking for can be passed on the command line as options or in a parameter file. Table 6-1 provides a list of the parameters that can be passed on the command line or in a parameter file.

Using a Parameter File

When configuring Database Control with emca, there are a lot of flags, options, and parameters that can be used for specific configuration reasons. In order to keep the typing to a minimal and make it easier configure, the option to use a parameter file is available.

To use a parameter file, include the -repFile command-line parameter on the command line when running emca. Listing 6-7 shows the contents of a parameter file used with the emca command.

Listing 6-7. Parameter File Contents

```
PORT=1521
SID=patty
DBSNMP_PWD=<pass>
SYSMAN_PWD=<pass>
```

After creating the parameter file, Listing 6-8 shows you how it can be referenced from the command line. Focus on the -repfile parameter.

Listing 6-8. EMCA with a Parameter File

```
$cd $ORACLE_HOME/bin
$ ./emca -config dbcontrol db -repos create -repFile input_path_to_file
```

The command listed in Listing 6-8 shows you how to specify a response file when executing the emca utility. Using a response file makes the configuration of the Database Control much easier and provides a repeatable approach for future configurations.

Controlling Database Control

At times, you will need to check to see if Database Control is running. The Enterprise Manager Control (emctl) command is used to check on the Database Control from the command line. Using the emctl command, you can check the status, and stop and start the Database Control.

Status of Database Control

Once Database Control is configured, the status can be checked using the command in Listing 6-9. Listing 6-9 also provides a sample of output from a successful status check.

Listing 6-9. Status of the Database Control

```
$ cd $ORACLE_HOME/bin
$ ./emctl status dbconsole
```

The output from the command is as follows:

```
[oracle@patty bin]$ ./emctl status dbconsole
Oracle Enterprise Manager 11g Database Control Release 11.2.0.3.0
Copyright (c) 1996, 2011 Oracle Corporation.  All rights reserved.
https://patty.enkitec.com:1158/em/console/aboutApplication
Oracle Enterprise Manager 11g is running.
------------------------------------------------------------------
Logs are generated in directory /u01/app/oracle/product/11.2.0.3/dbhome_1/patty_dboda/sysman/log
```

Stopping Database Control

There will be times where you need to stop Database Control. These times include when you need to do maintenance, reconfiguration, or scheduled outages of the database. To stop Database Control, you need to use the emctl command, as shown in Listing 6-10.

Listing 6-10. Stop Database Control

```
$ cd $ORACLE_HOME/bin
$ ./emctl stop dbconsole
```

When you stop Database Control, it is often a best practice to check the status afterward to verify that Database Control really is stopped. Listing 6-11 shows a stop command followed by a status check to verify that the stop actually occurred.

Listing 6-11. Examples of Stopping and Status

```
[oracle@patty bin]$ ./emctl stop dbconsole
Oracle Enterprise Manager 11g Database Control Release 11.2.0.3.0
Copyright (c) 1996, 2011 Oracle Corporation. All rights reserved.
https://patty.enkitec.com:1158/em/console/aboutApplication
Stopping Oracle Enterprise Manager 11g Database Control ...
   ... Stopped.

[oracle@patty bin]$ ./emctl status dbconsole
Oracle Enterprise Manager 11g Database Control Release 11.2.0.3.0
Copyright (c) 1996, 2011 Oracle Corporation. All rights reserved.
https://patty.enkitec.com:1158/em/console/aboutApplication
Oracle Enterprise Manager 11g is not running.
Deconfigure Database Console
```

Start Database Control

If Database Control is down, you will need it to be up in order to monitor the database instances that are running on your server. Starting Database Control is as easy as stopping the Database Control. To start Database Control, you use the start option to the emctl command. Listing 6-12 illustrates.

Listing 6-12. Start Database Control

```
$ cd $ORACLE_HOME/bin
$ ./emctl stop dbconsole
```

Again, it is a good practice to check the status to verify that Database Control came up successfully. Listing 6-13 shows a start command followed by a status check.

Listing 6-13. Examples of Starting and Status

```
[oracle@patty bin]$ ./emctl start dbconsole
Oracle Enterprise Manager 11g Database Control Release 11.2.0.3.0
Copyright (c) 1996, 2011 Oracle Corporation. All rights reserved.
https://patty.enkitec.com:1158/em/console/aboutApplication
Starting Oracle Enterprise Manager 11g Database Control .... started.
------------------------------------------------------------------
Logs are generated in directory /u01/app/oracle/product/11.2.0.3/dbhome_1/patty_dboda/sysman/log

[oracle@patty bin]$ ./emctl status dbconsole
Oracle Enterprise Manager 11g Database Control Release 11.2.0.3.0
Copyright (c) 1996, 2011 Oracle Corporation. All rights reserved.
https://patty.enkitec.com:1158/em/console/aboutApplication
Oracle Enterprise Manager 11g is running.
------------------------------------------------------------------
Logs are generated in directory /u01/app/oracle/product/11.2.0.3/dbhome_1/patty_dboda/sysman/log
```

Up to this point, you have taken a look at how to check the status, how to stop, and how to start Database Control. In some environments, there will be times when you either need to create or re-create Database Control in order to reconfigure it. In the next section, you will take a look at how to reconfigure the Database Control.

Reconfiguring the Database Console

With the Oracle 11g Release 2 version of the Database Control, there have been occasions in which the control needs to be rebuilt or reconfigured. Reconfiguring of the Database Control often corrects any issues that may have occurred in the repository for the control. To reconfigure the Database Control, you need to invoke the Enterprise Manager Configuration Assistant (emca) with the recreate option. The following emca command (see Listing 6-14) will reconfigure the Database Control and re-create the repository for the database on the Oracle Database Appliance.

Listing 6-14. recreate Command

```
$ cd $ORACLE_HOME/bin
$ ./emca -config dbcontrol db -repos recreate -cluster
```

When reconfiguring Database Control, the emca command will ask you for a few parameters. These parameters can be passed on the command line or in a parameter file. These parameters can be found in Table 6-1. The output in Listing 6-15 is from reconfiguring Database Control for a cluster database on the Oracle Database Appliance. The output has been shortened to highlight the areas that are of concern when reconfiguring Database Control.

Listing 6-15. Output from emca Reconfigure of Database Control

```
STARTED EMCA at Oct 9, 2013 4:47:58 AM
EM Configuration Assistant, Version 11.2.0.3.0 Production
Copyright (c) 2003, 2011, Oracle. All rights reserved.

Enter the following information:
Database unique name: dboda
Service name: dboda
Listener ORACLE_HOME [ /u01/app/11.2.0.3/grid ]:
Password for SYS user: come
Database Control is already configured for the database dboda
You have chosen to configure Database Control for managing the database dboda
This will remove the existing configuration and the default settings and perform a fresh
configuration
----------------------------------------------------------------------
WARNING : While repository is dropped the database will be put in quiesce mode.
----------------------------------------------------------------------
Do you wish to continue? [yes(Y)/no(N)]: y
Password for DBSNMP user:
Password for SYSMAN user:
Cluster name: dboda_cluster
Email address for notifications (optional):
Outgoing Mail (SMTP) server for notifications (optional):
ASM ORACLE_HOME [ /u01/app/11.2.0.3/grid ]:
ASM port [ 1521 ]:
ASM username [ ASMSNMP ]:
ASM user password:
Oct 9, 2013 4:48:41 AM oracle.sysman.emcp.util.GeneralUtil initSQLEngineRemotely
WARNING: Error during db connection : ORA-12514: TNS:listener does not currently know of service
requested in connect descriptor
```

```
------------------------------------------------------------------

You have specified the following settings

Database ORACLE_HOME ................ /u01/app/oracle/product/11.2.0.3/dbhome_1

Database instance hostname ............... Listener ORACLE_HOME ................
/u01/app/11.2.0.3/grid
Listener port number ................ 1521
Cluster name ................ dboda_cluster
Database unique name ................ dboda
Email address for notifications ..............
Outgoing Mail (SMTP) server for notifications ..............
ASM ORACLE_HOME ................ /u01/app/11.2.0.3/grid
ASM port ................ 1521
ASM user role ................ SYSDBA
ASM username ................ ASMSNMP


-------------------------------------------------------------
-------------------------------------------------------------
WARNING : While repository is dropped the database will be put in quiesce mode.
-------------------------------------------------------------
Do you wish to continue? [yes(Y)/no(N)]: y
Oct 9, 2013 4:48:49 AM oracle.sysman.emcp.EMConfig perform
INFO: This operation is being logged at /u01/app/oracle/cfgtoollogs/emca/dboda/
emca_2013_10_09_04_47_58.log.
   .
   .
   .
   .
INFO: >>>>>>>>>> The Database Control URL is https://patty.enkitec.com:1158/em <<<<<<<<<<<
Oct 9, 2013 4:57:56 AM oracle.sysman.emcp.EMDBPostConfig showClusterDBCAgentMessage
INFO:
**************** Current Configuration  ****************
  INSTANCE          NODE          DBCONTROL_UPLOAD_HOST
 ----------        ----------    ----------------------

 dboda              patty          patty.enkitec.com
 dboda              selma          patty.enkitec.com


Oct 9, 2013 4:57:56 AM oracle.sysman.emcp.EMDBPostConfig invoke
WARNING:
********************** WARNING  **********************
```

Management Repository has been placed in secure mode wherein Enterprise Manager data will be encrypted. The encryption key has been placed in the file: /u01/app/oracle/product/11.2.0.3/ dbhome_1/patty_dboda/sysman/config/emkey.ora. Ensure this file is backed up as the encrypted data will become unusable if this file is lost.

```
**********************************************************
Enterprise Manager configuration completed successfully
FINISHED EMCA at Oct 9, 2013 4:57:56 AM
```

Deconfiguring Database Control

Deconfiguring is as simple as what you did to originally configure. Simply invoke emca using the parameter –deconfig. The -deconfig option will begin the process of deconfiguring l. Listing 6-16 shows how to deconfigure Database Control for the current database on the Oracle Database Appliance.

Listing 6-16. Deconfigure the Database Control

```
$ cd $ORACLE_HOME/bin
$ ./emca -deconfig dbcontrol db
```

When the deconfiguration begins, the emca utility will ask you for the ORACLE_SID value associated with the Database Control you are deconfiguring. Provide that ORACLE_SID value; then emca will ask if you really want to deconfigure Database Control. This is a confirmation prompt, and an answer is needed. Once the deconfiguration is complete, the database console will not be usable or accessible for the associated database.

Listing 6-17 shows output from a typical deconfiguration operation.

Listing 6-17. Deconfiguration Output

```
STARTED EMCA at Oct 8, 2013 9:24:18 AM
EM Configuration Assistant, Version 11.2.0.3.0 Production
Copyright (c) 2003, 2011, Oracle.  All rights reserved.

Enter the following information:
Database SID: bc11gtst

Do you wish to continue? [yes(Y)/no(N)]: y
Oct 8, 2013 9:24:28 AM oracle.sysman.emcp.EMConfig perform
INFO: This operation is being logged at /opt/oracle/cfgtoollogs/emca/bc11gtst/
emca_2013_10_08_09_24_17.log.
Oct 8, 2013 9:24:29 AM oracle.sysman.emcp.util.DBControlUtil stopOMS
INFO: Stopping Database Control (this may take a while) ...
Enterprise Manager configuration completed successfully
FINISHED EMCA at Oct 8, 2013 9:25:04 AM
```

Why might you wish to deconfigure Database Control? One answer boils down to using Enterprise Manager instead. When faced with monitoring more than just the single database or a single cluster database, many organizations begin to look at implementing Oracle Enterprise Manager, a product widely used for monitoring more than one database in an enterprise environment. By contrast, Database Control is traditionally used for a single database or a single cluster database within the environment. Thus, the need to manage multiple databases via Enterprise Manager is one reason you might choose to deconfigure Database Control.

With Oracle Enterprise Manager being used, there is no need to have Database Control configured. This is due to the overhead that will be contributed by running Database Control along with the Oracle Management Agent needed by Oracle Enterprise Manager. When using the Oracle Database Appliance as the Oracle Enterprise Manager repository and management server, deconfiguring Database Control is *required*.

Supporting Oracle Enterprise Manager

Up until this point, you have reviewed how to manage the Oracle Database Appliance with Oracle Database Control. As mentioned earlier, the database console only supports and can be configured against a single database or Real Application Cluster (RAC). As the Oracle Database Appliance becomes more commonplace in enterprises, these engineered systems will need to be monitored, just as many other resources are today.

Oracle Enterprise Manager provides and allows for a single point of monitoring. Oracle Enterprise Manager further allows for the Oracle Database Appliance to be managed just like any other commodity resource.

■ **Note** Currently, the Oracle Database Appliance does not have an engineered system plug-in to manage the hardware layer as Exadata does. The lack of a plug-in makes managing the Oracle Database Appliance like managing any other commodity hardware.

Now that it has been established that the Oracle Database Appliance is managed just the same as any commodity hardware-driven Real Application Cluster, how do we enable Oracle Enterprise Manager to monitor and manage the Oracle Database Appliance? Just as any other resources that Oracle Enterprise Manager can monitor and manage, the Oracle Database Appliance needs to have the Oracle Management Agent installed on both nodes of the appliance.

The Oracle Management Agent is one of the three core management pieces of the Oracle Enterprise Manager. It is the only management piece that is required to be installed on monitored targets. The Oracle Management Agent, once installed, takes an unmanaged host and makes it a managed host that can be interacted with through Oracle Enterprise Manager. The agent works with plug-ins to provide management capabilities for a wide range of targets on the host.

When managing the Oracle Database Appliance with Oracle Enterprise Manager, ensure that a management agent is installed on each node of the appliance.

■ **Note** Out of the box, the Oracle Database Appliance ships with Oracle Enterprise Linux (64-bit). Depending on the configuration of your Oracle Enterprise Manager, additional management agents may need to be downloaded to the software library.

Let's take a look at how to add the Oracle Database Appliance as a target to Oracle Enterprise Manager. Begin by going to **Setup ➤ Add Target ➤ Add Targets Manually**, as shown in Figure 6-1.

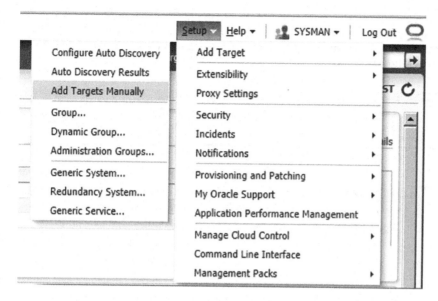

Figure 6-1. Set up targets manually

Since we want to add the Oracle Database Appliance to Oracle Enterprise Manager, we need to add the host targets. The host targets for Oracle Database Appliance are the two internal servers that make up the Real Application Cluster within the Oracle Database Appliance. Figure 6-2 shows that we selected Add Host Targets. Once you've made that selection, click the Add Host button.

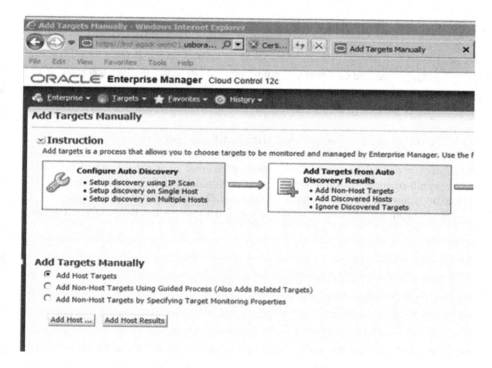

Figure 6-2. Add Targets Manually

On the next screen, we need to specify the two hosts that we want to add to the Oracle Enterprise Manager. We also need to specify their operating system. The Oracle Database Appliance ships with Oracle Enterprise Linux (64-bit); you need to make sure to select the correct operating system. Figure 6-3 shows the input screen that should be displayed when adding a new host target(s).

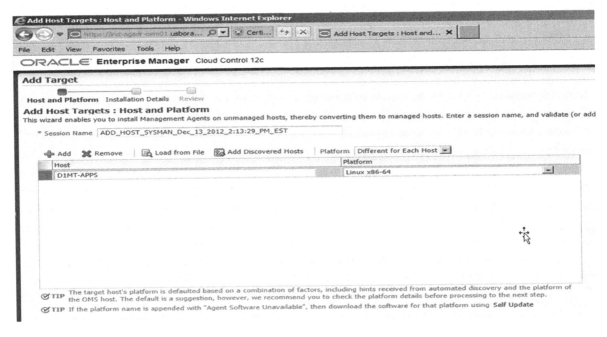

Figure 6-3. *Add Host Targets*

■ **Note**   If the Oracle Enterprise Manager is installed on a host that is not Linux (64-bit) based, then you will need to download the correct agent software from Oracle through Oracle Enterprise Manager.

After filling in the host and platform information, you are taken to the Installation Details page shown in Figure 6-4. On this page, you add the specifics related to the hosts you are adding. You are adding an Oracle Database Appliance; the Installation Base Directory on both hosts will be the same. All the other installation details should be filled in; if not, provide the necessary information. The option for Named Credentials needs to be populated with either an existing credential, or create a new one by clicking the plus (+) button. Once all the installation details are provided, installation of the Oracle Management Agent can continue. Figure 6-4 illustrates how the installation details should look when filled out.

Figure 6-4. *Agent Installation Details*

Once all the information is provided for Installation Details, as shown in Figure 6-4, click Next to advance the wizard. This will take you to the Review screen in Figure 6-5. From there, you can see all the items you have entered through the wizard. Click Deploy Agent to begin the deployment of the agent.

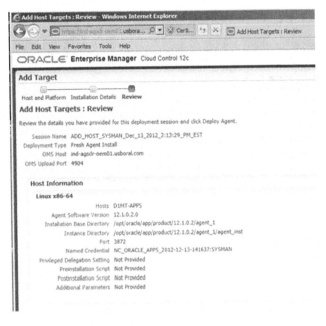

Figure 6-5. *Add Target Review screen*

Once the deployment begins, it can be monitored on the Add Host Status screen. This screen is shown in Figure 6-6.

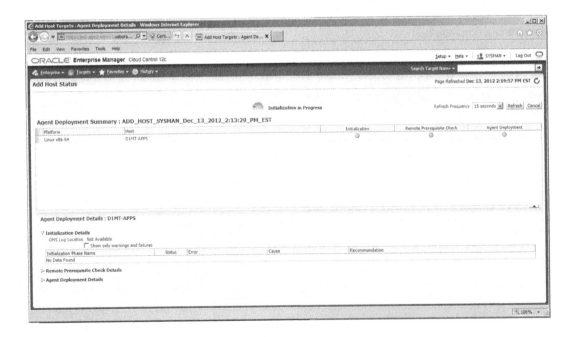

Figure 6-6. *Add Host Status*

■ **Note** To manage the databases, listeners, and Automatic Storage Management (ASM) instances on the Oracle Database Appliance, the database plug-in needs to be deployed on the Oracle Management Server and Oracle Management Agents on the Oracle Database Appliance. The plug-in will be deployed automatically when the agent is deployed through Oracle Enterprise Manager.

Summary

In this chapter, we discussed two methods—both configured on an Oracle Database Appliance—for monitoring the Oracle Database. The first method uses Oracle Database Control. We discussed Oracle Database Control, including how to configure it, manage it, and deconfigure it. The second method uses the Oracle Enterprise Manager. We discussed how it relates to the Oracle Database Appliance, how to install management agents to enable it to monitor the appliance, and what can be expected from using it with the appliance.

■ ■ ■

## CHAPTER 7

Diagnosing the Oracle Database Appliance

The Oracle Database Appliance (ODA) is a self-sufficient device, and care has been taken to provide a variety of checks and balances to allow for optimal operation of the appliance, as well as the databases that reside on it. It is very important to understand the diagnostic capabilities built into the Appliance itself and apply them as needed to solve various trivial and nontrivial activities.

The ODA now has had two hardware iterations and multiple software iterations to improve and add various features. The ODA software updates have brought together many diagnostic capabilities. Some have been added to the standard Oracle Appliance Kit (OAK) command set, whereas others are accessible via preinstalled tools and through capabilities available in the hardware and the operating system. We will be looking at bare-metal appliance install diagnostics in this chapter. Virtualization diagnostics will be covered in Chapter 10.

ODA diagnostics can be looked at in two ways:

- Proactively

- Reactively

This chapter will look at various techniques available to the ODA admin team to understand and debug various issues. Database-related diagnosis is not in the scope of this book, and all standard database monitoring and diagnostics techniques still apply to a database running on the ODA.

Proactive Diagnostics

An ODA is a server, and as such it is very important that care be taken in handling and performing various functions on the device. There are multiple ways to proactively ensure that the ODA is performing to the satisfaction of the customer. Oracle provides a set of one-button utilities that are embedded in the OAK framework. OAK provides a complete set of utilities to allow users to perform various activities, from deployment to diagnostics. It is discussed in detail in various chapters of this book.

Validation

The first set of diagnostics that we will look at is validation. The ODA comes with prebuilt validation functionality that has evolved with each version of the software. Validation is the first step in proactive diagnostics and should be executed at install, and then again after every software patch or change to ensure that the system is performing as expected. A baseline should be established and maintained to ensure consistency is there. Depending on the workload and the version of software on the ODA, there might be additional validation built into the utility as the platform matures.

Validation is part of the OAK command set and can be accessed through the `oakcli validate` command. There are multiple parts of `oakcli validate`, and we will look at them in detail. To see what `oakcli validate` provides, we can look at the help first.

```
[root@oda1 bin]# ./oakcli validate -h
Usage:
 oakcli  validate [-V | -l | -h]
 oakcli  validate [-v] [-f absolute output_file_name] [-a | -d | -c check1[,check2]]
            ARGUMENTS:
                    -v      verbose output
                    -f      output_file_name.The output is sent to the file instead of
                            standard output
                    -a      run all checks
                    -d      run only default checks.
                    -c      check1[,check2] run specific checks
                    -l      list the checks and description
                    -V      Print the Version
                    -h      print help
            EXAMPLES:
            oakcli validate -l
            oakcli validate -a
            oakcli validate -c DiskCalibration
            oakcli validate -c SystemComponents,NetworkComponents,asr
```

The OAK validate checks depend on the version of the software that is installed. ODA 2.6 added Automatic Service Request (ASR) validation to ensure that ASR is installed and configured in the appropriate manner. Executing a `validate` command without any options will result in the following checks being made:

- System components
- OS disk storage
- Shared storage
- Network components
- Storage topology (X3-2 only)

Disk calibration and ASR (new in 2.6) are not executed by default. The storage topology step (#5) validates the shared disk array and the optional storage shelf that was introduced with ODA X3-2. That step will be executed by default on the ODA X3-2 platform only.

Listing 7-1 shows a brief description of the ODA V1 validate commands that are available as of OAK 2.6.

Listing 7-1. Validation Options for ODA V1

```
[root@oda1 bin]# ./oakcli validate -l
Checkname               Description
=========               ===========
*SystemComponent        Validate system components based on ilom sensor data readings
*OSDiskStorage          Validate OS disks and filesystem information
*SharedStorage          Validate Shared storage and multipathing information
DiskCalibration         Check disk performance with orion
*NetworkComponents      Validate public and private network components
asr                     Validate asr components based on asr config file and ilom
                        sensor data readings

* -- These checks are also performed as part of default checks
```

Listing 7-2 shows that there are added validation commands in ODA X3-2 vs. its predecessor, ODA V1. In ODA X3-2, storage is external. This means that it's important to ensure that external storage connectivity is properly validated.

Listing 7-2. Validation Options for ODA X3-2

```
[root@odax32 bin]# ./oakcli validate -l

Checkname           Description
=========           ===========
*SystemComponent    Validate system components based on ilom sensor data readings
*OSDiskStorage      Validate OS disks and filesystem information
*SharedStorage      Validate Shared storage and multipathing information
DiskCalibration     Check disk performance with orion
*NetworkComponents  Validate public and private network components
*StorageTopology    Validate external JBOD connectivity
asr                 Validate asr components based on asr config file and ilom
                    sensor data readings
```

■ **Note**   Disk calibration does not work on ODA X3-2 due to an internal bug in ODA 2.6.

Validation checks are arranged into various subcategories. We will look at each subcategory and explain each set of checks individually.

System Component Checks

System components checks are key to ensuring a healthy ODA. As database administrators, we tend to ignore looking at the health of the hardware itself. OAK provides validations to the system components in a manner that is easy for people who are not very proficient in understanding hardware-related metrics.

Since the system components on ODA V1 and X3-2 are different, the validation will provide different results on both appliances. The checks comprise the following entities:

- Software inventory
- System information
- BIOS information
- Controller information
- System ILOM and BMC firmware version
- Power supply and cooling unit status
- Processor and memory status
- OS disk status
- Expander and shared disk status (ODA V1 only)
- Temperature of various components

Listing 7-3 displays the output that is expected from running a system components check on the ODA V1. This output will differ depending on the version of OAK software that is running. This means the output in Listing 7-3 is provided as an example.

Listing 7-3. Validating ODA V1 System Components (ODA 2.6)

```
root@oda1 bin]# ./oakcli validate -c SystemComponents
INFO: oak system information and Validations
RESULT: System Software inventory details
 Reading the metadata. It takes a while...
 System Version  Component Name        Installed Version     Supported Version
 --------------  --------------        -----------------     -----------------

 2.6.0.0.0
                 Controller            11.05.02.00           Up-to-date
                 Expander              0342                  Up-to-date
                 SSD_SHARED            E12B                  Up-to-date
                 HDD_LOCAL             SA03                  Up-to-date
                 HDD_SHARED            0B25                  Up-to-date
                 ILOM                  3.0.16.22.b r78329    Up-to-date
                 BIOS                  12010310              Up-to-date
                 IPMI                  1.8.10.5              Up-to-date
                 HMP                   2.2.6.1               Up-to-date
                 OAK                   2.6.0.0.0             Up-to-date
                 OEL                   5.8                   Up-to-date
                 TFA                   2.5.1.4               Up-to-date
                 GI_HOME               11.2.0.3.6(16056266,  Up-to-date
                                       16083653)
                 DB_HOME               11.2.0.3.6(16056266,  Up-to-date
                                       16083653)
                 ASR                   4.4                   Up-to-date
RESULT: System Information:-
        Manufacturer:ORACLE CORPORATION
        Product Name:SUN FIRE X4370 M2 SERVER
        Serial Number:XXXXXXXXXXX
RESULT: BIOS Information:-
        Vendor:American Megatrends Inc.
        Version:12010310
        Release Date:08/14/2012
        BIOS Revision:1.3
        Firmware Revision:1.3
SUCCESS: Controller p1 has the IR Bypass mode set correctly
SUCCESS: Controller p2 has the IR Bypass mode set correctly
INFO: Reading ilom data, may take short while..
INFO: Read the ilom data. Doing Validations
RESULT: System ILOM Version: 3.0.16.22.b r78329
RESULT: System BMC firmware version  3.0
RESULT: Powersupply PS0 V_IN=206 Volts I_IN=2 Amps V_OUT=12.16 Volts I_OUT=30.80
        Amps IN_POWER=420 Watts OUT_POWER=390 Watts
RESULT: Powersupply PS1 V_IN=208 Volts I_IN=2 Amps V_OUT=12.16 Volts I_OUT=30.20
        Amps IN_POWER=420 Watts OUT_POWER=370 Watts
```

```
SUCCESS: Both the powersupply are ok and functioning
RESULT: Cooling Unit FM0 fan speed F0=7700 RPM F1=6300 RPM
RESULT: Cooling Unit FM1 fan speed F0=7600 RPM F1=6500 RPM
SUCCESS: Both the cooling unit are present
RESULT: Processor P0 present Details:-
        Version:Intel(R) Xeon(R) CPU         X5675  @ 3.07GHz
        Current Speed:3066 MHz  Core Enabled:6  Thread Count:12
SUCCESS: All 6 memory modules of CPU P0 ok, each module is of Size:8192 MB Type:DDR3
        Speed:1333 MHz manufacturer:Samsung
RESULT: Processor P1 present Details:-
        Version:Intel(R) Xeon(R) CPU         X5675  @ 3.07GHz
        Current Speed:3066 MHz  Core Enabled:6  Thread Count:12
SUCCESS: All 6 memory modules of CPU P1 ok, each module is of Size:8192 MB Type:DDR3
        Speed:1333 MHz manufacturer:Samsung
RESULT: Total System Memory is 98929480 kB
SUCCESS: All OS Disks are present and in ok state
SUCCESS: All expander present and ok status
SUCCESS: All shared Disks are present and in ok state
RESULT: Temperature System Board=37 degrees C||Riser Board=35 degrees
        C||Power Supply=31 degrees C
```

Listing 7-4 provides an example of an issue being uncovered through validation. The example shows that there was a problem with a power supply, and all power was being drawn from only one power supply rather than from two, as is normally the case.

Listing 7-4. Uncovering a Problem Through a Validation Check

```
Validation failure RESULT: Powersupply PS0 V_IN=Disabled I_IN=Disabled V_OUT=0.88
Volts I_OUT=2 Amps IN_POWER=Disabled OUT_POWER=Disabled
RESULT: Powersupply PS1 V_IN=206 Volts I_IN=3.75 Amps V_OUT=12.08 Volts I_OUT=4.40
Amps IN_POWER=720 Watts OUT_POWER=670 Watts
```

There are differences in components between ODA V1 and ODA X3-2. This can be seen in Listing 7-5's results. The ODA X3-2 hardware is very different from, and newer than, the hardware in ODA V1.

Listing 7-5. Performing an ODA X3-2 System Component Check (X3-2)

```
[root@odax32 bin]# ./oakcli validate -c SystemComponents
INFO: oak system information and Validations
RESULT: System Software inventory details
 Reading the metadata. It takes a while...
System Version  Component Name     Installed Version    Supported Version
--------------  --------------     -----------------    -----------------
2.6.0.0.0
                Controller         11.05.02.00          Up-to-date
                Expander           000F                 Up-to-date
                SSD_SHARED         9432                 Up-to-date
                HDD_LOCAL          A31A                 No-update
                HDD_SHARED         A31A                 Up-to-date
                ILOM               3.1.2.10 r74387      Up-to-date
                BIOS               17021300             Up-to-date
                IPMI               1.8.10.5             Up-to-date
```

HMP	2.2.6.1	Up-to-date
OAK	2.6.0.0.0	Up-to-date
OEL	5.8	Up-to-date
TFA	2.5.1.4	Up-to-date
GI_HOME	11.2.0.3.6(16056266, 16083653)	Up-to-date
DB_HOME	11.2.0.3.6(16056266, 16083653)	Up-to-date
ASR	4.4	Up-to-date

```
RESULT: System Information:-
        Manufacturer:Oracle Corporation
        Product Name:SUN FIRE X4170 M3
        Serial Number:111FML11T
RESULT: BIOS Information:-
        Vendor:American Megatrends Inc.
        Version:17021300
        Release Date:06/19/2012
        BIOS Revision:13.0
        Firmware Revision:3.1
SUCCESS: Controller p1 has the IR Bypass mode set correctly
SUCCESS: Controller p2 has the IR Bypass mode set correctly
INFO: Reading ilom data, may take short while..
INFO: Read the ilom data. Doing Validations
RESULT: System ILOM Version: 3.1.2.10 r74387
RESULT: System BMC firmware version  3.1
RESULT: Powersupply PS0 V_IN=206 Volts IN_POWER=100 Watts OUT_POWER=110 Watts
RESULT: Powersupply PS1 V_IN=206 Volts IN_POWER=130 Watts OUT_POWER=120 Watts
SUCCESS: Both the powersupply are ok and functioning
RESULT: Cooling Unit FM0 fan speed F0=6800 RPM F1=4300 RPM
RESULT: Cooling Unit FM1 fan speed F0=7300 RPM F1=3900 RPM
SUCCESS: Both the cooling unit are present
RESULT: Processor P0 present Details:-
        Version:Intel(R) Xeon(R) CPU E5-2690 0 @ 2.90GHz
        Current Speed:2900 MHz  Core Enabled:8  Thread Count:16
SUCCESS: All 8 memory modules of CPU P0 ok, each module is of Size:16384 MB Type:DDR3
        Speed:1600 MHz manufacturer:Hynix Semiconductor
RESULT: Processor P1 present Details:-
        Version:Intel(R) Xeon(R) CPU E5-2690 0 @ 2.90GHz
        Current Speed:2900 MHz  Core Enabled:8  Thread Count:16
SUCCESS: All 8 memory modules of CPU P1 ok, each module is of Size:16384 MB Type:DDR3
        Speed:1600 MHz manufacturer:Hynix Semiconductor
RESULT: Total Physical System Memory is 264405228 kB
SUCCESS: All OS Disks are present and in ok state
RESULT: Power Supply=30 degrees C
```

ODA X3-2 does not have an expander, but it does have an external disk shelf. Validation of the shared disks is thus done using the validate command's –c switch. This is demonstrated in Listing 7-6.

Listing 7-6. Validating ODA X3-2 Storage Topology

```
[root@odax32 bin]# ./oakcli validate -c StorageTopology
It may take a minute. Please wait...
INFO    : ODA Topology Verification
INFO    : Running on Node0
INFO    : Check hardware type
SUCCESS : Type of hardware found : X3-2
INFO    : Check for Environment(Bare Metal or Virtual Machine)
SUCCESS : Type of environment found : Bare Metal
INFO    : Check number of Controllers
SUCCESS : Number of Internal LSI SAS controller found : 1
SUCCESS : Number of External LSI SAS controller found : 2
INFO    : Check for Controllers correct PCIe slot address
SUCCESS : Internal LSI SAS controller   : 50:00.0
SUCCESS : External LSI SAS controller 0 : 30:00.0
SUCCESS : External LSI SAS controller 1 : 40:00.0
INFO    : Check if JBOD powered on
SUCCESS : 1JBOD : Powered-on
INFO    : Check for correct number of EBODS(2 or 4)
SUCCESS : EBOD found : 2
INFO    : Check for External Controller 0
SUCCESS : Controller connected to correct ebod number
SUCCESS : Controller port connected to correct ebod port
SUCCESS : Overall Cable check for controller 0
INFO    : Check for External Controller 1
SUCCESS : Controller connected to correct ebod number
SUCCESS : Controller port connected to correct ebod port
SUCCESS : Overall Cable check for controller 1
INFO    : Check for overall status of cable validation on Node0
SUCCESS : Overall Cable Validation on Node0
INFO    : Check Node Identification status
SUCCESS : Node Identification
SUCCESS : Node name based on cable configuration found : NODE0
INFO    : Check JBOD Nickname
SUCCESS : JBOD Nickname set correctly : Oracle Database Appliance - E0
```

Storage topology validation provides checks on connectivity confirmation, which should be run directly after an ODA install to ensure that all cables are connected properly. You should also run it regularly to ensure that disk connectivity has no problems.

OS Disk Storage

After validating the system, it is also important to look at the disks from the OS perspective and ensure that all disks are functioning properly. You can also ensure that RAID levels are OK on the box. Setup is similar between ODA V1 and X3-2, but ODA X3-2 has more disk space available to the OS.

■ **Note** Virtualized ODAs show virtual disks mapped to various physical disks. Bare-metal ODAs show one-to-one physical mappings.

Listing 7-7 shows an example of validating the disk storage for an ODA device.

Listing 7-7. Validating ODA OS Disk Storage (V1 & X3-2)

```
[root@odax32 bin]# ./oakcli validate -c OSDiskStorage
INFO: Checking Operating System Storage
SUCCESS: The OS disks have the boot stamp
RESULT: Raid device /dev/md0 found clean
RESULT: Raid device /dev/md1 found clean
RESULT: Physical Volume   /dev/md1 in VolGroupSys has 370206.05M out of total 599986.80M
RESULT: Volumegroup   VolGroupSys consist of 1 physical volumes,contains 4 logical volumes, has 0
volume snaps with total size of 599986.80M and free space of 370206.05M
RESULT: Logical Volume   LogVolOpt in VolGroupSys Volume group is of size 60.00G
RESULT: Logical Volume   LogVolRoot in VolGroupSys Volume group is of size 30.00G
RESULT: Logical Volume   LogVolSwap in VolGroupSys Volume group is of size 24.00G
RESULT: Logical Volume   LogVolU01 in VolGroupSys Volume group is of size 100.00G
RESULT: Device /dev/mapper/VolGroupSys-LogVolRoot is mounted on / of type ext3 in (rw)
RESULT: Device /dev/mapper/VolGroupSys-LogVolOpt is mounted on /opt of type ext3 in (rw)
RESULT: Device /dev/md0 is mounted on /boot of type ext3 in (rw)
RESULT: Device /dev/mapper/VolGroupSys-LogVolU01 is mounted on /u01 of type ext3 in (rw)
RESULT: / has 7242 MB free out of total 29758 MB
RESULT: /opt has 46985 MB free out of total 59516 MB
RESULT: /boot has 65 MB free out of total 99 MB
RESULT: /u01 has 80271 MB free out of total 99194 MB
```

It is very important to keep an eye on the operating system space. Lack of nonshared disk space for various components like the RDBMS or the operating system causes serious disruption of service on the appliance. Depending on the configuration (bare metal or virtualized), the disk sizing and the spare disk space will be different. This will be explained in detail in Chapter 10.

Shared Storage

Each ODA has storage that is shared between both nodes of the appliance. In ODA V1, the shared storage is built into the appliance using storage expanders, whereas ODA X3-2 uses an external shelf to add a shared disk to the appliance.

Validating shared storage is very important in ensuring that all paths are available and that there are no issues in the shared disk. Depending on your disk group, redundancy level (NORMAL or HIGH) disks can go bad and should be replaced. Disk behavior can be monitored via the syslog or ASM Alert Log, but it is important to validate and ensure that all paths to the disk are up and functional.

Listing 7-8 provides an example of storage validation. You can see the active disk paths, as well as the names of the logical and physical disk devices.

Listing 7-8. ODA Shared Storage Validation (V1 & X3-2)

```
[root@odax32 bin]# ./oakcli validate -c SharedStorage
INFO: Checking Shared Storage
RESULT: Disk HDD_E0_S00_373737408 path1 status active device sda with status active path2
        status active device sdy with status active
SUCCESS: HDD_E0_S00_373737408 has both the paths up and active
RESULT: Disk HDD_E0_S01_373737516 path1 status active device sdb with status active path2
        status active device sdz with status active
```

```
SUCCESS: HDD_E0_S01_373737516 has both the paths up and active
....
....
SUCCESS: HDD_E0_S18_373750584 has both the paths up and active
RESULT: Disk HDD_E0_S19_373760780 path1 status active device sdt with status active path2
        status active device sdar with status active
SUCCESS: HDD_E0_S19_373760780 has both the paths up and active
RESULT: Disk SSD_E0_S20_805834037 path1 status active device sdu with status active path2
        status active device sdas with status active
SUCCESS: SSD_E0_S20_805834037 has both the paths up and active
RESULT: Disk SSD_E0_S21_805834107 path1 status active device sdv with status active path2
        status active device sdat with status active
SUCCESS: SSD_E0_S21_805834107 has both the paths up and active
RESULT: Disk SSD_E0_S22_805834081 path1 status active device sdw with status active path2
        status active device sdau with status active
SUCCESS: SSD_E0_S22_805834081 has both the paths up and active
RESULT: Disk SSD_E0_S23_805834056 path1 status active device sdx with status active path2
        status active device sdav with status active
SUCCESS: SSD_E0_S23_805834056 has both the paths up and active
```

Any devices that are not in a successful state should be evaluated immediately. Any reported issues should be looked at, and an Oracle support ticket should be immediately opened to resolve any problem that is found.

Network Components

The ODA comes with public as well as private interfaces to allow network connectivity to the outside world, and internal network connectivity for the server nodes and the cluster to communicate. There is a difference between the ways a virtualized ODA sees network components in comparison to a bare-metal installation. ODA V1 has 2x 1GbE interfaces for the interconnect, 2x3 1GbE interfaces for public connectivity, as well as a two-port 10GbE SFP+ interface. ODA X3-2 went in a different direction with all 10GbE ports (copper) All ports are set up as active/passive at the operating system.

Listing 7-9 shows the output that one will see from a component validation on an ODA V1.

Listing 7-9. Validating ODA V1 Network Components

```
[root@oda1 bin]# ./oakcli validate -c NetworkComponents
INFO: Doing oak network checks
RESULT: Detected active link for interface eth0 with link speed 1000Mb/s -- Interconnect
RESULT: Detected active link for interface eth1 with link speed 1000Mb/s -- Interconnect
WARNING: No Link detected for interface eth2    -- unused network
WARNING: No Link detected for interface eth3    -- unused network
RESULT: Detected active link for interface eth4 with link speed 1000Mb/s -- 1Gbe network Active
RESULT: Detected active link for interface eth5 with link speed 1000Mb/s -- 1Gbe network Passive
WARNING: No Link detected for interface eth6
WARNING: No Link detected for interface eth7
RESULT: Detected active link for interface eth8 with link speed 10000Mb/s -- 10Gbe Network Active
RESULT: Detected active link for interface eth9 with link speed 10000Mb/s --10Gbe Network Passive
INFO: Checking bonding interface status
WARNING: Bond interface bond0 has the following current status:down
RESULT: Bond interface bond0 is down configured in mode:fault-tolerance (active-backup)
        with current active interface as None
```

```
        Slave1 interface is eth2 with status:down Link fail count=0 Maccaddr:00:21:28:e7:c2:f0
                Slave2 interface is eth3 with status:down Link fail count=0
Maccaddr:00:21:28:e7:c2:f1
RESULT: Bond interface bond1 is up configured in mode:fault-tolerance (active-backup)
        with current active interface as eth5
        Slave1 interface is eth4 with status:up Link fail count=1 Maccaddr:00:1b:21:cb:03:29
                Slave2 interface is eth5 with status:up Link fail count=0 Maccaddr:00:1b:21:cb:03:28
WARNING: Bond interface bond2 has the following current status:down
RESULT: Bond interface bond2 is down configured in mode:fault-tolerance (active-backup)
        with current active interface as None
        Slave1 interface is eth6 with status:down Link fail count=0 Maccaddr:00:1b:21:cb:03:2b
                Slave2 interface is eth7 with status:down Link fail count=0
Maccaddr:00:1b:21:cb:03:2a
RESULT: Bond interface xbond0 is up configured in mode:fault-tolerance (active-backup)
        with current active interface as eth8
        Slave1 interface is eth8 with status:up Link fail count=0 Maccaddr:00:1b:21:bb:6e:7c
                Slave2 interface is eth9 with status:up Link fail count=0
Maccaddr:00:1b:21:bb:6e:7d
SUCCESS: eth0 is running 192.168.16.24
SUCCESS: eth1 is running 192.168.17.24
```

The naming convention for Ethernet devices in terms of bonds differs between the virtualization model and the bare-metal model. In ODA V1, xbond0 is the collective name for the 10GbE interfaces, whereas bond0 through bond2 represent the 1GbE interfaces. ODA X3-2 abandons the xbond vs. bond naming convention because all ports are copper-enabled 10GbE ports, including the interconnect. Listing 7-10 shows how the configuration looks. The detected active link will show the actual speed the switch has allowed for the port—not what that port can theoretically achieve, but what it currently is achieving. In Listing 7-10, the switch that is serving eth2 to eth5 only supports 1GbE, which is what is displayed.

Listing 7-10. Validating ODA X3-2 Network Components

```
[root@odax32 bin]# ./oakcli validate -c NetworkComponents
INFO: Doing oak network checks
RESULT: Detected active link for interface eth0 with link speed 10000Mb/s
RESULT: Detected active link for interface eth1 with link speed 10000Mb/s
RESULT: Detected active link for interface eth2 with link speed 1000Mb/s
RESULT: Detected active link for interface eth3 with link speed 1000Mb/s
RESULT: Detected active link for interface eth4 with link speed 1000Mb/s
RESULT: Detected active link for interface eth5 with link speed 1000Mb/s
INFO: Checking bonding interface status
RESULT: Bond interface bond0 is up configured in mode:fault-tolerance (active-backup)
        with current active interface as eth2
        Slave1 interface is eth2 with status:up Link fail count=0 Maccaddr:00:10:e0:23:8d:84
        Slave2 interface is eth3 with status:up Link fail count=0 Maccaddr:00:10:e0:23:8d:85
RESULT: Bond interface bond1 is up configured in mode:fault-tolerance (active-backup)
        with current active interface as eth4
        Slave1 interface is eth4 with status:up Link fail count=0 Maccaddr:00:10:e0:23:8d:86
        Slave2 interface is eth5 with status:up Link fail count=0 Maccaddr:00:10:e0:23:8d:87
```

Since ODA X3-2 does not support SFP+ Fiber based networking, switch support for copper-based 10GbE is needed to attain 10GbE speeds. ODA X3-2 shows only the interfaces that are active. This is in contrast to ODA V1, which shows the unused network in a manner similar to the active network.

Disk Calibration

The ODA comes with a disk calibration utility to check disk performance. Disk calibration is done using Orion (Oracle I/O numbers), which is an Oracle utility used to mimic Oracle workloads on systems. Orion can also be used to simulate ASM striping and to provide performance metrics like MBPS, IOPS, and I/O latency.

I/O metrics can change depending on the workload on the system. ODA V1 has 20 SAS disks and 4 SSD disks, and the results of a performance calibration can be seen. These results will vary depending on the state of the system and the workload being performed on the system. On a new system with no workload, you should see SAS disks performing about 4000 read RIOPS. ODA X3-2 currently doesn't support executing disk calibration, and currently the official numbers are 7000 RIOPS.

Listing 7-11 shows the execution of a disk calibration validation on ODA V1.

Listing 7-11. Validation of ODA V1 Disk Calibration

```
[root@oda1 bin]# ./oakcli validate -c DiskCalibration
INFO: Doing oak disk calibration checks
INFO: About to run random read IOPS throughput tests for SASDisk
RESULT: Random read throughput across all 20 SASDisk = 3950 IOPS
INFO: About to run random read IOPS throughput tests for SSDDisk
RESULT: Random read throughput across all 4 SSDDisk = 15661 IOPS
INFO: About to run random read MBPS throughput tests for SASDisk
RESULT: Random read throughput across all 20 SASDisk = 1965 MBPS
INFO: About to run random read MBPS throughput tests for SSDDisk
RESULT: Random read throughput across all 4 SSDDisk = 972 MBPS
INFO: Completed IOPS tests for individual disks of type SASDisk
INFO: Completed MBPS tests for individual disks of type SASDisk
INFO: Completed IOPS tests for individual disks of type SSDDisk
INFO: Completed MBPS tests for individual disks of type SSDDisk
INFO: Completed all single disk tests
INFO: Calibration results for SASDisk
RESULT: Random read throughput of HDD_E1_S10_979877715 is 303 IOPS 160 MBPS
RESULT: Random read throughput of HDD_E1_S06_979677567 is 308 IOPS 167 MBPS
RESULT: Random read throughput of HDD_E0_S05_979864071 is 309 IOPS 164 MBPS
RESULT: Random read throughput of HDD_E1_S14_979871167 is 313 IOPS 165 MBPS
RESULT: Random read throughput of HDD_E1_S15_979869315 is 295 IOPS 163 MBPS
RESULT: Random read throughput of HDD_E1_S11_979853103 is 306 IOPS 166 MBPS
RESULT: Random read throughput of HDD_E0_S08_979867223 is 305 IOPS 164 MBPS
RESULT: Random read throughput of HDD_E1_S18_979672443 is 305 IOPS 163 MBPS
RESULT: Random read throughput of HDD_E0_S16_979672427 is 304 IOPS 164 MBPS
RESULT: Random read throughput of HDD_E0_S04_979846015 is 298 IOPS 160 MBPS
RESULT: Random read throughput of HDD_E1_S02_979865471 is 301 IOPS 158 MBPS
RESULT: Random read throughput of HDD_E0_S01_979676399 is 294 IOPS 158 MBPS
RESULT: Random read throughput of HDD_E0_S00_979802375 is 303 IOPS 160 MBPS
RESULT: Random read throughput of HDD_E1_S03_979773239 is 304 IOPS 160 MBPS
RESULT: Random read throughput of HDD_E0_S13_979854143 is 301 IOPS 168 MBPS
RESULT: Random read throughput of HDD_E1_S19_979877275 is 312 IOPS 167 MBPS
RESULT: Random read throughput of HDD_E1_S07_979781771 is 311 IOPS 168 MBPS
RESULT: Random read throughput of HDD_E0_S12_979804175 is 310 IOPS 163 MBPS
RESULT: Random read throughput of HDD_E0_S17_979865419 is 306 IOPS 163 MBPS
RESULT: Random read throughput of HDD_E0_S09_979670555 is 311 IOPS 164 MBPS
INFO: Calibration results for SSDDisk
RESULT: Random read throughput of SSD_E1_S23_805674868 is 4138 IOPS 328 MBPS
```

```
RESULT: Random read throughput of SSD_E0_S20_805674815 is 4144 IOPS 328 MBPS
RESULT: Random read throughput of SSD_E0_S21_805674571 is 4143 IOPS 328 MBPS
RESULT: Random read throughput of SSD_E1_S22_805674882 is 4146 IOPS 328 MBPS
```

The results can vary depending on the workload currently performing on the ODA. The results in Listing 7-11 are from a very low workload time period, and thus are very close to the I/O speeds that Oracle advertises in its marketing material.

■ **Note** ODA X3-2 Disk Calibration results are broken and the command shows that the action is unsupported and not working as of the ODA 2.7 software release.

Automatic Service Requests

ASR is a feature of the ODA that allows for hardware failures to be reported to the Oracle Corporation via a Service Request. Results are reported back to the user. This allows for an expedited resolution for common hardware failures.

ASR is completely integrated into My Oracle Support (MOS), which allows for ease of creation of Service Requests for any hardware-related issuesthat is, hardware faults due to hardware failure. The ODA is a hardware component that is registered as an asset with MOS during the setup and deployment of an ODA. A local ASR service per ODA can be used. Alternatively, if an organization has multiple ODAs and other Oracle hardware that it is managing, it is advisable to have an external, centralized ASR server.

Oracle added validation and testing of ASR in ODA 2.6. This software upgrade brought forward the ability to not only validate ASR connectivity and ensure that ASR is setup right, but also to test various scenarios to ensure that alerts are actually being generated.

Automatic Service Requests provide the ability to automatically open Oracle service requests for specific hardware faults. ASR is an optional utility that can be set up during deployment of the ODA or after. In ODA 2.5 and above, ASR deployment can use the built-in ASR packages or a standalone ASR server to manage the fault management process. Prior to ODA 2.5, the only official option was to use the ASR built into the box, and thus connect each ODA to the Internet to provide ASR capability.

Let's look at the ASR validation process. The ASR validation process is the same for ODA V1 and X3-2, but in ODA X3-2, the ILOM and the server nodes have different serial numbers, which is not the case in a V1 box. The validation process checks for a number of things:

- Is ASR installed?

- Are SNMP traps set on the ILOM to point to the ASR server?

- Are the assets registered in an ASR server?

- Can an event be tested?

Listing 7-12 shows the output that is expected from a server that has ASR running on the ODA box.

Listing 7-12. Running an ASR Validation

```
root@odab1 bin]# ./oakcli validate -c asr
INFO: oak Asr information and Validations
RESULT: /opt/oracle/oak/conf/asr.conf exist
RESULT: ASR Manager ip:x.x.x.x
RESULT: ASR Manager port:1162
SUCCESS: ASR configuration file validation successfully completed
RESULT: /etc/hosts has entry 141.146.156.46 transport.oracle.com
```

```
RESULT: ilom alertmgmt level is set to minor
RESULT: ilom alertmgmt type is set to snmptrap
RESULT: alertmgmt snmp_version is set to 2c
RESULT: alertmgmt community_or_username is set to public
RESULT: alertmgmt destination is set to x.x.x.x
RESULT: alertmgmt destination_port is set to 1162
SUCCESS: Ilom snmp confguration for asr set correctly
RESULT: notification trap configured to ip:x.x.x.x
RESULT: notification trap configured to port:1162
SUCCESS: Asr notification trap set correctly
INFO: IP_ADDRESS HOST_NAME SERIAL_NUMBER ASR     PROTOCOL SOURCE PRODUCT_NAME
INFO: ---------- --------- ------------- ------- -------- ------ ------------------------
INFO: x.x.x.x    oda1-ilom 9243FMW000    Enabled SNMP     ILOM   SUN FIRE X4370 M2 SERVER
INFO: x.x.x.x    oda2-ilom 9243FMW000    Enabled SNMP     ILOM   SUN FIRE X4370 M2 SERVER
INFO: x.x.x.x    oda1      9243FMW000    Enabled SNMP     FMA    SUN FIRE X4370 M2 SERVER
                                                                 x86/x64 System
INFO: 1x.x.x.x   oda2      9243FMW000    Enabled SNMP     FMA    SUN FIRE X4370 M2 SERVER
                                                                 x86/x64 System
INFO: Please use My Oracle Support 'http://support.oracle.com' to view the activation status.
SUCCESS: successfully set asr log level to Fine.
RESULT: Registered with ASR backend.
RESULT: test connection successfully completed.
RESULT: submitted test event for asset:
RESULT: bundle com.sun.svc.asr.sw is in active state
RESULT: bundle com.sun.svc.asr.sw-frag is in resolved state
RESULT: bundle com.sun.svc.asr.sw-rulesdefinitions is in resolved state
RESULT: bundle com.sun.svc.ServiceActivation is in active state
SUCCESS: ASR diag successfully completed
```

As part of the test, a message that confirms a successful check is e-mailed. It is very important to ensure that this e-mail message is received by the ASR administrator. The administrator's e-mail address is set up when the assets are activated, and can be checked by logging in at `http://support.oracle.com`. Figure 7-1 shows a sample image of a successfully sent e-mail message.

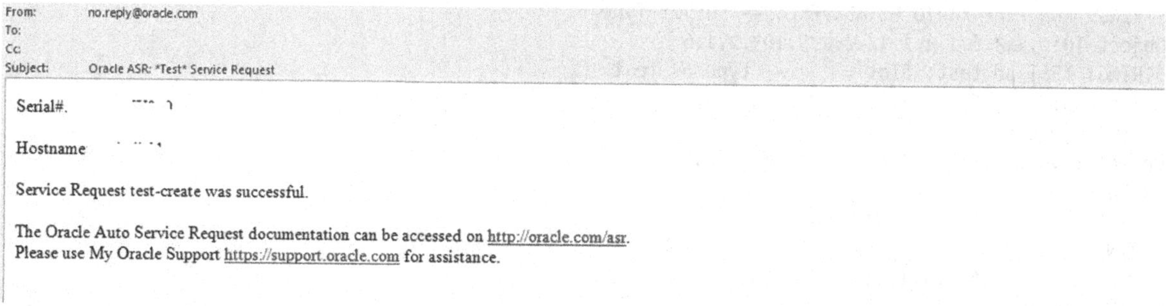

From: no.reply@oracle.com
To:
Cc:
Subject: Oracle ASR: *Test* Service Request

Serial#.

Hostname

Service Request test-create was successful.

The Oracle Auto Service Request documentation can be accessed on http://oracle.com/asr.
Please use My Oracle Support https://support.oracle.com for assistance.

Figure 7-1. *E-mail confirming ASR validation of Service Request (SR) create*

Oracle has added testing capabilities to ODA 2.6 to allow simulations for bad disks and other hardware events. This is very important because, in the past, simulating and confirming that the ASR was actually working was not a very easy task. The addition of testing capabilities makes that task much easier.

You can run an ASR test by executing the command oakcli test asr. Listing 7-13 shows an example of the questions asked in response to that command.

Listing 7-13. Running an ASR Test

```
[root@odax32 bin]# ./oakcli test asr
Please select one of the following to generate ASR test trap[1 .. 4]:
1        => Generate snmptrap test alert from ilom management
2        => Generte disk alert test
3        => Generate TESTSRCREATE snmptrap
4        => Generate test trap using 'oakcli test pd_xx BAD'
```

The options in Listing 7-13 provide a menu you can use to execute various tests. Output is either written to a log file or a test SR is created and an e-mail (similar to that shown in Figure 7-1) is generated. We can look at the options in detail. Listing 7-14 shows an example of the data that is displayed via the log file.

Listing 7-14. Log File for ASR Tests

```
Setting Asr log level to Fine. Wait ...
ASR log level is already set to Fine
Generated and sent test trap successfully using disk alert test
Please check the log files "/var/opt/SUNWsasm/log/sw-asr-accepted.log.*"
Jun 28, 2013 11:14:21 AM com.sun.svc.asr.sw.snmp.common.ControlObject writeAcceptedEventLog
FINE: Trap received from:
x.x.x.x:37491
, community: public
Object ID: .1.3.6.1.2.1.1.3.0
TimeTicks: 30 days, 4 hours, 59 minutes, 26 seconds.
Object ID: .1.3.6.1.6.3.1.1.4.1.0
Object ID: .1.3.6.1.4.1.42.2.175.103.2.0.43
Object ID: .1.3.6.1.4.1.42.2.175.103.2.1.1
STRING: Oracle Database Appliance
Object ID: .1.3.6.1.4.1.42.2.175.103.2.1.14
STRING:  <Serial Number>  -- Serial Number of ODA Machine
Object ID: .1.3.6.1.4.1.42.2.175.103.2.1.15
STRING: SUN FIRE X4370 M2 SERVER    -- Server Type
Object ID: .1.3.6.1.4.1.42.2.175.103.2.1.6
STRING: TEST pd_test; Slot =     -- type of test
Object ID: .1.3.6.1.4.1.42.2.175.103.2.1.7
STRING: NULL
Object ID: .1.3.6.1.4.1.42.2.175.103.2.1.8
INTEGER: 0
Object ID: .1.3.6.1.4.1.42.2.175.103.2.1.17
STRING: 1
Object ID: .1.3.6.1.4.1.42.2.175.103.2.1.18
STRING: NULL
Object ID: .1.3.6.1.4.1.42.2.175.103.2.1.10
Object ID: .0.0
Object ID: .1.3.6.1.4.1.42.2.175.103.2.1.9
STRING: SUN FIRE X4370 M2 SERVER      ; <server name> Disk TEST_Alert problem:
                                DISKALRT-OTEST. - Final SNMP String.
```

ODA Configuration Audit Tool

Part of the proactive checks portfolio is ODA Configuration Audit Toolkit (odachk). Oracle has been building best practices in their engineered and nonengineered systems portfolio for a while, and these checks include racchk, exachk, and now for ODA—odachk.

The odachk utility is a complete auditing and assessment tool developed by Oracle's RAC Assurance team to provide best-practice checks for RAC and Clusterware. The tool also provides various OS-specific checks. While every version of the check can add more options and features., the following categories are key:

- OS kernel parameters

- OS packages

- Many other OS configuration settings important to RAC

- CRS/grid infrastructure

- RDBMS

- ASM

- Database parameters

This list is pretty comprehensive, and these .checks are updated every 90 days to ensure freshness of the tests. The updates also provide the addition of newer best practices, and solutions to known problems. The odachk utility should be run at least on a monthly basis, and also before and after any change to the system, to ensure that no problems have arisen in the environment. The utility also provides pre- and post-upgrade checks that allow for upgrading to 11.2.0.3 from 11.2.0.2 to ensure that all best practices are met.

Listing 7-15 provides an example of getting the version of the odachk, as well as getting help from the odachk utility. The odachk is updated very frequently and each version of the ODA software can contain a new version of the utility.

Listing 7-15. ODA Checks

```
[root@odax32 odachk]# ./odachk -v
ODACHK  VERSION: 2.2.1_20130415
[root@odax32 odachk]# ./odachk -h
Usage : ./odachk [-abvhpfmsuSo:c:rt:]
        -a      All (Perform best practice check and recommended patch check)
        -b      Best Practice check only. No recommended patch check
        -h      Show usage
        -v      Show version
        -p      Patch check only
...
```

The odachk .packs a lot of information into its output, and due to the volatile nature of checks, it is independent on the OAK framework. The command executable is typically found at /opt/oracle/oak/odachk. You should only run the utility as the Oracle RDBMS software owner. Running as any other user will net a message like the following:

```
odachk found that oracle software owner exists and its being run by root.
```

Let's look at a typical run of odachk. Listing 7-16 shows such a run, along with its output.

Listing 7-16. ODA Check Execution

```
Checking ssh user equivalency settings on all nodes in cluster
Node odax322 is configured for ssh user equivalency for oracle user
Searching for running databases . . . . .
. . . . . . . . . .
List of running databases registered in OCR
1. dodx32
. . . . . .
. . . . .
9. All of above
10. None of above
Select databases from list for checking best practices. For multiple databases, select 9 for All or
comma separated number like 1,2 etc [1-10][9].1
Searching out ORACLE_HOME for selected databases.
. . . . . . . . . .
Checking Status of Oracle Software Stack - Clusterware, ASM, RDBMS
. . . . . . . . . . . . . . . . . . . . . . . . . . . . . . . . .
-----------------------------------------------------------------------------
                             Oracle Stack Status
-----------------------------------------------------------------------------
Host Name CRS Installed ASM HOME  RDBMS Installed  CRS UP  ASM UP   RDBMS UP DB Instance Name
-----------------------------------------------------------------------------
dodax31   Yes           Yes       Yes              Yes     Yes      Yes      dodx321
dodax32   Yes           Yes       Yes              Yes     Yes      Yes      dodx322
-----------------------------------------------------------------------------
97 of the included audit checks require root privileged data collection . If sudo is not configured
or the root password is not available, audit checks which  require root privileged data collection
can be skipped.
1. Enter 1 if you will enter root password for each  host when prompted
2. Enter 2 if you have sudo configured for oracle user to execute root_odachk.sh script
3. Enter 3 to skip the root privileged collections
4. Enter 4 to exit and work with the SA to configure sudo  or to arrange for root access and run the tool later.
Please indicate your selection from one of the above options[1-4][1]:- 2
*** Checking Best Practice Recommendations (PASS/WARNING/FAIL) ***
Log file for collections and audit checks are at
/opt/oracle/oak/odachk/odachk_062913_120441/odachk.log
Starting to run odachk in background on dodax32.
```

The end result will be a run of all the checks and the creation of a zip file. The zip file is created in case you decide the results need to be uploaded for evaluation and analysis. .You'll also get an HTML file for your own evaluation and analysis. Figure 7-2 shows an example of all the files that are generated.

Name	Ext		Size	Changed
⬆ [ ]				6/29/2013 12:09:43 PM
odachk_timings.out			803 B	6/29/2013 12:09:43 PM
odachk_results.xml			49,213 B	6/29/2013 12:09:42 PM
odachk_exceptions.xml			4,242 B	6/29/2013 12:09:42 PM
odachk	' ' 1_062913_120441.html		342 KiB	6/29/2013 12:09:42 PM
odachk_brows		0441.html	1,439 KiB	6/29/2013 12:09:42 PM
odachk.rep			12,327 B	6/29/2013 12:09:42 PM
upload_odachk_result.sql			50,843 B	6/29/2013 12:09:41 PM
odachk_summary.rep			6,224 B	6/29/2013 12:09:41 PM
odachk_cwc_summary_pass.rep			1,036 B	6/29/2013 12:09:41 PM
odachk_cwc_summary_fail.rep			289 B	6/29/2013 12:09:41 PM
odachk_cwc_pass.rep			1,744 B	6/29/2013 12:09:41 PM
odachk_cwc_fail.rep			289 B	6/29/2013 12:09:41 PM
odachk.log			378 KiB	6/29/2013 12:09:41 PM
o_misc_clusterwide_checks.out			125 B	6/29/2013 12:09:41 PM
o_audit_resul'	1.out		8,642 B	6/29/2013 12:09:41 PM
mb_db_tmp.out			70 B	6/29/2013 12:09:41 PM
c_actual.out			315 B	6/29/2013 12:09:41 PM
9EC87FB8BF2F4ED8E040E50A1EC03015_report.out			36 B	6/29/2013 12:09:41 PM
8FC4FA469BAA945EE040E50A1EC06AC6_report.out			22 B	6/29/2013 12:09:41 PM
8FC307D9A9CEF95FE040E50A1EC01580_report.out			22 B	6/29/2013 12:09:40 PM
8BEFA88017530395E040E50A1EC05E99_report.out			58 B	6/29/2013 12:09:40 PM
8955120D63FCAC2DE040E50A1EC006CA_report.out			36 B	6/29/2013 12:09:40 PM

Figure 7-2. ODAchk files generated

The HTML file contains a lot of sections. The first section is a cluster summary and the table of contents, such as what's shown in Figure 7-3. It provides information about the cluster being examined and what is contained within the report.

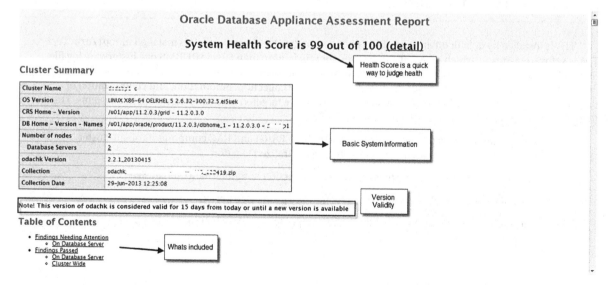

Figure 7-3. ODA check cluster summary

The report is comprehensive and looks at a lot of metrics to ensure that the system is working optimally. A findings report .is displayed first, showing potential issues on the database server. Figure 7-4 provides an example.

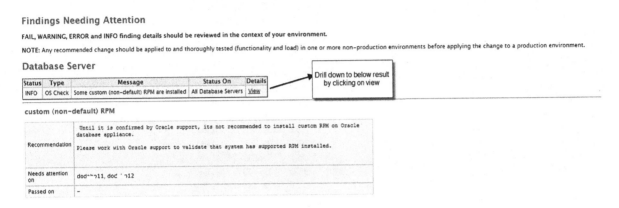

Figings Needing Attention

FAIL, WARNING, ERROR and INFO finding details should be reviewed in the context of your environment.

NOTE: Any recommended change should be applied to and thoroughly tested (functionality and load) in one or more non–production environments before applying the change to a production environment.

Database Server

Status	Type	Message	Status On	Details
INFO	OS Check	Some custom (non-default) RPM are installed	All Database Servers	View

Drill down to below result by clicking on view

custom (non-default) RPM

Recommendation	Until it is confirmed by Oracle support, its not recommended to install custom RPM on Oracle database appliance. Please work with Oracle support to validate that system has supported RPM installed.
Needs attention on	dod--n11, dod ' n12
Passed on	-

Figure 7-4. ODA check findings report

Each finding should be validated depending on the environment. Take care to ensure that the system is working within .predefined parameters. Run the odachck utility often to ensure that the system has no issues and that everything is working correctly.

Trace File Analyzer

Trace File Analyzer (TFA) is a new utility introduced in ODA 2.5. It is installed and working automatically in the background to proactively capture information from various log files during real-time or user-initiated scans.

■ **Note**   TFA is also an independent utility[1] from the Oracle RAC Assurance team. It is available for install on most platforms that are supported by Oracle RAC.

TFA is installed by default on an ODA. TFA is not part of the OAK framework. It is installed in /opt/oracle/tfa. TFA is software-agnostic, which means it can be used for much more than Oracle RDBMS or Clusterware log files. Since TFA is an independent utility, it has a faster software cycle, with updates as frequent as the ODAchk tool.

TFA provides a variety of functions that revolve around the collection, automation, and centralization of diagnostic data. In essence, TFA provides an easy way to achieve targeted data collection from live systems. The following are some of the features .that TFA provides:

- Encapsulation of diagnostic data collection for all CRS/GI and RAC components on all cluster nodes into a single command executed from a centralized location

- The ability to trim diagnostic files during data collection to reduce data upload size

- The ability to isolate diagnostic data collection to a given time period

- The ability to centralize collected diagnostic output to a single server in the cluster

---

[1]MOS Note 1513912.1 is the master note for TFA

- The ability to isolate diagnostic collection to a particular product component (for example, ASM, RDBMS, Clusterware)

- The ability—known as Real Time Scan—to scan alert logs in real time for conditions that indicate a problem (DB Alert Logs, ASM Alert Logs, Clusterware Alert Logs, etc.)

- Automatic Data Collection based on Real Time Scan findings

- On Demand Scan (user initiated) of all log and trace files for conditions that indicating a problem

- Automatic Data Collection based on On Demand Scan findings

TFA syntax can be seen by executing the `tfactl` command .without any options. Listing 7-17 provides what can be done with `tfactl`.

Listing 7-17. tfactl Help

```
[root@odax32 bin]# ./tfactl
Usage : /opt/oracle/tfa/tfa_home/bin/tfactl <command> [options]
<command> =
        status      Check the status of TFA across nodes in cluster
        add         Add a directory or host to TFA
        change      Change permission of directory in TFA
        modify      Modify TFA parameters
        set         Turn ON/OFF various TFA features
        remove      Remove a directory from TFA
        print       Print requested details
        run         Run inventory or scan
        diagcollect Collect logs from across nodes in cluster
For help with a command: /opt/oracle/tfa/tfa_home/bin/tfactl <command> -help
For debug output use -verbose option
```

The Oracle Database Appliance has TFA installed as part of the ODA patching. Startup of TFA is handled by the oakd process. To ensure that TFA is running at any point in time, you can validate with `tfactl`, as shown in Listing 7-18.

Listing 7-18. tfactl Status

```
root@odax32 bin]# ./tfactl status
.---------------------------------------------.
| Host    | Status of TFA | PID   | Port |
+---------+---------------+-------+------+
| odax32  | RUNNING       | 18839 | 5000 |
| odax32  | RUNNING       | 18637 | 5000 |
'---------+---------------+-------+------'
```

We will examine some of the key features of TFA, starting with a display of the various information that TFA is collecting. Execute the command `tfactl print` to look at various pieces of information about TFA, as shown in Listing 7-19.

Listing 7-19. tfactl Print

```
[root@odax32 bin]# ./tfactl print -h
Usage: /opt/oracle/tfa/tfa_home/bin/tfactl print [directories|hosts|actions|inventory|invrunstat
|repository|...]
  Prints requested details.
```

```
Options:
  config           Print current tfa config settings
  log              Print last ten lines in TFA log
  directories      Print all the directories to Inventory
  hosts            Print all the Hosts in the Configuration
  actions          Print all the Actions requested and their status
  inventory        Print all the files in the Inventory
  invrunstat       Print inventory run statistics
  repository       Print the zip file repository information
```

There are many pieces of information that the .tfactl print command provides. The key parameters can always be checked by displaying the config information. Listing 7-20 shows the ODA default setup.

Listing 7-20. ODA Default Setup for tfactl

```
# ./tfactl print config
.------------------------------------------------------------------.
| Configuration Parameter                                | Value   |
+--------------------------------------------------------+---------+
| TFA Version                                            | 2.5.1.4 |
| Allow auto diagcollection by events                    | true    |
| Allow Real Time Scan                                   | true    |
| Allow On Demand Scan                                   | true    |
| Real Time Scan running                                 | true    |
| Allow events found during Real Time Scan to fire diagcollection | false |
| Allow events found during On Demand Scan to fire diagcollection | false |
| Allow trimming of files during diagcollection          | true    |
| Trace Level                                            | 1       |
| Repository current size (MB) in podadb01               | 0       |
| Repository maximum size (MB) in podadb01               | 10240   |
'--------------------------------------------------------+---------'
```

Attributes can be changed if needed. For example, you can change the settings so that a diagnostic collection is automatically triggered on certain events during a real-time scan. Listing 7-21 shows how to make that change.

Listing 7-21. Modifying Diagnostic Event Triggers with tfactl

```
./tfactl set firediagcollectRT=true
Successfully set firediagcollectRT=true
.------------------------------------------------------------------.
| Configuration Parameter                                | Value   |
+--------------------------------------------------------+---------+
| TFA Version                                            | 2.5.1.4 |
| Allow auto diagcollection by events                    | true    |
| Allow Real Time Scan                                   | true    |
| Allow On Demand Scan                                   | true    |
| Real Time Scan running                                 | true    |
| Allow events found during Real Time Scan to fire diagcollection | true  |
| Allow events found during On Demand Scan to fire diagcollection | false |
| Allow trimming of files during diagcollection          | true    |
| Trace Level                                            | 1       |
| Repository current size (MB) in podadb01               | 0       |
| Repository maximum size (MB) in podadb01               | 10240   |
'--------------------------------------------------------+---------'
```

If you want to look at the directories that the TFA tool is monitoring, you can execute the `tfactl print directories` command. You'll get a long list of directories. Listing 7-22 provides an example subset.

Listing 7-22. tfactl Print Directories

```
./tfactl print directories
```

odax32		
Trace Directory	Component	SubComponent
/etc/oracle Permission: public Added by: root	CRS	CRS
/opt/oracle/oak/log/odax32/oak Permission: public Added by: root	ODA	ODA
/opt/oracle/oak/osw/archive Permission: public Added by: root	OS	OS
/u01/app/11.2.0.3/grid/OPatch/crs/log Permission: public Added by: root	CRS	CRS
/u01/app/11.2.0.3/grid/cfgtoollogs/opatch Permission: public Added by: root	INSTALL	INSTALL
/u01/app/11.2.0.3/grid/oc4j/j2ee/home/log Permission: public Added by: root	CRSOC4J	CRSOC4J
/u01/app/grid/diag/asm/+asm/+ASM2/trace Permission: public Added by: root	+asm	+ASM2
/u01/app/grid/diag/tnslsnr/dodax32/listener/trace Permission: public Added by: root	TNS	TNS
/u01/app/oracle/cfgtoollogs Permission: public Added by: root	CFGTOOLS	CFGTOOLS
/u01/app/oracle/diag/rdbms/dodabp1/dodax32/trac e Permission: public Added by: root	dodax32	dodax32
/u01/app/oracle/product/11.2.0.3/dbhome_1/cfgtoollogs/opatch Permission: public Added by: root	CFGTOOL	CFGTOOL

```
+---------------------------------------------------+----------+-------------+
| /u01/app/oracle/product/11.2.0.3/dbhome_1/install | INSTALL  | INSTALL     |
| Permission: public                                |          |             |
| Added by: root                                    |          |             |
+---------------------------------------------------+----------+-------------+
| /var/log                                          | OS       | OS          |
| Permission: public                                |          |             |
| Added by: root                                    |          |             |
'---------------------------------------------------+----------+-------------'
```

The team behind TFA keeps adding and removing directories in the inventory as needed. They also provide a way to manually add directories if needed. However, adding a directory is not recommended on the ODA unless doing so has been discussed with Oracle Support.

The add directive is used to add directories or hosts. The TFA process is also intelligent, to avoid duplication. Listing 7-23 shows an example of a directory that already exists attempting to be added. This tfactl will respond by not adding the directory.

Listing 7-23. tfactl Add Directory

```
# tfactl  add  directory /opt/oracle/oak/log
No new directories were added to TFA
```

TFA also provides a manual way to collect diagnostics information and allows for information to be trimmed as needed. Listing 7-24 shows examples of collecting all diagnostics, as well as diagnostics for specific timeframes.

Listing 7-24. tfactl Diagnostic Collection Examples

```
# tfactl diagcollect -all
Allows for diagcollect to be run an zip be collected in the initiating node
#tfactl diagcollect -crs node1,node2 -since 9h
Allows for diagcollect to be run for crs only and zip copied to initiating node
#tfactl diagcollect -for "Jun/29/2013 21:00:10"
        Collect diagnostics for all files for all nodes and collect only for timestamp listed.
```

The TFA team determines the events that cause diagnostic collection. These events are listed in detail in the TFA User Guide, accessible via MOS Note 1513912.1. Listing 7-25 provides a subset of the events that can trigger a tfactl collection.

Listing 7-25. tfactl Diagnostic Collection Event Triggers

```
Search for:
.*ORA-297(01|02|03|08|09|10|40).*
In Files :
Alert Logs - ASM and RDBMS
Error Description:
29701, unable to connect to Cluster Synchronization Service
29702,error occurred in Cluster Group Service operation
29703, error occurred in global enqueue service operation
29708, error occurred in Cluster Synchronization Services
29709, Communication failure with Cluster Synchronization Services
29710, Current operation aborted by Cluster Synchronization Services
29740 ,evicted by instance number %s, group incarnation %s
29770,global enqueue process %s (OSID %s) is hung for more than %s seconds
```

TFA is still a new tool and a work in progress. It bridges the gap between problem and collection, and it allows for the automatic collection of important events on multiple layers (database, grid/Clusterware) to provide all the right information to Oracle Support, which is what makes TFA different from the active diagnostics repository (ADR).

Miscellaneous Tools

So far, we've looked at a lot of the built-in tools in the ODA portfolio. There will be more tools, like Oracle Enterprise manager, which will be discussed in subsequent chapters, but it is important to mention other tools that are important in proactively diagnosing various issues with the ODA. Oracle Linux comes with anacron installed which is a variant of cron and allows more flexibility in running jobs, and there are various jobs built into anacron that run on a daily, weekly, or monthly basis. These jobs include the following functions:

- Log rotation of various files

- A log watch script that checks various logs, and generates a report and mails it to the root unix account.

- Weekly RAID checks

The log rotation of files is handled via the logrotate daemon and uses logrotate.conf to determine various configuration parameters that are used for managing log files. Listing 7-26 shows a default logrotate.conf file.

Listing 7-26. Logrotate.conf

```
root@farshad-linux]# cat /etc/logrotate.conf
# see "man logrotate" for details
# rotate log files weekly
weekly
# keep 4 weeks worth of backlogs
rotate 4
# create new (empty) log files after rotating old ones
create
# use date as a suffix of the rotated file
dateext
# uncomment this if you want your log files compressed
#compress
# RPM packages drop log rotation information into this directory
include /etc/logrotate.d
# no packages own wtmp and btmp -- we'll rotate them here
/var/log/wtmp {
    monthly
    create 0664 root utmp
        minsize 1M
    rotate 1
}
/var/log/btmp {
    missingok
    monthly
    create 0600 root utmp
    rotate 1
}
# system-specific logs may be also be configured here.
```

Log rotation can also be controlled by including attributes for the files that need to be included in log rotation in the /etc/logrotate.d directory. These can include various directives, depending on the type of log file that is being rotated. Listing 7-27 provides an example of an HTTP service log-file rotation with post-rotate directives as well.

Listing 7-27. Logrotate.d. Httpd

```
[root@farshad-linux logrotate.d]# vi httpd
/var/log/httpd/*log {
    missingok
    notifempty
    sharedscripts
    delaycompress
    postrotate
        /sbin/service httpd reload > /dev/null 2>/dev/null || true
    endscript
```

Logwatch is another facility that gives a daily synopsis of what the system looks like. Listing 7-28 provides an example of what a logwatch output looks like.

Listing 7-28. Logwatch

```
:
#################### Logwatch 7.3 (03/24/06) ####################
        Processing Initiated: Sat Jun 29 04:02:01 2013
        Date Range Processed: yesterday
                            ( 2013-Jun-28 )
                            Period is day.
      Detail Level of Output: 0
              Type of Output: unformatted
          Logfiles for Host: odax32
 ##################################################################
 --------------------- SSHD Begin ------------------------

Users logging in through sshd:
   root:
      10.10.7.51: 1 time

 --------------------- SSHD End --------------------------
 --------------------- Disk Space Begin ------------------------

Filesystem            Size  Used Avail Use% Mounted on
/dev/mapper/VolGroupSys-LogVolRoot
                      30G   19G  9.2G  67% /
/dev/md0              99M   48M   47M  51% /boot
/dev/mapper/VolGroupSys-LogVolU01
                      97G   32G   61G  34% /u01
/dev/mapper/VolGroupSys-LogVolOpt
                      59G   24G   32G  43% /opt


 --------------------- Disk Space End ----------------------
 #################### Logwatch End ######################
```

A script to validate RAID is also available and run weekly to ensure the RAID configurations of the box. Listing 7-29 shows a snippet of the raid-check script.

Listing 7-29. Raid Check Script

```bash
#!/bin/bash
#
# This script reads it's configuration from /etc/sysconfig/raid-check
# Please use that file to enable/disable this script or to set the
# type of check you wish performed.

# We might be on a kernel with no raid support at all, exit if so
[ -f /proc/mdstat ] || exit 0
```

All the scripts listed are enabled by default on the ODA, but the output is e-mailed to the internal root account using the mail utility. In order to look at the outputs, you need to log on to the box as the root user and execute the mail utility or set up mail redirection as described in MOS Note 405229.1.

Reactive Checks

Proactive checks have been the focus of this chapter so far. Things can happen, however, and it is important to understand various reactive procedures that are needed or embedded in the ODA. Diagnostics are a very complex process, and thus not all forms of reactive checks can be covered as part of this section, but we do cover some of the more useful ones.

Diagnostic Collection

The ODA provides an easy way to collect and manage various diagnostic information in the form of the oakcli manage diagcollect command. The command allows for easy access to all log files and diagnostic information across various ODA, Clusterware, ASM, and RDBMS log files, and on multiple nodes. Listing 7-30 shows how to get the help text for the command.

Listing 7-30. ODA Diagnostic Collection Utility

```
./oakcli  manage diagcollect -h
Usage:
oakcli manage diagcollect [options]
options:
  --all                    - For collecting all diag info (Default option),
                             excluding adr, chmos
  --crs                    - For collecting crs diag information
  --patch                  - For collecting ODA Patching logs
...
```

Diagnostic information can be trimmed and, depending on the type of problem, only specific information can be collected or excluded. Diagnostic data when paired with TFA can help provide Oracle with a lot of information, which in turn can help debug and diagnose a problem pretty quickly.

Disk Failures

As part of hardware operations, it is very common for various components to fail. Due to the nature and operational factors of disks, failure should always be seen as imminent, and that is why ODA provides double or triple software mirroring. Such mirroring allows for failures to occur without data loss.

Diagnosis of a failed disk is very important, and providing the right level of information helps in the expedited replacement of a disk. Listing 7-31 displays how to execute odasundiag.sh, which is a diagnostics command built specifically for the ODA so that an Oracle engineer can get pertinent diagnostic information about the disk failure and create a Field Service Task to either send a replacement disk or have a service engineer replace it.

Listing 7-31. ODA Sun Diagnostics Script

```
# /root/Extras/odasundiag.sh
```

The file generated when the command in Listing 7-31 is executed will need to be uploaded to My Oracle Support as part of a service request. This will allow for the support personnel to determine the problem and provide a resolution. If the resolution is disk replacement, it can be handled by the customer or by Oracle's field services team.

ASR, if set up, will also open a service request to Oracle and provide base data so that a Field Service Request is opened to replace a disk.

If you need to replace a drive, you can ease the job of finding the offending drive by turning on the locator beacon. Listing 7-32 displays the command to locate a disk.

Listing 7-32. Locate a Disk

```
# ./oakcli locate  disk e0_pd_00 on
Disk: e0_pd_00 and to: ON
```

Executing this command causes an LED to be turned on, which is used to ensure that the correct disk is being removed and replaced. This is useful for hardware engineers and ensures that only the right part is replaced.

Summary

This chapter focused on various proactive and reactive measures to keep an ODA healthy and to diagnose various issues. The ODA is meant to be a fully self-sufficient solution, and as such, provides tools such as built-in validation, ODA configuration audit toolcheck., and Trace File Analyzer to provide fully proactive diagnostics. Problems can still happen, however, and tools such as ODA diagnostic collection utility help in the transmission and collection of data for quicker problem resolution. ASR is an optional utility that provides automatic failure detection and SR creation for Oracle x86 systems, including the ODA.

CHAPTER 8

■ ■ ■

Patching the Oracle Database Appliance

Patching is one of the biggest challenges a modern IT organization faces today. Patching is a regular task that most probably involves most of the support team's efforts after supporting functional and business requests. It involves a lot of effort to plan, verify, test, and execute patching activities. Patching is an ongoing activity that addresses existing problems and reduces risk of facing potential problems discovered by other product users. Patching also simplifies work, with Oracle Support in troubleshooting issues your team has faced or will possibly face in the near future. The good news is that the Oracle Database Appliance significantly reduces the amount of effort necessary to keep a database system on the current level. This chapter explains how the Oracle Database Appliance addresses the never-ending patching challenge and makes it significantly less resource consuming.

Introduction to Patching

The Oracle Database Appliance takes a very simple and practical approach to patching. A single patch delivers updates for all system components. The patching process is automated and fully scripted. It takes just a few commands to patch the whole system, starting from the internal hard-drive firmware and ending with Oracle Database patches. Oracle Corporation releases patches and patch bundles on a quarterly basis. This simplifies your planning process.

Conventional Systems Limitations

What is so special about patching you ask? Just install a new version of software and you are done. Right? Would that it were that simple. The problem is that a modern server is a complex system. It contains many separately updatable components, starting from the BIOS and lights-out adapter, and ending with the operational system. Furthermore, a database system doesn't consist of a server only. There are other important components that need regular software updates. There are network components, internal storage, external storage, and more. The storage could be a complex system by itself. To make a long story short, a database system consists of a dozen or more components that need to be patched on a regular basis.

Updating a single component is a relatively simple task. However, each of the components interacts with others. To make sure that all will operate without issues, an administrator or a group of administrators should verify the compatibility of all components at their current version level. The lights-out adapter version should be compatible with the current BIOS version; disk and network card drivers should be compatible with the operational system version, and so on.

Often, different groups within the organization are responsible for patching different system components. A storage team, for example, is responsible for storage components, whereas a network team maintains network components like switches used in clustered environments. A system administration team is responsible for operational system patching. The patching process typically is divided into separate phases in which each group plans, tests, and executes their own patching separately from the other groups.

In preparation to a patching exercise, the group doing the patching should ensure that changes they are going to introduce in the system will not impact other components, such as the operational system, cluster services, and others. To ensure compatibility and supportability, the group needs to ensure and verify that the new version they are going to install is compatible with components that are managed by other groups. The planning phase can take significant time just because of the need to verify the complex interdependencies. The complexity brings with it the risk of error and subsequent downtime.

With the approach of patching one component at a time, an organization needs to introduce significantly more downtime than if it has the ability to patch all system components in one go. Each patching effort requires system downtime. Each downtime involves more coordination between different groups within the organization. Applications that are dependent on the component to be patched need to be stopped, increasing the amount of downtime needed. After the patching is completed, the system components need to be started one by one and verified. After all components have been started, a "smoke" test needs to be performed before releasing the system for end users to use. All these steps add time to the downtime necessary for each component's patching. However, if we are able to patch all components in one go, then we significantly reduce the overall downtime necessary to keep a system up to date.

The same applies to the efforts necessary for system and application testing. In the ideal case, each change should be tested started from lower technical layers and ending with application and business testing. Multiple patching phases require more testing efforts from different groups within an organization than when we patch all components at once.

Another challenge that many IT groups face is the fact that many patching activities involve manual steps. Manual steps introduce space for human errors and makes the patching process even longer than it could be. Some organizations may decide to invest time and resources into automating the patching steps and make those as human-independent as possible. However, the fact that different system components are produced by different vendors makes the task of streamlining a patching process a challenge. Each component may use different patching technology. For many organizations, it may not be economically justifiable to invest in patch automation, and instead they accept and manage the risks related to manual patching.

There is a planning challenge involved in the traditional system-patching life cycle. Different component vendors release patches at different points in time. This lack of coordination in timing makes it almost impossible to make patching a regular routine. It would greatly simplify planning if all component vendors released patches at well-known intervals and synchronized with each other. This way, IT groups within the organization could establish well-known patching cycles with well-known steps.

These and other challenges make a modern clustered database system's patching a very complex, time- and resource-consuming process. The challenges increase overall IT costs and reduce efficiency, whereas modern businesses are demanding precisely the opposite outcome.

Oracle Database Appliance Benefits

The Oracle Database Appliance simplifies and streamlines the patching process significantly. In fact, this is one of the most valuable Oracle Database Appliance advantages over traditional clustered systems. The Oracle Database Appliance patches are released on a quarterly basis and cover all system components, starting from firmware and ending with the Oracle Database software. The so-called "One Button" patching process is fully automated and involves a few simple steps.

The fact that the system is engendered, put together, and supported by one company makes it possible to combine all the patching activities into one set of scripts. This simplifies planning as well. Oracle releases Oracle Database Appliance patches on a quarterly basis. An organization may choose the frequency at which it would like to apply those patches. Predictability of patch releases and their application makes it much easier to schedule patching cycles and associated testing, preparation, downtime, and other activities.

The patching process consists of three phases, and those phases provide a certain level of flexibility. For example, an application and a functional team may decide to adopt a six-month patching cycle, and the infrastructure group still could patch the infrastructure components on a three-month basis. Such an approach of skipping alternating patches to the database may reduce application testing activities if an organization decides that such is necessary.

Patching Flow

The following two subsections discuss the overall flow of patching in the ODA environment. The first section gives the general sort of flow one might normally encounter. The second section specifically focuses on the three steps specific to the ODA.

General Patching Flow

Figure 8-1 represents the Oracle Database Appliance general patching process flow. It isn't too different from a traditional system's patching cycle. As with any system, testing the patch's application process is an important step in the Oracle Database Appliance patching life cycle. Your team should get comfortable with the patching process steps, document them, and measure the downtime necessary each time you patch. The functional team should do a reasonable amount of testing in the test and development environments before moving patches to the production system.

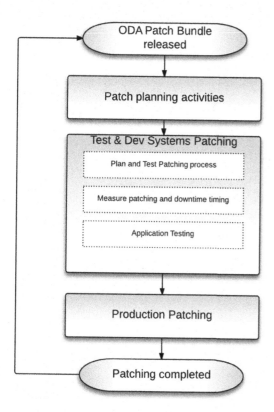

Figure 8-1. Patching in the general case

I have seen organizations that because of limited budgets and other constraints purchase just one Oracle Database Appliance as a production system, and then run test and development environments on some other platform. While such is a possible setup, I suggest to avoiding it. The problem in such a case is that it isn't possible to test and verify an Oracle Database Appliance patch before you apply it in a production environment. My suggestion is to purchase at least two Oracle Database Appliances and test the patch process on a test environment before applying it on the production Oracle Database Appliance(s).

Someone may think that Oracle tests all patches and therefore it is not necessary to do in-house patch testing. The problem is that even with the Oracle Database Appliance, each system may be slightly different. Some clients may decide to skip some of the patches. Some may decide to customize the configuration just a bit. Some may use a different network setup. My recommendation is to test the patch on your particular setup in a test environment, and make all possible efforts to apply the patch in the same way on the production environment.

Specific ODA Steps

Figure 8-2 illustrates the Oracle Database Appliance's patching steps. There are three main steps involved. We'll describe them briefly in this section, and then in more detail in later sections. Depending on your business requirements, each of the three main patching steps can be separated in time from the others.

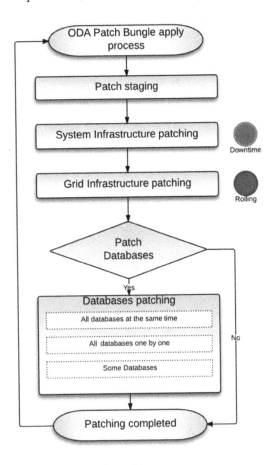

Figure 8-2. *ODA's patching steps*

System infrastructure components like disks, firmware, BIOS, and the operational system are patched first. The "System Infrastructure" patching step requires full system downtime. All database instances and the Grid Infrastructure processes are stopped during the patching.

Each quarterly release, the Oracle Database Appliance patch bundle may contain patches for different sets of system infrastructures components. For example, a given release might contain patches for the Storage Expander, ILOM, BIOS, and OVM. As mentioned, it is possible to skip some of the patch bundles. Helpfully, each of the Oracle Database Appliances patch bundles is cumulative. An ODA customer may skip one or several patch bundles. However, the number of system components to be patched in such a case is potentially higher than would be the case when you patch each bundle. Patching downtime can increase depending on the number of system components to be updated.

Based on our current experience, the total downtime for "System Infrastructure" patching generally falls between 45 and 80 minutes. The Oracle Database Appliance's nodes may be rebooted as part of the update of components like OS, OVM, or storage. It is essential for critical systems to have a test run on a test environment to measure the total downtime from the patch bundle and to verify whether node reboots are required.

After the system infrastructure is updated, the Grid Infrastructure needs to be patched. At the time of writing, all Oracle Database Appliance patch bundles apply Grid Infrastructure updates in a rolling fashion. This means that one of the two nodes is available during the update, and all the database services are up and running on the other node. No downtime is involved.

The next and final stage is the databases upgrade. Several options are available for how to approach this task. Some organizations may decide to skip the database-patching step each alternate quarter, and patch databases once in six months, thus saving time on application testing while still keeping their system infrastructure up to date. Other organizations may patch their databases at the same time as they apply infrastructure patches. Some organizations may separate the infrastructure and databases updates. Such separation allows one to take the whole system down for just the infrastructure patching, and then bring the system up and complete the remaining updates in a rolling fashion. The ODA provides the flexibility, allowing you to choose your own approach to patching depending on your organizational requirements.

Timing

There are two aspects to timing. The first is the question of how often to patch. We've touched on that already by mentioning that some organizations apply only every alternating patch. The other aspect to consider is how long an individual patch application takes. If one is to apply a patch, one should have an idea as to how long the target system will be offline.

How Often to Patch

Oracle releases Patch Set Updates (PSU) and Security Patch Updates (SPU)—the SPUs are better known as Critical Patch Updates (CPU)—for Oracle Database products on a quarterly basis. The SPU is a smaller set of changes focused on critical issues only. PSUs include SPUs plus additional fixes. Oracle suggests choosing one of the following practices:

- Apply SPUs on top of a base release to minimize the amount of change applied between one main release and the next.

- Implement PSUs on a regular basis to make sure that all critical and security fixes are applied.

The Oracle Database Appliance adopts the PSU's patch cycle. An Oracle Database Appliance patch bundle is released shortly after a PSU patch is released. It is worth mentioning that Oracle Database is just one component that is included in the Oracle Database Appliance patch bundles. However, it is one of the main components. Therefore, Oracle's adoption of the PSU patch cycle for the ODA makes a lot of sense.

Oracle's regular patch releases simplify your patch planning and aid in flexibility. Some customers may find quarterly patching too aggressive and choose to skip applying one or more of the Oracle Database Appliances patch bundles. The important point here is that the regular patch releases allow organizations to introduce regular, well known, and planned patching cycles into their environments. That simplifies a lot of things, including the scheduling of human resources for implementation and testing, making the patching a well-known routine rather than a one-off activity triggered by a critical problem in a production system. The resulting, regular application of patches proactively protects database systems from potentially dangerous issues and unnecessary downtime. Stability of the production environment is improved.

How Long It Takes to Patch

Table 8-1 gives you an approximate idea of the timing involved in each patching step. The table also indicates whether a given step requires full system downtime, and whether it requires a reboot. Table 8-1 is just a general guide to give you the lay of the land. You should measure patching time yourself. Measure it for each phase in a test system before you apply a patch to a production system.

Table 8-1. *Downtime Estimates by Phase*

Phase	Full Downtime	Requires Reboot	Approximate Time (min)
System Infrastructure	Yes	Possible	45–80*
Grid Infrastructure	No (rolling upgrade)	No	45–60
Databases	No (rolling upgrade)	No	10–20**

* Depends on the number of components to be updated by the patch bundle
** Depends on the number of databases that are involved

Please note that each of the patching steps can be separated in time. It is not necessary to perform all three steps in quick succession. The database upgrade phase allows some flexibility. You can execute the steps individually at time intervals that are comfortable for your business.

ODA Patching Options

Different options are available to you depending upon your business needs. Read the following sections to learn more about your options and when they might be best used.

New Appliances

If you received a new Oracle Database Appliance from the factory, chances are that it isn't running the latest version of the Oracle Database Appliance software and firmware. You need to update it to the latest patch level. There are two options you can employ to get there:

- The first and recommended option is to use a process similar to the update process described earlier in the "Patching Flow" section. You need to follow the steps described in the latest Oracle Database Appliance patch README file.[1]

---

[1]Information about the latest Oracle Database Appliance patch available from the My Oracle Support Note 888888.1

- The other option is to use the Oracle Database Appliance's Bare Metal Restore option as described the My Oracle Support note titled "Oracle Database Appliance Bare Metal Restore Procedure" (Doc ID 1373599.1).

The first option takes care of all system infrastructure components. In the Bare Metal Restore case, you should implicitly update system infrastructure components such as BIOS and firmware after you unpack the bundle on the Oracle Database Appliance. The instructions for updating system infrastructure are provided later in this chapter in the "Executing Patching" section. You can also find them in the README file.

The Oracle Database Appliance comes with a bare metal system infrastructure version preinstalled by default. Through a reimaging process, you can convert to a virtual setup. If you intended to use the virtual option, you must reimage the Oracle Database Appliance using instructions provided in the following My Oracle Support note: "Step by Step Instructions on Installing Virtualized Image on Oracle Database Appliance" (Article ID 1520579.1).

Default Patching Option

The default patching option is a straightforward process that can be executed in approximately two hours. It assumes that you have a standard Oracle Database Appliance configuration, with minimal deviation from the recommended configuration and less restrictive downtime requirements. This option is to be taken as the base option for the more fixable options described in the next sections.

Steps Separated in Time

To minimize the length of a downtime interval, and to allow yourself a clear focus and a more granular control over the patching process, you may wish to separate the three steps of patching the System Infrastructure, Grid Infrastructure, and the RDBMS. Each step can be executed separately, and with several weeks between them if that's what you need.

This approach of separating the steps requires more planning and more implementation effort. The only step that requires complete system downtime, however, is the System Infrastructure patching. The other two steps (Grid Infrastructure and RDBMS) can be executed in rolling fashion by running services on one of the two nodes while the second node is being patched.

By separating steps in time, you can make sure that a previous step is completed successfully before going on to the next. The time needed per step is shorter than the time needed for the default approach of doing all steps in one go. However, the tradeoff is that the process becomes more complicated.

Delayed RDBMS Update

Based on the circumstances and business requirements, you may decide to update some databases while leaving others on the same appliance running at a prior version.

The standard ODA upgrade option works on a *per Oracle Home* basis. All databases that belong to a particular Oracle Home are upgraded at the same time. The Oracle Database Appliance also supports multiple Oracle Homes— you can have as many Oracle Homes as you want or have resources for. The Oracle Database Appliance currently supports 11.2.0.2 and 11.2.0.3 Oracle Home versions. Each Oracle Database Appliance bundle patch upgrades the fifth version number of the Oracle Database version. For example, upgrading from Oracle Database Appliance bundle patch 2.6 to bundle patch 2.7 upgrades from Oracle Database version 11.2.0.3.6 to 11.2.0.3.7.

There are two options available if you would like to patch databases one by one. The first option is to configure each database to be run from a separate Oracle Home. This way, during the patching process you can specify what Oracle Home and associated database you would like to patch. If there are several databases running from the same

Oracle Home, you need to separate those by making additional Oracle Home copies and moving those databases from the original Oracle Home to a new and separate Oracle Home that you have created. In the following example, we create additional Oracle Homes and move two databases to be started from a newly created, separate Oracle Home:

```
# On 2.6
# Show all current Oracle Homes
oakcli show dbhomes –detail
# Create a new Oracle Home
oakcli create dbhome -version 11.2.0.3.6
oakcli show dbhomes –detail
# Reconfigure a dataabse to be executed from a new Oracle Home
srvctl modify database -d DOG -o /u01/app/oracle/product/11.2.0.3/dbhome_2
# Restart the database
srvctl stop database -d DOG
srvctl start database -d DOG
oakcli create dbhome -version 11.2.0.3.6
srvctl modify database -d CAT -o /u01/app/oracle/product/11.2.0.3/dbhome_3
srvctl stop database -d CAT
srvctl start database -d CAT
```

The other option is to patch databases manually. In this case, you need just two Oracle Homes. You need one for the source and one for the target version of the database engine. Furthermore, you need to execute all the patching steps yourself, and you'll be moving databases between the Oracle Homes yourself, too. The following steps are involved:

1. Create an Oracle Home for the new version of the RDBMS.

2. Stop the database that you are updating.

3. Reconfigure the database to be started from the newly created Oracle Home.

4. Start the database and run upgrade steps.

5. Release the database to users.

This manual approach doesn't require you to create a separate Oracle Home for each database. You can update all the databases using just two Oracle Homes. However, this approach requires more manual steps than the first approach shown earlier. You use traditional database upgrade steps just as you would for a regular Oracle system, thereby losing the automatic database upgrade functionality provided by the Oracle Database Appliance.

Data Guard to Minimize Downtime

If your business demands the shortest possible downtime, you look at using an additional Oracle Database Appliance in a Data Guard configuration. This approach allows you to avoid downtime associated with System and Grid Infrastructure updates. Here is the process:

1. Establish a standby database configuration[2] between the primary and secondary Oracle Database Appliances.

2. Stop the redo log application process on the secondary/standby Oracle Database Appliance.

3. Update the System and Grid Infrastructure components of the standby Oracle Database Appliance.

---

[2] Please note that Data Guard configuration is out of scope of that book. You can reference an Oracle White Paper "Deploying Oracle Data Guard with Oracle Database Appliance" for additional information.

4. Do not update the standby database Oracle Home just yet. Instead, reestablish the redo log application process.

5. Switch your applications to use the secondary Oracle Database Appliance, thus switching over to the standby database. At this point, the primary Oracle Database Appliance can be taken offline to update infrastructure components.

6. Update your database to the latest version using the rolling update approach. This way, there is just a short switchover time when applications need to be repointed from the primary to the secondary Oracle Database Appliance. There is no application downtime associated with the infrastructure update activities.

Use of Data Guard as just described requires a bit more effort in planning, preparation, and implementation. However, the Data Guard approach provides a minimal switchover time as opposed to the hours of downtime and limited mode operations during the Grid Infrastructure and database patching steps when performed in their normal manner.

Virtual Oracle Database Appliance

We aren't going to spend too much time talking about the virtual machine (VM) option here. However, it is worth mentioning that a VM environment isn't too different from a patching perspective. There is just one additional component to patch during the System Infrastructure patching phase, and that is the Oracle VM Server.

If a patch bundle delivers an Oracle VM Server patch, then all virtual machines must be stopped, the main Oracle VM Server host's (so-called Dom0 host) operational system must be patched, and the whole server must be restarted.

As with any patching, you should spend time carefully looking through the patch bundle's README file to make sure that you complete all the additional steps related to VM configuration. Some of the earlier patch bundles came with instructions for patching-related activities that are specific to the VM configuration.

The other important thing to know is that all patching activities—for example, patch staging, unpacking, apply, and so forth—are to be executed from within the so-called Oracle Database Appliance Base Virtual Machine. Oracle engineers carefully design VM patches to make sure that they can be successfully applied from a running VM before restarting the Oracle VM Server.

The two items I've just mentioned are the only important differences between the bare metal patching process and the VM configuration patching process. Keep in mind that the system requires a small amount of full downtime for the System Infrastructure patching phase in either configuration. Therefore, there is no significant difference in that regard. The VM option may require perhaps ten minutes more downtime than the bare metal option, because the Oracle VM Server is an additional element that must be patched.

Preparation

The first step in the patching process is preparation. It's an important step unless you enjoy all-nighters. Don't shortchange it. Among other generic activities associated with traditional system patching, the following are some things to check, and then to do during the planning part of the ODA patching process.

Verify the Release Level

Before you update an Oracle Database Appliance to the latest release, you should be sure you know the current release that you are running. The easiest way to retrieve the information is to execute an oakcli command, as follows:

```
[root@s1 ~]# oakcli show version
Version
-------
2.6.0.0.0
```

The Oracle Database Appliance consists of over a dozen different software components. While you can use each component's interface to find out its current version, the easiest way to find all components' versions is to issue the oakcli command with the -details switch, as follows:

```
[root@s1 ~]# oakcli show version -detail
Reading the metadata. It takes a while...
```

System Version	Component Name	Installed Version	Supported Version
--------------	---------------	------------------	----------------
2.6.0.0.0			
	Controller	11.05.02.00	Up-to-date
	Expander	0342	Up-to-date
	SSD_SHARED	E12B	Up-to-date
	HDD_LOCAL	SA03	Up-to-date
	HDD_SHARED	0B25	Up-to-date
	ILOM	3.0.16.22.b r78329	No-update
	BIOS	12010310	No-update
	IPMI	1.8.10.5	Up-to-date
	HMP	2.2.6.1	Up-to-date
	OAK	2.6.0.0.0	Up-to-date
	OEL	5.8	Up-to-date
	OVM	3.1.1	Up-to-date
	TFA	2.5.1.4	Up-to-date
	GI_HOME	11.2.0.3.6(16056266, 16083653)	Up-to-date
	DB_HOME	11.2.0.3.6(16056266, 16083653)	Up-to-date
	ASR	Unknown	4.4

```
[root@s1 ~]#
```

Review the Patch Notes

Before you start downloading a patch, it is a good idea to review related notes for information about known issues. This is specifically true for such a relatively new product as the Oracle Database Appliance. For some releases, there are some specific steps to complete. The steps are subject to change, and therefore the patching instructions provided in this chapter are for reference only. You should confirm those instructions by reading a patch bundle's notes.

The My Oracle Support note "Oracle Database Appliance - 2.X Supported Versions & Known Issues (Doc ID 888888.1)" is a good starting point. The note contains useful information relative to patching, starting with the "Latest Releases" section, in which you find references to the latest patches and versions available. The note ends with a "Known Issues" section—also very important to read.

Review the known issues section and make notes if any of the known issues affect your configuration. The same note points you to the latest patch bundle available. Look for the patch with the name "ORACLE DATABASE APPLIANCE PATCH BUNDLE". In version 2.7, that bundle is "Oracle Database Appliance Patch 2.7.0.0.0 Patch 16760967." Figure 8-3 shows how the bundle is mentioned in the note.

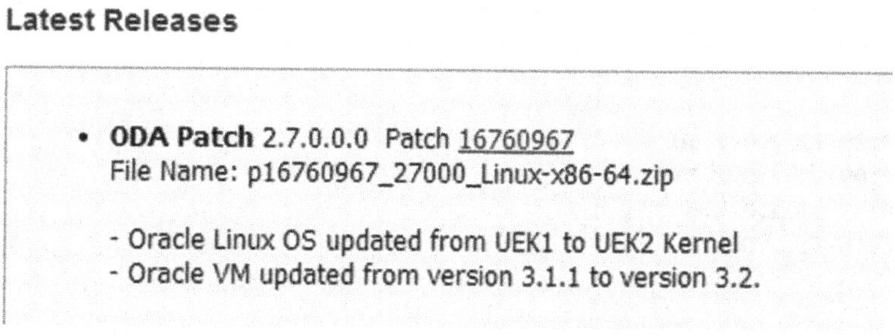

Latest Releases

- **ODA Patch** 2.7.0.0.0 Patch 16760967
  File Name: p16760967_27000_Linux-x86-64.zip

  - Oracle Linux OS updated from UEK1 to UEK2 Kernel
  - Oracle VM updated from version 3.1.1 to version 3.2.

Figure 8-3. A patch bundle listed in the "Latest Release" section of a patch note

Before downloading a patch, study the README that accompanies it, and pay close attention to the main installation steps applicable to your configuration and to the "Known Issues" section. Note the issues and any related corrective actions.

Let me give an example of why it is so important to read the known issues listing. There is a known issue in which ASM may not start successfully if one of the Oracle Database Appliance's hard drives has been replaced. This affects appliances running ODA versions prior to version 2.5. If your system is affected, contact Oracle Support to obtain a fix. Your system may not be affected by this particular issue. However, there are a few other issues that may be applicable to your configuration. It is important to do this homework before you start the actual patching process—unless that is, you enjoy staying up all night in a blind panic while trying to repair a broken system before your boss gets into the office the next morning.

Download the Patch Bundle Set

You may want use your workstation as a staging point when downloading a patch's zip file; or download from a staging server with direct access to My Oracle Support (https://updates.oracle.com). If My Oracle Support is accessible directly from the Oracle Database Appliance nodes, then you can download the patch file directly to the Oracle Database Appliance using the wget command.

Copy the file into a directory on both Oracle Database Appliance nodes. There is no particular directory that you must use; just use one that is in line with your organization's practice, or use your personal preferences. During the unpacking stage, the update patches are extracted and stored under a particular directory structure. Depending on the free space available in the root file system, it may not be practical to stage the patch file in the /tmp directory (as has been suggested in some patch bundles READMEs). In our example to follow, we use the /u01/patch_stage/2.7/ directory.

Unpack the Patch Bundle Set

The next step is to make the Oracle Appliance Kit (OAK) aware of what updates the patch bundle delivers, and to unpack those under the /opt/oracle/oak/pkgrepos/ file system. Execute the unpack command as the root user on each of the Oracle Database Appliance nodes. Use the following command as an example (please note that the command is subject to change, so you should always reference your patch's README file for the syntax to be used):

```
oakcli unpack -package /u01/patch_stage/2.7/p16760967_27000_Linux-x86-64.zip
```

Browse the Updates Repository

The unpack command extracts all the updates from the patch bundle file and puts them under OAK repository /opt/oracle/oak/pkgrepos/. You can browse the repository by listing the directories' content. To get an idea of which Oracle DB software versions are available in the repository, you could use the following commands:

```
[root@s1 DB]# cd /opt/oracle/oak/pkgrepos/orapkgs/DB
[root@s1 DB]# ls -l
total 16
drwxrwxrwx 3 root root 4096 Sep  1 13:20 11.2.0.2.10
drwxrwxrwx 4 root root 4096 Aug 31 14:09 11.2.0.2.11
drwxr-xr-x 3 root root 4096 Apr 24 09:57 11.2.0.3.6
drwxrwxrwx 4 root root 4096 Aug 21 16:16 11.2.0.3.7
[root@s1 DB]#
```

Alternatively, execute the following command to list the patch components (and their versions) stored in the repository:

```
[root@s1 ~]# tree /opt/oracle/oak/pkgrepos/ -L 3
/opt/oracle/oak/pkgrepos/
|-- System
|   |-- 2.6.0.0.0
|   |   |-- bin
|   |   |-- conf
|   |   `-- prereqs
|   |-- 2.7.0.0.0
|   |   |-- bin
|   |   |-- conf
|   |   `-- prereqs
|   |-- VERSION
|   `-- system_repos_metadata.xml
|-- orapkgs
|   |-- ASR
|   |   |-- 4.4
|   |   `-- 4.4.1
|   |-- DB
|   |   |-- 11.2.0.2.10
|   |   |-- 11.2.0.2.11
|   |   |-- 11.2.0.3.6
|   |   `-- 11.2.0.3.7
|   |-- GI
|   |   |-- 11.2.0.3.6
|   |   `-- 11.2.0.3.7
|   |-- HMP
|   |   |-- 2.2.6
|   |   `-- 2.2.6.2
|   |-- IPMI
|   |   `-- 1.8.10.5
|   |-- OAK
|   |   |-- 2.6.0.0.0
|   |   `-- 2.7.0.0.0
|   |-- OEL
```

```
|    |    `-- 5.9
|    |-- OPATCH
|    |    `-- 11.2.0.3.0
|    |-- OVS
|    |    `-- 2.7.0.0.0
|    `-- TFA
|         |-- 2.5.1.4
|         `-- 2.5.1.5
|-- rpms
|    |-- db4-4.3.29-10.el5_5.2.i386.rpm
|    |-- gdbm-1.8.0-28.el5.i386.rpm
|    |-- libXi-1.0.1-4.el5_4.x86_64.rpm
|    |-- libXp-1.0.0-8.1.el5.x86_64.rpm
|    |-- libstdc++-devel-4.1.2-54.el5.i386.rpm
|    |-- screen-4.0.3-4.el5.x86_64.rpm
|    `-- screenlog.0
`-- thirdpartypkgs
     `-- Firmware
          |-- Controller
          |-- Disk
          |-- Expander
          `-- Ilom

45 directories, 9 files
[root@s1 ~]#
```

The /opt/oracle/oak/pkgrepos/System/ directory contains metadata files that describe the content of the repository. The system_repos_metadata.xml file is an XML file that contains references to all patches staged. A VERSION file contains the current Oracle Database Appliance version number. There is a subdirectory for each Oracle Database Appliance patch bundle under the system directory. For example, there are subdirectories named 2.6.0.0.0, 2.7.0.0.0, and so forth. Each patch bundle directory contains files that describe specific patches and their locations within the repository.

There is also a conf/patch_metadata.txt file that contains references to all updates. The following is an example of a few records from the file:

```
...
GI_PATCHES=16742216
GI_PATCH_DIR=$OAK_REPOS_HOME/pkgrepos/orapkgs/GI/11.2.0.3.7/Patches

DB_PATCHES=16742216
DB_PATCH_DIR=$OAK_REPOS_HOME/pkgrepos/orapkgs/DB/11.2.0.3.7/Patches
...
```

You are not supposed to manually delete, copy, or adjust files in the repository. The OAK utility should be used to manage the files. However, it is useful to know the details. The details just described may be useful in the event of troubleshooting problems that might occur during the patch application.

Verify Target Versions

After you unpack the patch bundle under the updates repository on each node, it is relatively simple to get a list of the Oracle Database Appliance components that are going to be updated by the patch. Issue the following OAK command specifying the patching target version:

```
[root@s1 2.7]# /opt/oracle/oak/bin/oakcli update -patch  2.7.0.0.0 --verify

INFO: 2013-08-18 16:41:40: Reading metadata . It takes a while...
WARNING: 2013-08-18 16:41:50: exceptions.IndexError:list index out of range
           Component Name        Installed Version      Proposed Patch Version
           ---------------       ------------------     -------------------
           Controller            11.05.02.00            Up-to-date
           Expander              0342                   Up-to-date
           SSD_SHARED            E12B                   Up-to-date
           HDD_LOCAL             SA03                   Up-to-date
           HDD_SHARED            0B25                   Up-to-date
           ILOM                  3.0.16.22.b r78329     No-update
           BIOS                  12010310               No-update
           IPMI                  1.8.10.5               Up-to-date
           HMP                   2.2.6.1                2.2.6.2
           OAK                   2.6.0.0.0              2.7.0.0.0
           OEL                   5.8                    5.9
           OVM                   3.1.1                  3.2.3
           TFA                   2.5.1.4                2.5.1.5
           GI_HOME               11.2.0.3.6(16056266,   11.2.0.3.7(16619892,
                                 16083653)              16742216)
           DB_HOME               11.2.0.3.6(16056266,   11.2.0.3.7(16619892,
                                 16083653)              16742216)

[root@s1 2.7]#
```

In the preceding example, there are seven components to be updated, including Oracle Appliance Kit, Oracle VM Server, Oracle Grid Infrastructure, and others. The list of components to be updated by a patch bundle is a good starting point for creating a downtime estimate and an impact analysis. The number of components to be updated depends on the currently installed versions of software, patches, and firmware on the Oracle Database Appliance, and the target version you are planning to upgrade to.

Each Oracle Database Appliance patch bundle may deliver a different set of updates. As a rule of thumb, each new patch bundle delivers the latest version of Grid Infrastructure and Oracle Homes. All other components delivered depend on the other products release dates.

Patch Execution

With the preparation work behind you, it's time for the patch execution to begin. This is when the patch updates are applied. You'll upgrade system and then grid infrastructure in this step. Let's start with describing where ODA patching process stores log files. You can follow log files to get a good idea of which steps the patching utility is currently executing, and then troubleshoot any possible issues.

Upgrade Log Files

The OAK patching process has component-specific logging enabled for every component being patched. Resulting log files can be found in the /opt/oracle/oak/log/<hostname>/patch/<patch bundle number> directory on each of the nodes. As an example, you may find the following output:

```
[root@s1 DB]# cd  /opt/oracle/oak/log/s1/patch/2.7.0.0.0/
[root@s1 2.7.0.0.0]# ls -lptr
total 480
-rw-rw-rw- 1 root root    136 Aug 21 14:46 prepatch_63726.log
-rw-rw-rw- 1 root root  29851 Aug 21 15:23 gidbupdate_64341.log
-rw-rw-rw- 1 root root    962 Aug 21 15:24 postpatch_96328.log
-rw-rw-rw- 1 root root   1188 Aug 21 15:56 createdbhome_77208.log
-rw-rw-rw- 1 root root   2608 Aug 21 16:18 createdbhome_19153.log
-rw-rw-rw- 1 root root   3669 Aug 21 16:26 createdbhome_25925.log
-rw-rw-rw- 1 root root   1873 Aug 21 16:35 dbupgrade_82891.log
-rw-rw-rw- 1 root root    136 Aug 21 16:40 prepatch_99697.log
-rw-rw-rw- 1 root root   6891 Aug 21 16:42 gidbupdate_100387.log
-rw-rw-rw- 1 root root    136 Aug 21 16:49 prepatch_5847.log
-rw-rw-rw- 1 root root  32179 Aug 21 17:02 gidbupdate_6662.log
-rw-rw-rw- 1 root root  24107 Aug 21 17:08 prepatch_32337.log
-rw-rw-rw- 1 root root  12625 Aug 21 17:12 hmpupdate_6051.log
-rw-rw-rw- 1 root root   1156 Aug 21 17:13 oakupdate_6970.log
-rw-rw-rw- 1 root root   5230 Aug 21 17:15 tfa_7629.log
-rw-rw-rw- 1 root root 178928 Aug 21 17:26 ospatch_7330.log
-rw-rw-rw- 1 root root    181 Aug 21 17:26 asrupdate_345.log
-rw-rw-rw- 1 root root   1475 Aug 21 17:26 ipmiupdate_361.log
-rw-rw-rw- 1 root root  24435 Aug 21 17:26 storage_407.log
-rw-rw-rw- 1 root root    500 Aug 21 17:37 ipmiupdate_12318.log
-rw-rw-rw- 1 root root    511 Aug 21 17:37 hmpupdate_12078.log
-rw-rw-rw- 1 root root   1813 Aug 21 17:37 storage_12321.log
-rw-rw-rw- 1 root root   1281 Aug 21 17:37 ilombios_12513.log
-rw-rw-rw- 1 root root   2410 Aug 21 17:41 ovspatch_12553.log
-rw-rw-rw- 1 root root   1496 Aug 21 17:46 postpatch_23166.log
```

This directory is a good starting point. However, each separate component that is patched may generate an additional specific log file. For example, the operating-system upgrade utility yum would report activities in the /var/log/yum.log file. From a practical perspective, it is very useful to know where to look for additional information in case you need it.

Upgrade System Infrastructure

During the system infrastructure upgrade step, the whole cluster will be unavailable. All databases are going to be stopped by the patching utility, and will be down for the duration of the upgrade. They will be restarted at the end of the process.

You start the system infrastructure upgrade by issuing the following command from the first node. The command needs to be executed as the root user:

```
cd /opt/oracle/oak/bin/
oakcli update -patch 2.7.0.0.0 -infra
```

Depending on what components are updated by the patch, this phase might require a reboot of the servers. The Oracle Database Appliance nodes are going to be rebooted if the patch bundle updates components that require a reboot, like ILOM/BIOS or storage firmware.

Upgrade Grid Infrastructure

The Grid Infrastructure is a critical Real Application Cluster component. It provides services necessary to run Oracle Database in a cluster configuration and ensures that those and other related services are highly available. The patching utility upgrades the Grid Infrastructure in a rolling fashion. This means it stops and updates one Oracle Database Appliance node at a time while database instances are available on the other node (needless to say, this requires the databases to be in RAC mode, and both instances need to be up). The patching is started by the following command:

```
oakcli update -patch  2.7.0.0.0 -gi
```

Please note that in the current version, the patching utility doesn't give any notice at the time it stops instances. Therefore, applications that rely on the database services should be able to handle an instance failure and reconnect to the other instance. Otherwise, you will need to restart the applications and doing so would introduce a downtime. If the Grid Infrastructure patching process completes well, all database instances and other services should be left up and running on the both ODA nodes in exactly the same state as right before the patching.

Database Upgrade

At this stage, we do have all system-level infrastructure components updated to the target version. The next step is to update the databases running on the Oracle Database Appliance. The OAK utility simplifies this database upgrade process significantly. You literally upgrade a database or set of databases by running a single command. All the actual activities are done by the OAK utility in response to that one command.

There are two ways an administrator can plan and execute database upgrade activities. One is to implement the default upgrade process that upgrades all Oracle Homes and databases running on a system. The other is to execute a one-by-one approach to upgrading each database. The following sections describe each of these options.

Upgrading All Databases

To update all Oracle Homes and associated databases, run the following command under the root OS user. The command will update all databases to the latest version delivered by the patch bundle.

```
oakcli update -patch  2.7.0.0.0  --database
```

The OAK utility will ask you if you want to update all Oracle Homes or choose a particular home to update.

```
Found the following 11.2.0.3 homes possible for patching:

HOME_NAME                   HOME_LOCATION
---------                   -------------
OraDb11203_home1            /u01/app/oracle/product/11.2.0.3/dbhome_1
OraDb11203_home2            /u01/app/oracle/product/11.2.0.3/dbhome_2

[Please note that few of the above database homes may be already up-to-date. They will be
```

automatically ignored]

Would you like to patch all the above homes: Y | N ? :Y

You either update all the Oracle Homes listed, or a particular home and associated databases. The OAK utility will patch Oracle Homes and databases in a rolling fashion. At any single point in time, at least one database instance is available in case you are using RAC or RAC one-node options. A single instance is stopped for the duration of the patching session.

Upgrading One by One

If you would like to have more granular control over the databases that are going to be updated, you may want to configure each database to be associated with a separate Oracle Home rather run all databases under one Oracle Home. The following steps demonstrate how to upgrade one-by-one CAT and a DOG databases using OAK utility in a fully automated way:

```
# Show all current Oracle Homes
oakcli show dbhomes -detail
Oracle HomeName        Oracle Home Version             Oracle HomeLocation
Database Name    Database Type
---------------        --------------------            ----------------------------------------
---------------        -----------
OraDb11203_home1       11.2.0.3.7(16619892,16742216)   /u01/app/oracle/product/11.2.0.3/dbhome_1
CAT              RAC
OraDb11203_home2       11.2.0.3.7(16619892,16742216)   /u01/app/oracle/product/11.2.0.3/dbhome_2
DOG                    RACOneNode

# Update dbhome_1 that executes CAT database
oakcli update -patch 2.7.0.0.0 --database
...
Would you like to patch all the above homes: Y | N ? :N
...
Please enter the comma separated list of database home_names that you do NOT want to patch:
OraDb11203_home2

...
........done
# At this stage the CAT database is updated to the latest version. The DOG database is still on the
previous version.

# Update dbhome_2 that executes DOG database
oakcli update -patch 2.7.0.0.0 --database
...
Would you like to patch all the above homes: Y | N ? :N
...
Please enter the comma separated list of database home_names that you do NOT want to patch:
OraDb11203_home1

...
........done
```

If you would like to update databases one by one, you should ensure that each database is running under its own Oracle Home before you start applying an Oracle Database Appliance patch bundle. The Oracle Database Appliance doesn't allow you to create previous versions Oracle Homes after you installed the new System and Grid infrastructures. Therefore, it is important to separate databases to be executed under different Oracle Homes if you would like to patch them separately before you start applying an ODA patch bundle. For instructions on how to move an Oracle Database to be executed under a dedicated Oracle Home, please see the "Delayed RDBMS Update" section from earlier in this chapter. After the Infrastructure components are updated to a new version (in this case, 2.7), we update the Oracle Homes and their associated databases.

The other option to consider is to move databases one by one in between a previous Oracle Home version and a target Oracle Home representing the new version. Such moves must be done manually, executing patching steps necessary to update each database after you move it. In this case, you just follow generic Oracle database patch guidelines to update an Oracle database from the source Oracle Home version to the destination version. The advantage of this method is that you need just two homes: one for the source and another for the destination. If you script and test all upgrade steps carefully, the timing of the database patching steps may be comparable or even shorter than the OAK-automated update. However, you may find yourself investing significantly more effort by implementing that approach.

Summary

The Oracle Database Appliance patching is a straightforward process. It significantly reduces the amount of time and resources necessary to keep the Oracle clustered system up to the current patch version. In a simple case, it is possible to update all the system's components by executing three simple commands within a two-hour maintenance window. The fact that Oracle releases the Oracle Database Appliance patch bundles on a quarterly basis significantly simplifies maintenance efforts and the associated resource planning. With the Oracle Database Appliance, an organization doesn't need to involve several groups—such as storage, system administration, networking, and database administration—to keep the clustered system up to date. The ODA thus delivers a significant economic advantage over traditional systems.

█ █ █

## CHAPTER 9

Business Values for the ODA

In September 2011, Oracle announced the availability of the Oracle Database Appliance as an innovative, entry-level engineered system optimized for databases. The announcement promised easy deployments, pay-as-you-grow licensing, and single-vendor support.

When a new technology is introduced, and business interest builds, someone within a company will ask the question: "Is this a better solution than the way we do things today?". The first step in answering this question and overcoming resistance to change is investigating the business case for the new technology. The Oracle Database Appliance has become a very successful product in the Oracle engineered systems product line. This chapter outlines the business benefits offered by ODAs, which you can use to consider the business case for deploying an ODA solution and assessing any potential technology risks.

Business Challenges

Many companies face the same challenges in meeting an ever-expanding range of business pressures. IT departments are being asked to become agile and deliver infrastructure quickly, even before all of the business requirements have been fully developed. Project timelines are becoming shorter and multiphased. While projects may run late during the early stages, this doesn't mean that the project due date will necessarily be changed. Instead, later project phases may need to make up the slack with shorter timelines. Database departments are usually at the end of the infrastructure provisioning chain. DBAs are being asked to deploy new database infrastructure rapidly and to deliver business value to IT customers sooner. If a project is late by the time it's time for DBAs to do their work, the lead times effectively drop to zero. The old practices of following a cycle of gathering requirements, ordering hardware, and engaging multiple teams with numerous handoffs between them to build database infrastructure simply don't meet modern business timelines.

Many companies face costs pressures from static budgets. New external public cloud offerings are competing for their infrastructure budgets. For a number of years, there has been a slow shift to commodity hardware solutions to reduce costs. While hardware related costs have fallen from commodity solutions, the costs of building and supporting database infrastructure solutions remain high.

Companies often face challenges from shortages of people with high-end skill sets. In general, there isn't a shortage of IT people, DBAs, and other staff. However, the mantra that "good people are hard to find in any economy" does persist. Companies are always looking for people that can solve any technical problem, get work done quickly, and build specialized subject matter expertise quickly.

The rapid introduction of new technologies has placed additional pressures on the availability of people with high-end skill sets. The rapid introduction of these new technologies can require the support staff to get up to speed without a lot of hand-holding. Support staffs have to react quickly to the challenges at hand, and task completion has to be quick. There is little margin for errors or problems that delay projects. Common issues include:

- People's plates are literally full today. There is no time for "OJT"—on-the-job training—and research. Everything has to be jump-started.

- Hourly consulting costs on projects can be very high, adding to the cost pressures. This adds to the pressures for rapid deployment and efficiency.

Security compliance is becoming vital in an age where audits and industry regulations are governing the actions that companies have to take to secure their systems. It is very difficult to achieve compliance across your application and database portfolio in an environment where database servers and databases are custom built.

Enter the ODA

Oracle developed the Oracle Database Appliance, or ODA, to develop a solution to the business challenges mentioned in the preceding section. If the ODAs have an overarching theme, it is "Infrastructure Deployment for Dummies." While some people may be taken back by this term, it is actually meant as a testament to the simplicity and elegance of ODA deployments. The other ODA themes include the time and ease of deployment using a one-button process, the ease of RAC deployments, and the ease of management. After viewing the ODA setup poster, you know that Oracle is delivering a new way of doing business.

The current X3-2 ODA model is an engineered system. An engineered system is hardware and software designed to operate together as a single, integrated packaged solution. While a company can build its own commodity hardware solution, very few have the ability to build their own engineered systems. Most companies simply don't have the resources, or business benefits, to build their own engineered systems, let alone a system that is optimized for highly available Oracle databases.

The X3-2 ODA comes prepackaged with two servers with a total of 32 –2.9Gz Intel E5-2690 CPU cores. An ODA comes with a storage cell that contains 20 900G data drives totaling 18T of raw storage, which can be expanded by adding a second storage expansion rack with an additional 18T of raw storage, for a total of 36T of raw storage. ODAs are deployed with either double or triple mirroring (configurable at installation time), bringing the usable storage to approximately 6T with triple mirroring, or 9T with double mirroring, on a single storage cell. The ODA Getting Started Guide should be consulted for the exact sizing of the mirrored storage options and disk groups, based on the deployment options selected. The current X3-2 servers come with 256G of memory each. Four SSD drives with a total of 800G of storage are included for the online redo logs.

■ **Note**   ODA capacity is certain to change with every generation of the underlying Oracle server hardware product line. Almost as soon as a hardware model is released, Oracle starts development of the next generation replacement.

The first generation of the ODA was a fixed, self-contained appliance unit. For the X3-2 second-generation model, the server and storage units were modularized for the product line to take advantage of an Oracle product roadmap for releasing new hardware to follow the Intel product line developments.

ODAs offer an engineered system from a single supplier, with a single-issue escalation point. The management of the appliance is mainly self-contained and is integrated with Oracle's comprehensive Oracle Enterprise Manager (OEM) management and monitoring solution.

ODAs have been purchased and deployed by a large customer base, consisting of companies of every size. A number of Fortune 500 companies have reported that the majority of their databases can be deployed on ODAs from a resource sizing standpoint. Models with more capacity and higher performance can be expected in the future.

Virtualization is also available on ODAs to support the rapid deployment of databases and applications using Oracle Virtual Manager (OVM) templates. A template for WebLogic has been released, and Oracle has announced the availability of additional templates.

ODAs will maintain their place within the Oracle engineered system product lineup for the foreseeable future. In August 2013, Oracle expanded its engineered system product lineup to include a new offering called the Oracle Virtualized Compute Appliance, or OVCA. This system offers a generalized Oracle Virtual Machine (OVM) provisioning solution, whereas ODAs offer a lower-cost entry point and the virtualization has been optimized for running databases.

Fast, Simple Database Infrastructure Deployments

The first business benefit offered by ODAs is fast and easy database infrastructure and database instance deployments. Deploying an ODA does not require spec'ing equipment, provisioning Storage Area Network (SAN) infrastructure, deploying RAC private interconnect networks, installing an Operating System (OS), or installing RAC, ASM, the grid infrastructure, Oracle database software, or project managers to coordinate all of this work.

The deployment of an ODA simply requires the steps outlined in the setup poster and deployment documents. Once the server is on the network, and the deployment configuration file is built, the time to build the ODA is slightly less than one hour. The result is a two-node RAC cluster, including the configuration of the file systems, ASM storage, grid and database homes, a local OEM database control, and a starter database. Your company can be running on a RAC cluster in less than a day.

If the time to deployment matters to your company, then ODAs will meet the need to have fully deployed high-availability databases and virtualized application solutions within days of completing the server cabling and other network dependencies. An ODA can be deployed by the average DBA by just reading the documentation. If your company is deploying a larger portfolio of ODAs, then adding additional skill sets to your team may make sense.

After deploying our first ODA, we counted the number of pre-deployment, install, and post-deployment steps involved in building databases on our other build-it-yourself platforms. The number of steps to cover all of the bases for the database server, without creating the databases, was between 103 and 107. The equivalent number of steps on an ODA to accomplish the same result, and also deploy a RAC cluster, numbered only in the twenties. Needless to say, we estimated that the reduction in the build and setup time was geometric in nature. Every company should perform their own count of the number of steps and handoffs between teams required to build a database server and high-availability databases using their current build processes.

We experienced a similar reduction in the costs for deploying ODA database infrastructure. Every company has their methods and rules for defining organizational roles and responsibilities. Let's just say that you can build an ODA without the involvement of a SAN team and sysadmins if that aligns with your company's views on roles and responsibilities. There is also a reduction in the amount networking work required to deploy and ODA.

A number of companies we have talked to regarding what resources are needed to build an ODA vs. how things are done today at their company, report that this change in paradigm can result in some interesting internal discussions as they shift their strategy toward engineered systems. The shift in roles and responsibilities can be worked out up front, or they can slowly change over time, as companies become more familiar with the platform and gain more experience.

So that leads to the question: "How long does it take to deploy an ODA?". To answer this question, you have to realize that an ODA has dependencies just like any other engineered system. You still have to order the ODA and have it shipped. An ODA requires fairly simple network cabling, and you still need to complete any DNS and firewall requests. However, much of this work can be done in parallel, even before the ODA arrives. With careful planning, an ODA can be deployed very quickly, with the actual build work taking less than a day.

The author's first experience with an ODA was for a project that required high availability and a very fast deployment. We needed to order equipment and have a set of four RAC clusters running in two weeks. At the time, the ODA platform was new, but we decided to take a chance because this was our best option. We ordered four ODAs and asked for immediate shipment. The ODAs arrived on a Monday, and we racked and cabled them on Tuesday. Some Oracle people flew in on Wednesday morning to see if they could help out, since the platform was very new. We drove to the data center and built all four ODAs at the same time in parallel Wednesday afternoon—with Oracle looking over our shoulders.

The process went so well that we decided to take one of the ODAs and bare metal a brand-new running production ODA RAC cluster in front of the entire DBA department over lunchtime. We finished the deployment just as everyone finished their lunches. People knew that they were looking at a new paradigm in building database servers. Building four RAC clusters in parallel in an afternoon with just a couple of DBAs was unthinkable before that day. Table 9-1 lists many of the tasks that we no longer had to be concerned with as a result of deploying an ODA.

Table 9-1. *Work That Doesn't Have to Be Done to Deploy an ODA*

Task	Traditional	ODA
Spec equipment	Standards dependent.	Standardized hardware and software.
Cabling for external RAC network	On RAC systems.	Included in the hardware.
Provision SAN storage	In most cases.	Included in build.
IO virtualization	Standards dependent.	Included in build for virtualized systems.
Server partitioning	Standards dependent.	Not needed for databases, but can be done to accommodate nondatabase virtual containers.
OS install	In most cases.	Included in build.
Grid Infrastructure install	In most cases.	Included in build.
Database software install	In most cases.	Included in build.
Project management to coordinate team handoffs	Company dependent.	Included in build.

So what happened next? Today it isn't unusual to be approached by application teams or project managers with the question, "Can we put this database on an ODA?". You're in a good place when you are getting this type of question.

The ODA install process eliminates unpredictable, time-wasting setup issues and handoffs that result in additional coordination, dependencies, and delays. Deployment times are measured in days, not weeks or months. The ODA provides a lot of flexibility in meeting project requirements challenges, which is something that a lot of database and infrastructure departments have to deal with.

ODAs can be pre-deployed quickly to avoid the need to buy capacity before it is needed. They are the perfect platform for the majority of your Oracle databases in support of Infrastructure as a Service (IaaS), Databases as a Service (DBaaS), or cloud-based services in support of your company's IT strategy. When you get the question: "How are you provisioning your databases so quickly and efficiently in your DBaaS offering?"—you are in an even better place. ODAs won't meet every project requirement. There are limits to the number of IOPS, and the compute nodes can't be scaled beyond two at this time. However, you may find that ODAs will meet the requirements for the majority of your databases.

RAC Without Tears

Building RAC clusters that will be stable and meet high-availability requirements requires a great deal of up-front planning and work, as well as pre- and post-install checks to validate the environments. Besides the RAC install manuals, there are additional documents that have to be analyzed:

- The RAC generic (MOS 810394.1) and any platform specific starter kits
- The RAC FAQ (MOS 220970.1)
- Oracle's support note (MOS 1344678.1) giving steps to stabilize a cluster, with platform-specific extensions
- The RAC Information Center note (MOS 1452965.2)
- Your platform-specific RAC setup recommendations
- RAC Known Issues support documents

In addition, you'll need to consult any documentation you have that gives advice on setting up RAC to support other Oracle products, such as eBusiness Suite and ATG Web Commerce.

There are additional tools you'll need to learn if you are building your own RAC clusters. Oracle has built various tools to help in validating RAC environments, such as:

- RACcheck (MOS 1268927.1)

- Cluster Verify (MOS 316817.1)

- RDA MOS 314422.1 and 250262.1 for Database checks

And, of course, there are all of the OS-specific settings, package requirements, and checks. Going through all of this effort on a traditional platform is well worth the effort. If you are fortunate, all of this will be documented one time and someone will make the effort to keep up with all of the documentation updates and RACcheck results to keep the "do it yourself" documentation updated. However, doing this takes a lot of time, the right people, a lot of handoffs between departments, and a lot of resulting QA work to make sure the work was done right.

Documenting and distributing complex technical information and training people to understand the information is a challenge for most companies, especially smaller and midsize companies. Adding to challenges are all of the handoffs between multiple teams that are required to implement all of the requirements. Someone may forget to route the interconnect traffic to redundant RAC-only switches (which are also expensive), or forget to configure Jumbo frames on both the server and switches. There can be additional issues related to external vendor software supporting IO multipathing. Because all of these scenarios are very real, Oracle has found the need to invest in extensive RAC diagnostic facilities.

Oracle is helping to manage this complexity by extending RACcheck and other tools to catch setup issues. However, the conclusion is that there are real reasons the people in the Oracle RAC assurance group and Oracle support are very busy these days. Engineered systems and ODAs take a lot of the work to correctly deploy RAC off your shoulders.

ODAs provide an answer to all of these challenges by making RAC configurations self-contained. There are no external interconnect requirements or instructions for making RAC configuration changes outside the standard ODA deployment process. If you are concerned about the ability of your company to successfully complete all of the engineering work required to build truly high availability RAC clusters, then ODAs may help provide a solution. The expertise to successfully deploy RAC clusters is greatly reduced. This is a major advantage for companies of all sizes. ODAs extend the ability to successfully deploy two-node RAC clusters to the masses, which is part of the reason that ODAs are a solution for "RAC Without Tears."

RAC One, a two-node RAC cluster, or a single instance database can be deployed during an ODA install. ODAs deploy RAC clusters in a matter of hours and according to Oracle's best practices. Oracle builds the physical RAC interconnect into the appliance. The quarterly automated patching process simplifies the process for keeping the grid/clusterware and Oracle Homes patched with the latest PSU patches and bug fixes. These quarterly patches are tested as a complete unit, along with the OS and firmware changes, making ODAs a great solution for maintaining ongoing RAC stability.

■ **Note** The author has discussed RAC installations on non-ODA systems with a number of small companies. Many small and midsized companies simply don't have the resources to perform that sort of installation by themselves. This includes the technical resources to research all of the RAC requirements and the cost of buying additional equipment, such as dedicated RAC switches, for the interconnect traffic.

While ODAs do a great job deploying and supporting RAC clusters, the need for understanding good RAC design best practices for eliminating contention between nodes is still something that teams deploying RAC on any platform need to be aware of. Also, a two-node cluster requires that one server is able to handle the entire processing load during a node switchover. Supplementing RAC with Data Guard can alleviate the failover capacity concerns.

High Availability Without Tears

ODAs provide high availability through easy-to-install RAC and RAC One deployments. In addition to provisioning high availability on a single appliance, ODAs make it easy to deploy Data Guard to extend the high availability solution. These deployments can cross data centers to provide geographic protection. Oracle assists the Data Guard deployment process through OEM, one-button ODA Data Guard deployment scripts, and supplemental documentation focused on deploying Data Guard on ODAs. In addition to streamlined Data Guard deployments, ODAs support high availability through higher levels of stability because it is a packaged solution tested as a single unit.

The grid and database portions of ODA patches can be deployed in a rolling fashion. At the time of writing, the infrastructure portion of ODA patches requires the clusterware to be completely down on both nodes, but this may change in the future. RAC One provides high availability capabilities for both production and nonproduction instances that are designed to run on only one of the two ODA nodes, but can be failed over to the second ODA node.

ODAs jump-start high availability implementations by greatly reducing the expertise levels required to deploy a RAC solution. This includes eliminating the need to perform a RAC interconnect design, researching all of the RAC requirements and best practices, provisioning ASM, eliminating all single points of failure, and all other aspects of a well-architected RAC cluster.

High availability is also achieved from the deployment of standard, tested configurations and the choice of either double or triple mirroring all ASM disk extents. The loss of a disk doesn't take the system down. The ODA operating system also implements the Oracle Linux unbreakable kernel (UEK). ODAs are supported by a dedicated Oracle engineered system support team that has an in-depth knowledge of the platform.

The majority of the hardware components are redundant. An ODA has two server nodes and redundant power supplies. The system interconnects between the system components are redundant and are implemented by SAS cables in the current X3-2 model.

Disk replacements are easy to perform on an ODA. Simply flip a switch on the front of the storage unit, pull the drive out, slide the new drive in, and flip the switch back.

ODAs reduce the number of moving parts needed to implement high availability. Fewer moving parts and fewer handoffs result in higher availability in most cases.

There are a number of high availability deployment patterns:

- *Active-Active*. This pattern is implemented as RAC deployed on an ODA, providing the ability to load balance processing across two nodes and failover between the two servers.

- *Active-Passive*. This pattern is implemented through RAC One, RAC, and/or Data Guard. Processing is configured to run on a single node. Failover is supported by RAC One or RAC within an ODA. Failover across ODAs, including the ability to failover across geographic distances, is handled by Data Guard.

Achieving high availability requires additional designs, such as RAC services, and role-based services if Data Guard is part of the solution. The effectiveness of your high availability implementation will be directly proportional to the amount of design and testing that go into the solution.

Costs and Value Proposition

ODAs do not fit the traditional build vs. buy purchasing model. A company can certainly choose to build their own commodity hardware-based infrastructure. However, the typical company doesn't have the resources to build its own engineered system. Regardless, check out the Oracle "build vs. buy" ODA videos. You'll find some videos on the main Oracle ODA product page and Oracle's YouTube channel detailing the ease of deployment and the reasons why you want to give serious consideration to the value proposition of buying a better, prepackaged solution. Some of the videos have an element of humor, so they are very viewable. The content is dynamic, so we're not including any web links because they are subject to change. However, finding them is easy enough.

From a hardware perspective, you get a lot of resources when you purchase an ODA. For the current X3-2 model, this includes two servers with 256G memory each, with a total of 32 cores, and a lot of storage. The current storage volume is 18T of raw disk, which can be deployed as approximately 9T usable double mirrored, or 6T usable triple mirrored. The storage can be doubled again to 36T of raw storage with a storage expansion rack. The ODA Getting Started manual details the exact amount of usable storage, depending on the deployment options that are selected.

However, the secret sauce of the ODA is not the hardware. The secret sauce of an ODA is the software. The ingredients include RAC deployments in hours, the automated patching of all tiers (BIOS, firmware, OS, ILOM, grid, database) resulting in systems that are kept up-to-date, stable, and compliant. The ODA hardware—with the standard, embedded Oracle hardware support facilities and accompanied by a lot of value-added management software—offers a great value proposition. Benefits include the following:

- ODAs come with an embedded validation toolkit (oakcli—Oracle appliance kit command-line interface). oakcli contains a full set of diagnostic and management utilities to maintain the "keep it simple" management theme of ODAs.

- An ODA allows you to cap the licensing and resources that are deployed on the hardware in a "pay as you grow model" vs. paying for all of the capacity and licensing up front. Additional capacity is enabled through applying a key.

- The prepackaged software and deployment model provides the ability to deploy a standardized database platform across your database portfolio. ODAs are a solution to the traditional model of building servers and databases by hand, resulting in a data center full of "totem poles," where no two totem poles look the same.

There is no question that the ODA standardized deployment model lowers management and administration costs. This is in part due to the reduced number of build steps and the reduction in the number of people and teams that need to become involved, as well as reducing all of the handoffs between teams. After an ODA is deployed, the unified nature of the system and platform-specific automations lower ongoing administration costs. The ongoing administrative savings come from the combination of reducing the number of teams needed to support an ODA, the platform's stability, automated patching of all of the appliance components, a lower number of moving parts, server and component redundancy, appliance kit automation, and the embedded support facilities, including ASR and the ILOM.

The rapid setup and standardized model is an excellent building block for DBaaS or cloud services. The process to create new single instance, RAC One and RAC databases on an ODA has been reduced to 15 minutes. ODAs are engineered systems that can be deployed by companies of any size. ODAs often serve as low-cost lower-life cycle environments for Exadata, as well as an entry point and starting success story for companies that want to invest in Exadata in the long term.

Oracle is investing in the platform. New functionality is released every quarter, and the software changes are backward compatible to previous hardware generations. ODAs started as a small to midsized company solution, but then big companies started buying them. This helped to drive more momentum for the ODA product. Since ODAs are a single vendor product, intervendor handoffs are eliminated, and the testing of all components as a unit is self-contained within Oracle. From a troubleshooting standpoint, customers only have one vendor that needs to be contacted for all support issues. When a support call is initiated, it is handled by a specialized engineered system support team.

The ability to deploy infrastructure quickly, or pre-deploy infrastructure, has overall savings by getting projects launched quickly to achieve business benefits. ODAs come with sufficient resources to serve as a consolidation platform and support your internal shared services initiatives. ODAs also support the standard Oracle resource management facilities, such as instance caging and database resource management to support consolidation efforts.

In the end, companies need to decide how much work and overhead they want to take on by developing their own solution vs. buying a prepackaged solution like the ODA. A key benefit of the ODA is that it lets companies spend their time on core business functions instead of routine support tasks.

What about the *total cost of ownership* (TCO) numbers? Oracle publishes numbers—just like all vendors do for their competing products. Oracle's ODA TCO studies can currently be found on Oracle's main ODA product page. Oracle's numbers can be helpful in supporting your initial purchase. However, the best TCO numbers are the ones that you put together for your company as you gain experience with the platform.

Oracle Hardware

ODAs take advantage of the standard Oracle (formerly Sun) hardware facilities to administer the appliance and harden it from routine failures. The management facilities include the ILOM and Automatic Service Request (ASR) facilities. As you've seen previously in this book, ILOMs let you remotely administer the hardware, such as powering it down and up, and running a complete set of diagnostics. The ILOM functionality is so comprehensive that at the time of this writing, Oracle has published eight separate manuals to cover all of the facilities. Similarly, the ASR software provides phone-home capabilities to automatically issue alerts and upload hardware fault messages to Oracle to initiate the service request process.

The ODA hardware is both modular and resilient. The servers are modular, consisting of two separate units cabled together. Similarly, the storage is modular. The power supplies are redundant and field replaceable. The disk drives are hot replaceable.

The Oracle hardware is supported by a field services unit that will fix any hardware failures that are encountered. Backing up the field services unit is the Oracle support organization that will respond to service requests by assisting with diagnostics to determine the cause of the issue, and then dispatch the field services group to fix the problem.

Security and Compliance

The first security feature of ODAs is the inclusion of the quarterly PSU bug fix and security patching in the quarterly ODA release. The quarterly ODA patches are documented in MOS note 888888.1. Oracle will release the quarterly ODA releases approximately two to four weeks after Oracle releases the quarterly PSU patch set. Oracle follows this approach to include the latest security patches in each ODA release, and continues the process of testing all components of a patch set as a complete unit. The ease of the one-button patching process is a key enabler of keeping ODAs patched regularly to keep the systems compliant. Keeping systems patched with the most up-to-date security patches is a requirement of PCI (the credit card industry) and other security compliance certifications.

The second security implementation feature for ODAs is security scanning during the development release process. Oracle uses security scanning software from a third-party vendor to independently perform these checks. The scan results are used to upgrade the Oracle Linux package versions deployed on an ODA to keep the system compliant.

The third security mechanism for locking down ODAs is the ODA-specific Oracle-supplied STIG script (MOS notes 1456609.1 and 1461102.1). The STIG script is part of the US Department of Defense's Security Technical Implementation Guide (STIG) process. Running the STIG script is a two-step process. In first step, the script can be run in check mode to search for security violations. In the second step, the "fix" process allows these flagged violations to be corrected.

Some of the STIG security checks include the following list, developed by looking at the code. The list of security checks performed is not detailed in the MOS notes.

- Category 1: This is DOD speak for "You had better fix this."

    - Is the password for grub enabled?

    - Is the `sendmail decode` command commented out in `/etc/aliases`?

    - Is the privilege account `halt` present?

- Is the Ctrl-Alt-Del combination available to shut down the system?

- Is the RealVNC rpm installed on the server?

- Is support for a USB device found in the kernel?

- Category 2: This is DOD speak for "Document these and develop a plan to fix the issues."

  - Is single user mode boot-enabled without a password?

  - Is the pam-tally account configuration and login failure management tool configured to lock accounts after three consecutive login failures?

  - Does the system prohibit the use of past passwords?

  - How secure is the password strength? Is the password less than eight characters?

  - Is a delay configured to make users wait before trying to log in again after a login failure?

  - Do passwords have to be changed no less than every 60 days?

  - Can passwords changed be more than once every 24 hours?

  - Is `cron` access controlled?

  - Can you log into the system directly as root through `ssh`?

  - Is the `tcp dump` rpm installed on the system?

  - Do all of the file systems have the correct permissions?

  - Are there any unnecessary accounts present?

  - Is the `sendmail help` command enabled?

- Category 3: This is DOD speak for "Document the risk and decide what you want to do about it."

  - Are the UNIX man page permissions correct?

  - Is the `sendmail` version hidden?

There are some additional checks in the STIG scripts that even your seasoned sysadmins may need to look up and figure out. The purpose of the STIG scripts is to check your security setup practices rather than the ODA out-of-the-box security implementations. A search of "My Oracle Support (MOS)" only found STIG implementation documents for ODAs and Exadatas. This security implementation check script is another value-added proposition for ODAs.

The implementation of which STIG script fixes that you choose to implement will depend on your company's security standards. Not every company has the same security requirements as the US Department of Defense. However, security is an area where some companies choose to err on the side of caution. At the minimum, the STIG process performs an ODA-specific DOD security analysis.

Oracle also publishes Oracle Linux security manuals and the Oracle Linux group publishes additional blogs for steps to lock down your systems. While it isn't always easy to translate these steps directly to an ODA, they do serve as valuable guides for security lockdowns on your systems. While a full coverage of server security implementation is outside the scope of this chapter, additional steps can be taken to lock down your ODA systems, such as limiting access to ODAs through jump servers.

Virtualization

In March 2013, Oracle released support for the Oracle virtualization solutions on ODAs in software release 2.5. Oracle has since been enhancing the virtualization capabilities of ODAs with every release. Virtualization on ODAs is a major business case for the use of ODAs. The Oracle virtual machine implementation on ODAs is currently unique because the virtualization has been optimized for databases. Expect virtualization to continue to be a major initiative for Oracle, including enhancing the capabilities on ODAs.

Oracle has simplified the management of ODA virtual machines by implementing VM management in oakcli, including the ability to clone, start, and stop VMs. oakcli has been enhanced to import templates. There is no separate VM manager needed to support virtualization on an ODA.

The ability to "pay as you grow" on the ODA platform means that additional capacity can be available on ODAs to run nondatabase applications and other infrastructure-support software. Oracle has coined the phrase "Solution in a Box" for ODA-packaged application solutions. Oracle is porting their software to ODA-specific VM templates. At the time of this writing, a WebLogic template has been released for ODAs, and a JD Edwards template had been announced. Additional templates for more Oracle software products are likely to come. Oracle's partners have jumped on the bandwagon by beginning to develop their own application "solutions in a box."

The business value proposition to maximize the use of the hardware and to rapidly deploy applications is huge. Companies of every size often deploy large consulting firms, system integrators, and consulting staffs to deploy complex software. Deploying applications on ODAs through VM templates offers the promise for major cost savings through the rapid deployment of standardized images. Oracle has stated that they will be releasing additional ODA VM templates in the future.

ODA Technical Solutions

ODAs are a technical "solution in a box." That solution includes a number of major components that you should be aware of. We introduce those in this section.

The Oracle Appliance Kit (oakcli) is a built-in appliance management jack-of-all-trades. The oakcli command reference can be found in MOS 1417879.1, the latest ODA version release notes, and the ODA Getting Started Guide. The ODA Release Notes and Getting Started Guide are generally more current than the MOS notes. New oakcli functionality is released quarterly, so you have to proactively check the quarterly release notes to keep up with the newest features.

Here are some of the things you can do with oakcli:

- ODA management

  - Deploy an ODA

  - Patch an ODA

  - Create a new database in approximately 15 minutes

  - Create new database software home from the current ODA release

  - Delete databases and database homes

  - Run a complete check of the system

  - Run a disk calibration

  - Configure and test ASR (Automatic Service Request)

  - Display the hardware details and versions

- Display software and firmware versions
- Display disks, disk groups, and other storage details
- Clean up patches that have been applied
- Activate cores when additional Oracle licenses are purchased

- Diagnostics

  - Run a complete check of the system
  - Locate a disk drive and light up its LED indicator to signal which specific disk drive needs to be replaced
  - Run disk diagnostics
  - Run an ODAchk health check
  - Collect and package diagnostic information

- Virtualization

  - Create or clone an ODA virtual machine
  - Configure resources on an ODA virtual machine
  - Start and stop ODA_Base (the database partition on a virtualized ODA) or another ODA virtual machine
  - Display the information for ODA VM templates
  - Deploy/import an Oracle VM template
  - Create CPU pools for ODA virtual machines
  - Display all of the details for one or all of virtual machines on an ODA
  - Apply IPs to an ODA virtual machine
  - Open a VM console to manage an ODA VM

Oracle also provides additional ODA diagnostic utilities as part of the ODA software product set. The main utility is ODAchk (MOS 1485630.1). This is an ODA-specific version of RACcheck. Oracle recommends that you deploy the latest version of ODAchk, so you have to check the MOS note as new versions are released following changes to the RACcheck and Exadata Exachk tools.

ODAs ship with the standard top, vmstat, and sar server resource monitoring utilities. ODAs also ship with the detailed server resource collection utility OSWatcher (MOS 301137.1 and 461053.1). Two additional standard RAC utilities common to self-install platforms are also included with the ODA RAC software:

- Cluster Health Monitor (MOS 736752.1 and 1328466.1)—Granular resource monitoring
- Trace file analyzer utility (MOS 1513912.1) —Real-time event capture

ODAs ship with a set of database templates designed for performance and consolidating DBs on ODAs. The Database templates sizing is documented in the Getting Started Guide. The templates range in size from very small, small, medium, large, extra-large, and extra-extra large. Besides configuring memory, redo log sizes, and the starting DB size, the templates determine the number of databases that can be deployed on an ODA.

The following are some other software utilities and tools to be aware of:

- ODAs come with two utilities that allow GUI-based tool sessions to be started. They are VNC Server and StartX from the ILOM remote console.

- Server software includes the previously discussed ILOM and ASR facilities. These server management utilities are an extra Oracle hardware value-added proposition vs. generic commodity hardware.

- ODAs pre-deploy a utility called Logwatch, which monitors file system space and authentication failures and logins through `ssh`. It is automatically scheduled.

- ODAs can run other proactive support tools (MOS 1459344.1). A good example is `oratop` (1500864.1), which produces a one-panel display of overall database and database server activity.

ODAs have a unique "worst case" recovery capability. When all is lost, and the server OS disk configurations are out of action and the databases can't be started, ODAs provide the ability to rebuild the appliance all over again using a bare metal restore, as long as the source of the problem isn't a major hardware failure. An ODA can be rebuilt in about two hours using this method. Of course, you will need a backup of your database and any additional objects that need to be restored to get the ODA in an operational state, such as exports and the OCR for RAC services.

Finally, ODAs come with a license for Oracle's Secure Backup product to use in backing up ODAs.

ODA Performance

The current X3-2 ODA model runs the same compute node model as an Exadata. ODAs do lag the Exadata server node release cycle. Regardless, they are running the same CPU model most of the time. Exadatas support a memory expansion from 256G to 512G per server, but ODAs do not. Regardless, logical IO performance on an ODA is excellent.

Another source of ODA performance is that everything is self-contained within the appliance. RAC traffic doesn't leave the appliance and travel through an external network to communicate between the compute nodes. The two server nodes and storage units are all next to each other and are connected through high-speed SAS cables. There are no intervening switches, firewalls, or other external network layers.

ODA physical IO storage performance is good—in fact, better than the typical SAN fiber channel disk. Oracle has published X3-2 Physical IO benchmarks of 5 milliseconds at 3,500 IOPS on a single storage unit, and 7,000 IOPS with an additional storage expansion unit. Above those IOPS levels, the service levels decrease. Oracle's ODA X3-2 benchmarks show service levels of 6 to 7 milliseconds at 5,750 IOPS, and 11,500 with a storage expansion rack. These last numbers are still very good and compare nicely to the levels seen on a well-tuned Fiber Channel disk-based SAN. However, as the IOPS build above these levels, at some point performance will start to drop noticeably. Since ODAs come with a lot of memory, caching data in memory is a key scalability factor to avoid reaching the ODA IOPS limitations.

ODAs do not currently have the supported option to use PCI Flash or SSD. The four SSD drives that come with ODAs are only supported for use by the online redo logs. ODAs do support expanding storage to NFS, including Oracle's ZFS storage appliance. The use of DNFS (Direct NFS) to increase performance is supported. However, I'm not aware of any physical IO performance benchmarks that have been published for ODAs using an NFS storage extension. While ASM is not supported on the NFS extension, Oracle has announced that ODAs do support Hybrid Columnar Compression when the NFS mount is an Oracle ZFS storage appliance.

Since Oracle is investing in the ODA platform, the IOPS and disk performance may change with each new model. You will need to relook at the physical performance and IOPS limits when a new model that replaces the X3-2 is released.

Summary

ODAs are a high availability application and database infrastructure solution in a self-contained engineered appliance. ODAs offer low-cost hardware with lower setup and ongoing support costs than traditional database solutions. Deployments are automated and fast, including the creation of RAC One and two-node RAC cluster databases. The ODA patching process patches the OS, grid, and database components as a single unit using Oracle supplied software. ODAs come prepackaged with management and deployment software.

ODAs offer a unique "pay as you grow" Oracle licensing option. Applications and databases can be deployed on ODAs using Oracle's virtualization product.

CHAPTER 10

Virtualization and the ODA

The Oracle Database Appliance (ODA) is primarily designed as an appliance to support and deploy the Oracle database quickly and to provide a pay-as-you-go licensing model. The ODA hardware provides a lot of flexibility in deployment options, and the 4u rack size is ideal for a lot of small- and medium-sized businesses (SMBs) to deploy in a variety of situations. SMBs typically want to use consolidated hardware, and the ODA, while a good database platform, still requires added components to support a complete application stack. This led to the idea that virtualization might achieve a one-box solution that helps a variety of SMBs to meet the "less hardware" goal.

Virtualization has been added to the ODA via a software update, and as with other major ODA features, it requires a reimage of the platform in order to implement. Virtualization on the ODA allows usage of capacity that could potentially remain unused. This chapter will focus on the basics of virtualization with Oracle VM (OVM), the technology used to implement virtualization on the ODA, as well as talk about the ease of deploying virtual machines to expand the usefulness of the ODA.

Oracle Virtual Machine (OVM)

OVM is based upon the open-source Xen hypervisor and competes in the market with the likes of EMC VMware and Microsoft Hyper-V. Oracle has taken the Xen hypervisor as the core to its OVM technology and added significant enhancements, like support for a variety of operating systems, as well as management interface to make a product that is more enterprise-ready.

Oracle's acquisition of Sun Microsystems allowed it to further enhance the OVM product and create an OVM family of products that includes Oracle VM Server as well as Oracle VM VirtualBox. Oracle VM Server is the platform that runs virtual hosts and allows for the provisioning of multiple virtual hosts on a set of hardware, and has a server component as well a management component that is required for use. Oracle VM VirtualBox, on the other hand, is a desktop virtualization tool that extends the capabilities of your existing desktop software, and it doesn't require a hypervisor to manage it. Oracle provides Oracle VM Server as well as Oracle VirtualBox for free, but Oracle VM Server has support costs associated with it. Oracle also provides an extensive VM template library of its products, which allows rapid deployment of virtual machines. Oracle VM templates can be converted into Oracle VirtualBox templates as well.

OVM and the Database Appliance

The OVM implementation on the ODA is unique in the sense that it does not require an Oracle VM Manager. The design philosophy behind bringing virtualization on the ODA was to enhance the value of the ODA without adding extra infrastructure, as well as ensuring that the database in the database appliance was still the primary focus of the ODA. ODA patch release 2.5 added the support for virtualization, and all subsequent releases from there have added features toward making virtualization better and easier to manage and deploy.

Virtualization on the ODA creates some unique challenges in installation, as well as the configuration of the device. The default setup on the ODA is bare metal, which means all hardware has a one-to-one affinity to each component. In order to convert a running ODA to a virtualized model, a complete reinstall of the appliance has to happen. This is particularly important to note as an install decision, because data loss or an outage is required for conversion.

Installation of a Virtualized ODA

The default condition of an ODA that is shipped from the factory is the bare-metal state. The process of an ODA bare-metal installation is explained in detail in Chapter 2. This section will highlight some specific changes, as well the changes in the ODA offline configurator to handle virtualization.

Preparation for Virtualization

Virtualization on the ODA has changed a lot between versions. The initial version of the virtualized ODA platform supported only local VM repositories, and none of the virtual network setup was predefined. The evolution of virtualization has now led to access to local or shared repositories, as well as the possibility to set up VLANs, which are needed to segment databases and apps. ODA patch 2.8 allows shared repositories and a simplified way to set up VLANs.

Preparing for virtualization on the ODA requires making decisions that need to be made at the time of deployment of the appliance. Due to the volatile nature of the appliance software, sometimes it can be hard to make design choices without having to reverse course. There are a few decisions that need to be made prior to deployment:

- Bare metal or virtualized?

- Shared or local repository?

- How many CPUs for the Database VM or ODA_Base?

The key decision is to decide between bare metal or virtualization. Once either is selected, it is very hard to revert this decision back because doing so requires a complete reinstallation of the system. The local repository option allows 250GB in an ODA v1 and 350GB in an ODA X3-2 to be made available for template management. This is superseded by the shared repository option at the cost of losing space from the DATA and RECO diskgroups. The shared repository option allows for higher availability of the virtual machines. With local repositories, a VM will only start on the node it was registered; whereas in the shared repository mode, a VM can failover to a different node if one is unavailable.

The other important sizing consideration is ensuring that the Database VM is sized correctly. The ODA's primary focus is the database, such that a virtualized ODA contains a special, optimized VM called ODA_BASE that has exclusive access to the shared disk, which is needed to ensure optimal database performance. ODA_BASE is a prebuilt OVM template that has all the specific components that are needed for the Oracle Clusterware and the database.

The design is a very important aspect of virtualizing the ODA. Figure 10-1 shows a basic architecture of the appliance virtualized. Since the ODA is a set on two physical servers, there are two main components that need to be deployed on the ODA as part of a virtualization exercise:

- Dom0 or the Virtualization controller

- ODA_BASE or the customer VM specific for the ODA

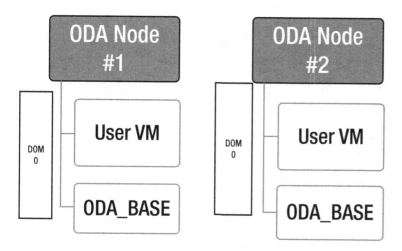

Figure 10-1. *Basic architecture of a virtualized ODA*

Domain 0, or Dom0, is the virtualization controller, which is a dummy operating system that has access to a hypervisor for the virtualized box. There is a Dom0 in both physical nodes; it is considered the piece that manages the visualized infrastructure of the ODA. Dom0 is used as the base operating system, and as such, nothing else should be installed on it. Dom0 does host the virtual template repository, however, and as such, all VM templates are imported from there.

The Database VM, also known as ODA_BASE, is a critical aspect of the appliance. ODA_BASE is a specially designed VM that has direct access to part of the ODA hardware. It has various drivers optimized for the ODA hardware that are already installed and configured for improved access to the hypervisor and the shared disks. The ODA_BASE template includes the cluster software binaries, database software binaries, as well as the custom database templates that are needed to create an Oracle database.

The other aspect of virtualization is installing an application or any other components in a separate visualized host. This is what is called a User VM. User VMs are not mandatory and an ODA can be virtualized and contain only a Dom0 and an ODA_BASE. Currently, there are space limitations on User VMs unless a shared VM repository is used. Shared repository support is a new feature in ODA 2.8, but prior to that, only 250GB was available on the ODA V1, and 350GB on the ODA X3-2 in local disk space on each physical machine. Also, User VMs did not have failover capabilities in previous releases of the ODA software.

Virtualization Deployment Considerations

It is very important to understand the changes in the ODA deployment strategy when used as a virtualized environment. Sizing and network changes need to be understood for the deployment. The appliance does not ship with virtualization installed unless an independent software vendor (ISV) creates a custom appliance that ships with virtualization enabled.

Table 10-1 and Table 10-2 look at the differences between the ODA V1 and the ODA X3-2 in terms of bare metal vs. virtualized interfaces. In a bare-metal environment, all network interfaces have a physical mapping and there is bonding at the Linux layer to provide High Availability to the network interfaces. It is very important to adhere to documentation and ensure that Eth0 is only used for the private interfaces.

Table 10-1. *Oracle Database Appliance V1 Network Setup*

Type	Physical Interface	Link Speed	Bare Metal Interface Name	Virtual Interface Name	Virtual Dom0 Bridge
Internal Dual 1GbE	Eth0	1GbE	Eth0	Eth0	Priv1
Internal Dual 1GbE	Eth1	1GbE	Eth1	Eth0	Priv1
Onboard Dual 1GbE	Eth2 and Eth3	1GbE	Bond1	Eth1	Net1
Onboard Dual Port	Eth8 and Eth9	10GbE	xbond0	Eth4	Net4
Quad Port Network Interfaces	Eth4 and Eth5	1GbE	Bond 2	Eth2	Net2
Quad Port Network Interfaces	Eth6 and Eth7	1GbE	Bond3	Eth3	Net3

Table 10-2. *Oracle Database Appliance X3-2 Network Setup*

Type	Physical Interface	Link Speed	Bare Metal Interface Name	Virtual Interface Name	Virtual Bridge Dom0
Onboard Dual Network Interfaces	Eth0	10GbE	Eth0	Eth0	Priv1
Onboard Dual Network Interfaces	Eth1	10GbE	Eth1	Eth0	Priv1
Onboard Quad Network Interfaces	Eth2 and Eth3	10GbE	bond0	Eth1	Net1
Onboard Quad Network Interfaces	Eth4 and Eth5	10GbE	Bond1	Eth2	Net1

It is very important to understand the physical and virtual connections and the differences, as shown in Tables 10-1 and 10-2. This information is required while deploying the ODA. The IP requirements shift slightly, as well between a bare-metal and a virtualized ODA. Table 10-3 shows the differences in IP requirements between a bare-metal ODA and a virtualized ODA. The addition of a Domain0 and User VMs are important factors in the IP requirement differences.

Table 10-3. *IP Requirements for ODA*

IP Type	Bare Metal IP #	Default Values	Virtualized IP #	Default Values
Host	2	User Defined	2	User Defined
Private IP	4	192.168.16.24 192.168.16.25 192.168.17.24 192.168.17.25	2	192.168.16.27 192.168.16.28
Dom 0	N/A	N/A	4	Two User Defined: 192.168.16.24 (Private) 192.168.16.25 (Private)
RAC VIP	2	User Defined	2	User Defined
SCAN VIP	2	User Defined	2	User Defined
ILOM IP	2	User Defined	2	User Defined
User VM IP*	N/A	N/A	1 per VM	User Defined

User VM IP dependent on number of VMs; a minimum of 1 IP/VM.

Deployment of the Virtualized ODA

Deployment of the virtual ODA requires the act of reinstallation of the appliance and then deploying the virtualized image on the ODA. Chapter 2 goes through the procedure of how to install the bare-metal version of the ODA in detail. In order for the ODA to become a virtual configuration, the appropriate patch needs to be downloaded from Oracle Support. Currently, Patch ID 16984856 can be downloaded to deploy a virtualized image.

The offline configurator has been enhanced to support building the configuration required for deployment of the virtualized ODA. Figure 10-2 is the initial entry to the configurator; due to the hardware configuration changes, it allows for various configuration selections.

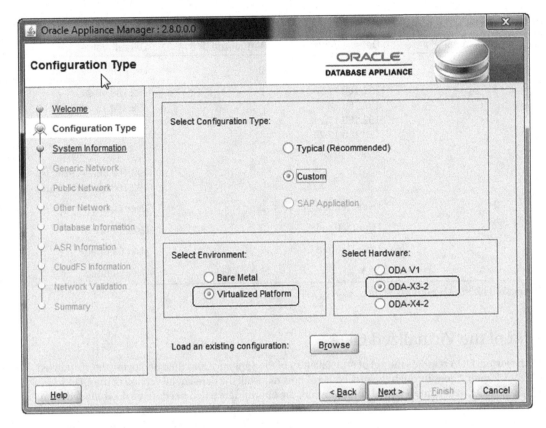

Figure 10-2. *Initial configuration selection screen*

The network mapping screen is where the virtual interfaces will be accessible; this in contrast to the physical interfaces that are available in a bare-metal configuration. Figure 10-3 shows the network interface change in a virtual environment in the ODA X3-2 case. The configuration screens are the same for ODA V1 and ODA X3-2, except that ODA V1 allows choosing between a 1Gbei and a 10GbE interface. All interfaces on the ODA X3-2 support 10 GbE.

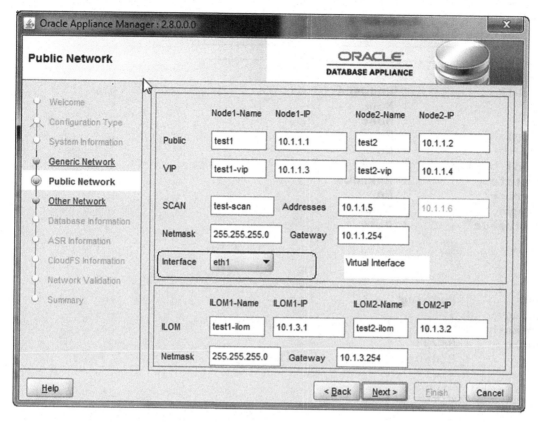

Figure 10-3. *Network configuration screen for ODA X3-2*

The configuration file that the configurator generates is used for the deployment process, which is started after the reimage completes. The reimage completes with the Dom0 being available and the Oracle VM Server installed. Figure 10-4 shows a screen of the Oracle VM Server running on Dom0.

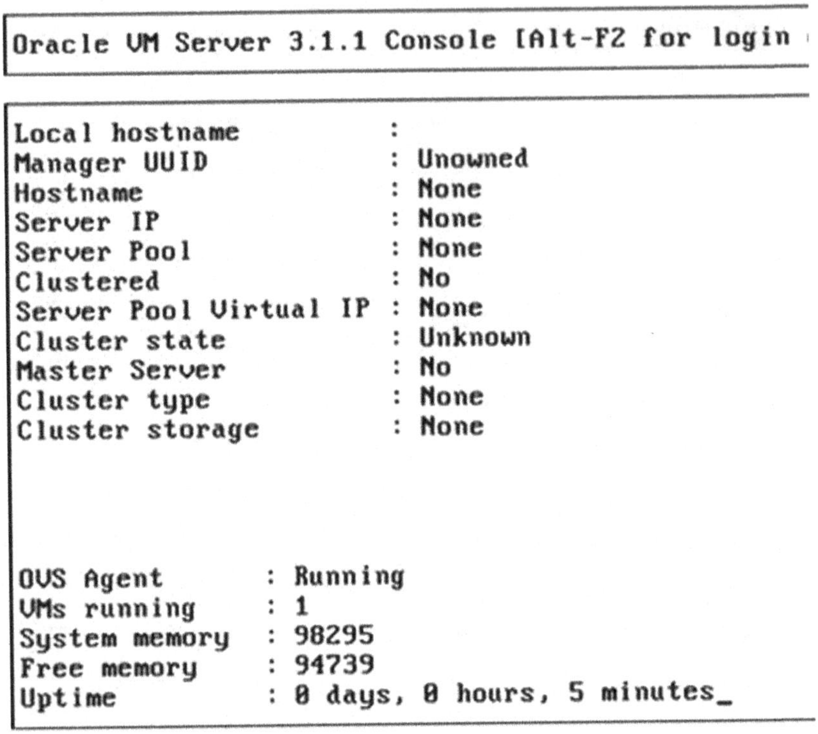

```
Oracle VM Server 3.1.1 Console [Alt-F2 for login
```

```
Local hostname          :
Manager UUID            : Unowned
Hostname                : None
Server IP               : None
Server Pool             : None
Clustered               : No
Server Pool Virtual IP  : None
Cluster state           : Unknown
Master Server           : No
Cluster type            : None
Cluster storage         : None



OVS Agent       : Running
VMs running     : 1
System memory   : 98295
Free memory     : 94739
Uptime          : 0 days, 0 hours, 5 minutes_
```

Figure 10-4. *Newly initialized Oracle VM Server on ODA*

Once the server reimaging is complete, a screen similar to the one shown in Figure 10-4 is available by using the remote access console from the ILOM. The offline configurator does not allow for adding an IP address to the Dom0, thus you need to log in via remote access on the ILOM and log in as root to configure the network, as shown in Listing 10-1.

Listing 10-1. Adding an IP to Dom0

```
/opt/oracle/oak/oakcli configure firstnet

Configure the network for the node(s)(local, global) [global]: <default is global for configuring
both nodes>
The network configuration for both nodes:
Domain Name:  your.company.com
DNS Server(s):  Primary Dns Server:  <enter your primary DNS server>
                Secondary Dns Server:  <enter your secondary DNS server>
                Tertiary Dns Server:  <enter your tertiary DNS server>
Node Name       Host Name
0               host1-dom0 <- enter your 1st hostname
1               host2-dom0 <- enter your 2nd hostname
Choose the network interface to configure (net1, net2) [net1]: <default is net1>
Configure DHCP on net1 (yes/no) [no]:
You have chosen static configuration on net1
Enter the IP address for net1 on Node 0: <enter your 1st hostname IP address>
Enter the IP address for net1 on Node 1: <enter your 2nd hostname IP address>
```

```
Netmask for net1: < enter your netmask >
Gateway Address for net1 [<Gateway IP>]:  <based on your IP and netmask, the proper gateway will
displayed>

Plumbing the IPs now on Node 0 ...
:::::::::::::::::::::::::::::::::::::::::::::::::::::
Plumbing the IPs now on Node 1 ...
:::::::::::::::::::::::::::::::::::::::::::::::::::::
dom0.xml                                        100% 860 0.8KB/s 00:00
```

The public IP addresses for dom0 on both physical servers are now configured. This allows access to the dom0 via any SSH client. At this stage, the ODA only has the dom0 accessible; this is the platform that is needed for ODA_BASE, which is the special ODA Database VM template required to run the Oracle Database Cluster.

Deployment of ODA_BASE

In order to deploy ODA_BASE, the template needs to be downloaded from My Oracle Support via patch 16985062. For version 2.8, the patch number can change; it is always recommended to use My Oracle Support note 888888.1. The files can be downloaded and then moved to the Dom0 that resides on Node 0 in /OVS. This allows the preparation of the template for deployment, as demonstrated in Listing 10-2.

Listing 10-2. Deployment of ODA_BASE on ODA X3-2

```
#cat oda_base_2.8.gz00 oda_base_2.8.gz01 > oda_base_2.8.tar.gz
# /opt/oracle/oak/bin/oakcli deploy oda_base
Enter the template location: /OVS/oda_base_2.8.tar.gz
Core Licensing Options:
        1. 2 CPU Cores
        2. 4 CPU Cores
        3. 6 CPU Cores
        4. 8 CPU Cores
        5. 10 CPU Cores
        6. 12 CPU Cores
        7. 14 CPU Cores
        8. 16 CPU Cores
        Selection[1 .. 8](default 16 CPU Cores) : 16
        ODA base domain memory in GB(min 8, max 244)[default xxx]   : 244
INFO: Using default memory size i.e. 244 GB
Additional vlan networks to be assigned to oda_base ? (y/n) [n]: n
INFO: Deployment in non-local mode
INFO: Verifying active cores on local node
INFO: Verified active cores on local node
INFO: Verifying active cores on remote node
INFO: Verified active cores on remote node
INFO: Running the command to copy the template /OVS/oda_base_2.8.tar.gz to remote node 1
oda_base_2.8.tar.gz           100% 4524MB  56.6MB/s   01:20
INFO: Spawned the process 24025 in the deployment node 0
INFO: Spawned the process 24026 in the node 1
templateBuild-2013-11-06-22-18/swap.img
templateBuild-2013-11-06-22-18/swap.img
templateBuild-2013-11-06-22-18/System.img
```

```
templateBuild-2013-11-06-22-18/System.img
templateBuild-2013-11-06-22-18/u01.img
templateBuild-2013-11-06-22-18/u01.img
Using config file "/OVS/Repositories/odabaseRepo/VirtualMachines/oakDom1/vm.cfg".
Started domain oakDom1 (id=40)
INFO: Deployment in local mode
INFO: Extracted the image files on node 0
INFO: The VM Configuration data is written to /OVS/Repositories/odabaseRepo/VirtualMachines/oakDom1/
vm.cfg file
INFO: Running /sbin/losetup /dev/loop0 /OVS/Repositories/odabaseRepo/VirtualMachines/oakDom1/System.
img command to mount the image file
INFO: Mount is successfully completed on /dev/loop0
INFO: Making change to the /OVS/Repositories/odabaseRepo/VirtualMachines/oakDom1/tmpmnt/boot/grub/
grub.conf file
INFO: Assigning IP to the first node...
INFO: Created oda base pool
INFO: Starting ODA Base...
INFO: Storing the odabase configuration information
Using config file "/OVS/Repositories/odabaseRepo/VirtualMachines/oakDom1/vm.cfg".
Started domain oakDom1 (id=1)
INFO: Deployment in local mode
INFO: Extracted the image files on node 1
INFO: The VM Configuration data is written to /OVS/Repositories/odabaseRepo/VirtualMachines/oakDom1/
vm.cfg file
INFO: Running /sbin/losetup /dev/loop0 /OVS/Repositories/odabaseRepo/VirtualMachines/oakDom1/System.
img command to mount the image file
INFO: Mount is successfully completed on /dev/loop0
INFO: Making change to the /OVS/Repositories/odabaseRepo/VirtualMachines/oakDom1/tmpmnt/boot/grub/
grub.conf file
INFO: Assigning IP to the second node...
INFO: Created oda base pool
INFO: Starting ODA Base...
INFO: Storing the odabase configuration information
#
```

At the end of the process, you will have a VM that can run the Oracle Database. This is the called ODA_BASE, and you can check the status of the VM by using the commands in Listing 10-3. The VM in the listing was created utilizing the maximum amount of resources.

Listing 10-3. Listing the Status of the VM on ODA X3-2

```
# xm list
Name                            ID     Mem   VCPUs   State   Time(s)
Domain-0                         0    2039      32   r-----  119019.9
oakDom1                          1  251904      32   -b----    2815.8

# /opt/oracle/oak/bin/oakcli show oda_base
ODA base domain
ODA base CPU cores       :32
ODA base domain memory   :244
ODA base template        :/OVS/oda_base_2.8.tar.gz
ODA base vlans           :['priv1', 'net1', 'net2']
ODA base current status  :Running
```

At this point in the process, we have deployed the ODA_BASE VM, and a small number of steps remain to actually get a database up and running. The ODA_BASE template can only be accessed via a vncserver through the dom0. The first VM can be accessed via port 5900 using VNC. This can be done via dom0 or via an external VNC client. The only difference in the deployment is the access to the VM. The rest of the deployment process is similar to a bare-metal deployment.

```
#vncsession dom0:5900
```

The VNC session now established allows access to ODA_BASE host. Once access is established, log in to the host and execute the deployment command with the file that was created with the offline configuration tool.

```
# /opt/oracle/oak/bin/oakcli deploy -conf /tmp/offlineconfig.param
```

The deployment process will complete the process of making the ODA_BASE accessible via the public network, as well as complete the install of the Clusterware and the Database Appliance Kit software.

Deployment of a User VM

The purpose of virtualizing the ODA is to allow using the resources on the appliance to build a complete environment. This can be accomplished by building various Application/User virtual machines on the appliance and making it one box that can host the database, as well as an app, on the same hardware.

Due to the nature of customization in the VM layer to accommodate the Database appliance, a VM can only be imported into the ODA using dom0. A variety of general-purpose VM templates are available at http://edelivery.oracle.com. This section will walk through the importing and configuring of the User VM template onto the ODA.

Virtual Image Repository

When the Virtualization option was first introduced on the ODA platform, there were specific limitations on what a User-defined VM could do. Some of the limitations included:

- No High Availability
- Local Repository Access only

The local repository limited VM sizes significantly, with only 250GB available in ODA V1 and 350GB available in ODA X3-2 for User VMs. Because each physical node was not aware of the others' repositories, VM failover was not possible and thus High Availability was not an option.

The newest version of the ODA software 2.8, among other enhancements, has added the ability to access the shared disk via an ASM Cluster File System (ACFS) mount and create a shared repository. This option not only allows the local space to be used for other uses, but also provides the option of High Availability for the VM itself.

The ODA_BASE is required for the shared repository because the ODA_BASE has access to the shared storage on the ODA. The process of creating the shared repository includes the process of creating the ACFS mount points, as well as the NFS export via the private network to dom0. All of this is accomplished via oakcli commands. Depending on the design, you can create one or many shared repositories at the cost of space in the DATA or RECO diskgroups.

While local repository access is available, using a shared repository is the recommended method in ODA 2.8 and going forward. The local repository is always created by default. Listing 10-4 shows how to create the shared repository and how to check the status.

Listing 10-4. Shared Repository Creation and Status

```
# oakcli create repo repo1 -dg data -size 20

# oakcli show repo
```

NAME	TYPE	NODENUM	STATE
odarepo1	local	0	N/A
odarepo2	local	1	N/A
repo1	shared	0	ONLINE
repo1	shared	1	ONLINE

```
#oakcli show repo repo1 -node 1

Resource: repo1_1
        AutoStart     :       restore
        DG            :     , DATA
        Device        :       /dev/asm/repo1-286
        ExpectedState :       Online
        MountPoint    :       /u01/app/repo1
        Name          :       repo1_0
        Node          :       all
        RepoType      :       shared
        Size          :       20720
        State         :       Online

# oakcli stop repo repo1 -node  1
```

User VM Creation

The repository creation is an important step toward getting a user-defined VM built. User-defined VMs are used to run any application or software that is independent of the Oracle Database. This can be any application, like WebLogic or even a Windows VM. The goal of providing virtualization as an option is to make the ODA a single box for deployment in scenarios such as stores or bank branches and reduce the number of infrastructure components to run a complete system.

User VMs are created using the process of cloning a VM template. Oracle provides a lot of commonly used templates at http://edelivery.oracle.com; the templates can be downloaded and imported into the repositories. Listings 10-5 through 10-8 show the process of importing a VM template in various ways. This process involves copying the file to the dom0 and importing it into a local or shared repository. Templates can also be imported from external template repositories.

Listing 10-5. Importing a VM Template to a Local Repository

```
#oakcli import vmtemplate ol6linux_64 -files /OVS/OVM_OL6_X86_64.tgz
```

Listing 10-6. Importing a VM Template into a Shared Repository

```
#oakcli import vmtemplate ol6linux_64 -files /OVS/OVM_OL6_X86_64.tgz -repo repo1
```

Listing 10-7. Importing a Template via an External Repository Template into a Shared Repository

```
#oakcli import vmtemplate ol6linux_64 -files 'http://vm.example.com/OEL6/OVM_OL6_X86_64.tgz'
-repo repo1
```

Listing 10-8. Importing a Template via a Template Assembly into a Shared Repository

```
#oakcli import vmtemplate ol6linux_64 -assembly
'http://vm.example.com/assemblies/OEL6/OVM_OL6_X86_64.ova' -repo repo1
```

At this point, we have only imported a VM template into the repository. We need to configure the VM template in order to be able to work with the configuration available to it on the ODA. Listings 10-9 through 10-11 show the various configuration settings that are available using the handy oakcli command set. For network related options, refer to Tables 10-1 and 10-2.

Listing 10-9. Configuring a VM Template Listing Configured Options for a VM Template

```
#oakcli show vmtemplate ol6linux_64
```

Listing 10-10. Adding a Network to the VM Template

```
#oakcli modify vmtemplate ol6linux_64 -addnetwork net1
```

Listing 10-11. Configure CPU, Memory on the Template

```
#oakcli configure vmtemplate ol6linux_64 -vcpu 4 -maxvcpu 8 -cpucap 10 -memory 3000M
-maxmemory 6G -os OTHER_LINUX
```

The configuration of the vmtemplate now allows the actual User VM to be created. In the examples, we have created a shared repository and an OL6 Linux VM template, assigned net1 as the network, and given a range of virtual CPUs and a CPU cap, as well as set memory boundaries. The values set in the template will be used by all VMs that are based on the template as the default values. Listings 10-12 through 10-18 show how to actually create the VM using the oakcli clone command, and then start it. In cases of shared repositories, we can configure High Availability options. Template values can also be overridden.

Listing 10-12. Creating and Configuring a User VM: Create a VM by Cloning from Template

```
#oakcli clone vm ol6test -vmtemplate ol6linux_64 -repo repo1 -node oda2
```

Listing 10-13. Override VM Template Values

```
#oakcli configure vm ol6test -vcpu 6 -memory 4G
```

Listing 10-14. Configure High Availability and Failover Values

```
#oakcli configure vm ol6test -prefnode oda2 -failover oda1
```

Listing 10-15. Start a VM

```
#oakcli start vm ol6test
```

Listing 10-16. Show the Status of All VMs

```
#oakcli show vm
```

Listing 10-17. Stop a VM

```
#oakcli stop vm ol6test
```

Listing 10-18. Access vmconsole

```
#oakcli show vmconsole ol6test
```

At this point, we have gone through the process of creating a vmtemplate and then cloning the vmtemplate to create a working VM called ol6test. We have assigned High Availability options as well as overridden some values that we didn't want to take from the template. Now we have a running VM on which we can deploy any application, as well as an ODA_BASE that is running the Oracle Database. This concludes the most basic configuration required for running a virtualized ODA.

Advanced VM Configuration and Patching

Configuring visualization on the ODA can be as simple as reimaging the ODA, creating a repository, importing a vmtemplate, and then cloning it to create a VM. There are advanced configuration techniques, however, that can be used to provide better control over the environment. We will briefly discuss some of the techniques used to provide stability and availability to the VM.

CPU Pools

One of the key benefits of the virtualization is controlling various resources and isolating workloads. The default configuration of creating a VM uses the unpinned CPU pool. This allows access to all the CPUs in the virtualized appliance to all the VMs , with the exception of ODA_BASE.

ODA_BASE is the Database VM, and as such, when it is created, a pool called odaBaseCpuPool is created. This pool contains the CPUs that only ODA_BASE has exclusive access to. If ODA_BASE exists, you will have two pools:

- default-unpinned-pool

- odaBaseCpuPool

The default-unpinned-pool is the pool that contains all the CPUs that are not part of the odaBaseCpuPool. In a simple configuration, all VMs will have access to the default pool. In cases where isolation is required, you can always create additional CPU pools to cage a VM. Listing 10-19 shows a configuration of CPU pools.

Listing 10-19. CPU Pools

```
#oakcli show cpupool -node 1

Pool                  Cpu List
default-unpinned-pool [12, 13, 14, 15, 16, 17, 18, 19, 20, 21, 22, 23]
       odaBaseCpuPool [0, 1, 2, 3, 4, 5, 6, 7, 8, 9, 10,11]
```

The CPU pools do not have to be uniform across the two nodes—with the exception of odaBaseCpuPool, which has to be the same across both nodes. Listing 10-20 shows how to create a CPU pool. Listings 10-21 and 10-22 show how to add CPUs and pin a VM to a CPU pool.

Listing 10-20. Creating and Managing a cpupool

```
#oakcli create cpupool unxpool -numcpu 6 -node 0
```

Listing 10-21. Add CPUs to a cpupool

```
#oakcli configure cpupool unxpool -numcpu 10 -node 0
```

Listing 10-22. Pin a VM to a CPU Pool

```
#oakcli configure vm ol6test -cpupool unxpool
```

The commands shown in these listings can only be applied to non-ODA_BASE cpupools. Due to the nature of ODA_BASE, a special command set needs to be used to manage CPUs. This is demonstrated in Listing 10-23.

Listing 10-23. Managing CPU in ODA_BASE

```
# /opt/oracle/oak/bin/oakcli configure oda_base

Core Licensing Options:
        1. 2 CPU Cores
        2. 4 CPU Cores
        3. 6 CPU Cores
        4. 8 CPU Cores
        5. 10 CPU Cores
        6. 12 CPU Cores
        7. 14 CPU Cores
        8. 16 CPU Cores
        Current CPU Cores      : 6
        Selection[1 : 6](default 16 CPU Cores) : 4
        ODA base domain memory in GB(min 8, max 96)(Current Memory 64G)[default
32]     :
INFO: Using default memory size i.e. 32 GB
Additional vlan networks to be assigned to oda_base? (y/n) [n]: Vlan network to be removed from
oda_base (y/n) [n]
INFO: Node 0:Configured oda base pool
INFO: Node 1:Configured oda base pool
INFO: Node 0:ODA Base configured with new memory
INFO: Node 0:ODA Base configured with new vcpus
INFO: Changes will be incorporated after the domain is restarted on Node 0
INFO: Node 1:ODA Base configured with new memory
INFO: Node 1:ODA Base configured with new vcpus
INFO: Changes will be incorporated after the domain is restarted on Node 1

#oakcli restart oda_base
```

The resulting command might ask for changes to system files, and a restart is needed to a new ODA_BASE to take effect. Restart ODA_BASE on both nodes, and this concludes discussion about cpu pools.

Virtual LANs

A new feature introduced in ODA version 2.8 software is the ability to create and manage virtual LANs in the ODA (VLAN). Virtual LANs need configuration on the switch level to allow VLAN tagging, but this feature allows network and security to create smaller chunks of the network and tag them for specific traffic types. Listings 10-24 and 10-25 show an example of creating a VLAN, as well as attaching it to a VM.

Listing 10-24. VLANs Creating a VLAN

```
#oakcli create vlan oda90 -vlanid 90 -if bond0 -node 0
#oakcli create vlan oda90 -vlanid 90 -if bond0 -node 1
```

Listing 10-25. Modifying a VM to Attach to a VLAN

```
# oakcli modify vm ol6test -addnetwork oda90
```

You're also able to add a VLAN to your ODA_BASE virtual machine. Listing 10-26 shows how. There you see the oakcli configure command being issued. Then you see the interaction triggered by the command. You'll be asked several questions. Respond by giving the correct values for your environment.

Listing 10-26. Adding a VLAN to ODA_BASE

```
/opt/oracle/oak/bin/oakcli configure oda_base
Core Licensing Options:
        1 2 CPU Cores

            ....

            ....
        8 16 CPU Cores
        Current CPU Cores       : 6
        Selection[1 : 6](default 12 CPU Cores) : 3
        ODA base domain memory in GB(min 8, max 88)(Current Memory 48G)[default 64]      : 48
INFO: Using default memory size i.e. 64 GB
Additional vlan networks to be assigned to oda_base? (y/n) [n]: y
Select the network to assign (oda90,oda91,oda92): oda90
Additional vlan networks to be assigned to oda_base? (y/n) [n]:
Vlan network to be removed from oda_base (y/n) [n]:
INFO: . . .
```

It is very important to have VLANs on both nodes if the shared repository option is used. This allows VM failover to work seamlessly.

Patching a Virtualized ODA

The patching process for a virtualized ODA is no different than the process for a bare-metal ODA. The unified patching does not support patching User VMs. The patch includes patches only for the ODA_BASE and the dom0. Any patching for User VMs is the responsibility of the administrator of the User VM.

Summary

Chapter 10 focused on the virtualization of the ODA. It only scratched the surface of the possibilities that are available with virtualization on the ODA. This includes OVM and the customization made for it to work on the ODA. ODA_BASE creation and the exclusive access it has to the shared disks to ensure performance is kept intact. We discussed the process to get a User VM up and running and looked at some of the advanced options that are available on the ODA. As the software evolves, so will the availability of options on and the customization of the ODA in the virtualization space.

■ ■ ■

## CHAPTER 11

e-Business Suite and the ODA

The Oracle Database Appliance is a preconfigured, highly available, engineered system running 11gR2 clusterware. Previous chapters of the book have explained the benefits of the ODA as the database and/or application platform. It's understandable why e-Business Suite (eBS) owners want to use it for their systems too. Unfortunately, the "out of the box" configuration of the ODA does not fully support e-Business Suite installations. This chapter will show how the standard configuration of ODA can be adjusted to comply with the specific requirements of e-Business Suite, and how to install or migrate e-Business Suite to ODA without sacrificing the ODA's flexibility and supportability.

Is ODA a Good Fit?

An obvious question is whether the ODA is a good fit for running Oracle's e-Business Suite. It's a good question, and the answer must consider a number of facets, including:

- Availability

- Storage capacity

- CPU capacity

- Memory

- Certification of eBS on the hardware

Availability is met by the RAC capability of the ODA. Typically, e-Business Suite is the core ERP system for a company, and in most cases, it is mission critical, which means it has to be highly available. The technical architecture of the ODA is built with high availability in mind. All components are redundant—from power supplies to network interfaces. The availability of the shared storage is arranged by configuring the disks in normal or high redundancy Automatic Storage Management (ASM) disk groups. If ODA is chosen as the platform for an e-Business Suite deployment, using a RAC (database) configuration, or at least RAC One Node, which is also supported for an e-Business Suite database, is recommended to fully utilize the capabilities of the ODA.

Storage capacity is easily met, at least for the typical case. An average e-Business Suite system rarely exceeds 2T size for the database.[1] The original ODA, depending on the storage configuration, provides up to 6T of space for the database. The ODA X3-2 provides up to 9T of the storage space, and even up to 18T with the storage expansion shelf added. In most cases, this is more than enough. As always, proper capacity planning is recommended before migration to a new platform.

---

[1]This figure is based on the author's experience working at The Pythian Group Inc. and supporting more than 15 e-Business Suite systems.

CPU needs are also easily met. The original ODA has two Intel Xeon X5675 6-core CPUs and the X3-2 has two Intel Xeon E5-2690 CPUs installed on each server node, which respectively provides 24 and 36 CPU cores per ODA. In many cases, e-Business Suite databases have up to 8 CPU cores per database node, but this depends heavily on the number of users and workload patterns of the environment. Make sure to estimate the required number of CPUs based on the characteristics of your environment and use the flexible licensing to enable only the required number of cores for the database.

Memory is potentially an issue, depending upon which ODA machine you are running, which version of e-Business Suite you use, and your virtualization choices. The original ODA came with 96G of RAM installed on each server node; the X3-2 was upgraded to 256G of RAM on each server. This is a sufficient amount of memory for the e-Business Suite database in most cases. However, if the virtualized deployment option is chosen, the amount of memory has to be split between the ODA Base (database), the management domain (Dom0), and the other virtual machines. With the original ODA, the amount of available memory may become a problem.

As you might expect, Oracle certifies its own software on its own hardware. Oracle Database Appliance is an Oracle Linux 5.6+ server cluster running Oracle grid infrastructure and database versions 11.2.0.2+. Both the OS and the database versions are certified for running the Oracle e-Business Suite R12.1 database; however, 11.2.0.3 is mandatory[2] for the R12.2 database version. Two deployment options for the application tier are possible:

- Virtualized ODA that uses the ODA's integrated Oracle VM and Oracle Linux 6 virtual servers for application tier hosts. This configuration is fully certified for e-Business Suite.

- Use of an external application tier. This approach is certified if built according to the requirements listed on My Oracle Support Certification Service.

e-Business Suite System Architecture on ODA

From a system architecture point, the ODA is nothing else than a "box" containing two servers, which can be configured for a database workload only, or for other types of workloads if a virtualized configuration is used. With the virtualization configuration, the ODA can also host multiple application servers; for a typical e-Business Suite configuration, two are needed to ensure better availability figures. Additional VMs can be added for more advanced configurations, that is, if external-facing modules (iSupplier, iRecruitment, iStore) are configured. Given the size and characteristics of the ODA platform, there are a number of possible system architectures that fully or partially utilize the ODA. Following are a few of the questions one has to answer to come up with the e-Business Suite architecture involving the use of an ODA:

- Which ODA configuration to use—bare metal or virtualized? If bare metal is used, the application tier servers will not reside on ODA.

- What's the configuration of the database—RAC, RAC One Node,[3] or single node? This decision affects the license costs and the availability characteristics of the database. For the best availability, RAC is recommended.

- Is an external load balancer available for use? (An ODA does not provide load balancer functionality). If it's not available, you may need to implement a software load balancing or failover functionality for the application tier on the ODA. Another option is to not use the load balancing at all. Is that a suitable configuration?

- What is the planned size of the application tier file system? Should it be shared between nodes? One of the options for the shared file system is to use the Oracle Automatic Storage Management Cluster File System (ACFS) on ODA; another option is to use an external NFS share, which introduces an external dependency.)

---

[2]Check the Certification Service on My Oracle Support for up-to-date requirements.
[3]RAC One Node is supported without explicit certification (`https://blogs.oracle.com/stevenChan/entry/rac_one_node_ebs`).

One of the architectures for deploying e-Business Suite fully on an ODA is visualized in Figure 11-1. This architecture uses Oracle Real Application Clusters for the database, SCAN listeners for the database connections, Oracle ACFS volume-mounted on virtual application servers to provide a shared application tier file system, one virtualized application tier node on each ODA physical server, and a virtual IP for user connections to the system assigned to one of the application tier nodes. The coming sections of the chapter will explore the details on how to deploy e-Business Suite system into this complex, 100% ODA-based architecture.

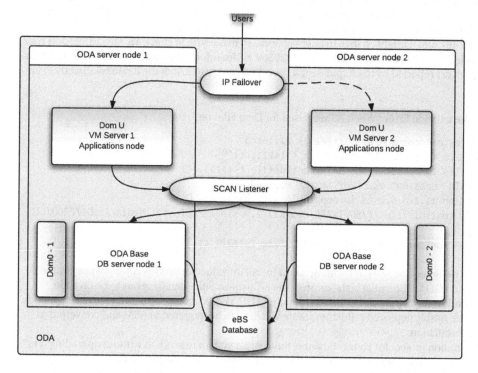

Figure 11-1. *e-Business Suite architecture on a virtualized ODA*

Configuring the ODA for e-Business Suite

The first step of configuring the ODA for e-Business Suite starts even before buying one. It's not enough to read a book that explains how to install e-Business Suite on ODA. Your system is unique. The first step is to plan. You know the characteristics of the system and you can tell if the HW specification of the ODA meets your requirements. Planning ahead is crucially important with the Oracle Database Appliance, as there are configuration items that can be set at the installation time and can't be changed later, like environment type (bare metal or virtualized platform) and ASM disk redundancy level.

Deploying e-Business Suite on ODA

The current most up-to-date version of e-Business Suite is Release 12.2, which became generally available in September 2013. Choose this version when starting implementation of e-Business Suite, as it introduces a number of technical improvements compared to R12.1. These improvements include online patching and use of Weblogic server in the technology stack of the application tier. On the opposite side, most of existing e-Business Suite R12.1 owners will be reluctant to upgrade their systems to R12.2 so soon after the date of general availability, so the migrations of Release 12.1 to ODA will still be common.

For new implementations, the R12.2 Rapid Install process has been improved by packaging RMAN backups of the e-Business Suite database and adding options to deploy the RAC or single node configuration using ASM or file system to store the data files. This provides more flexibility compared to the only native deployment option that was available for R12.1—the single node database with data files on a file system. Unfortunately, you will not be able to use these new capabilities to deploy the R12.2 environment into the ODA's RAC on ASM, because the e-Business Suite database has been prepackaged with the `compatible=11.2.0` parameter. In addition, the database compatibility of ASM disk groups on ODA is set to 11.2.0.2. This behavior was observed while using the latest available version of the Rapid Install StartCD (12.2.0.46), and it might change in later versions, so make sure to check My Oracle Support note "Oracle E-Business Suite Release Notes, Release 12.2 (Doc ID 1320300.1)" for information about the StartCD updates.

Listing 11-1 shows the errors reported by the Rapid Install process if you try to install the database directly to an ASM disk group on ODA.

Listing 11-1. Release 12.2 Installation Errors When ASM Is Used for Data Files on ODA

```
RMAN-03002: failure of restore command at 10/17/2013 22:16:46
ORA-19504: failed to create file "+DATA/controlfile_tst1221.ctl"
ORA-17502: ksfdcre:3 Failed to create file +DATA/controlfile_tst1221.ctl
ORA-15001: diskgroup "DATA" does not exist or is not mounted
ORA-15204: database version 11.2.0.0.0 is incompatible with diskgroup DATA
ORA-19600: input file is control file  (/SOFTWARE/eBS/R12.2.2/stage/EBSInstallMedia/AppDB/PROD/
backup_controlfile.ctl)
ORA-19601: output file is control file  (+DATA/controlfile_tst1221.ctl)
```

The inability to deploy the system on ASM by running Rapid Install introduces a serious complication for the installation process of R12.2 on ODA. The initial installation of the e-Business Suite database has to be on a file system and, as the only shared storage option for a RAC database on ODA is ASM, you're also limited to a single node configuration. This means the freshly deployed e-Business Suite will have to be migrated to ASM and converted to RAC immediately after the installation.

If you're planning a migration project for your e-Business Suite R12.1 system to an ODA without upgrading it to R12.2, then the complexity of the whole project depends on the current state of the system. The target state is clear—an 11.2 database running on Linux x86-64, and an Oracle Linux 5 or 6 for the application tier in case you choose to deploy as virtual machines on ODA. Although it's technically possible to build the application tier using Red Hat Enterprise Linux as the OS on the VMs, it's not recommended in order to preserve the "one throat to choke" support.[4] The contents of this chapter will explain how to configure the ODA to be capable of running the e-Business Suite R12.2, but the same configuration of the ODA is also able to run e-Business Suite 12.1.

The deployment process of the e-Business Suite R12.1 database tier on ODA in a bare metal (nonvirtualized) configuration has been very well explained in My Oracle Support note "Implementing Oracle E-Business Suite 12.1 Databases on Oracle Database Appliance (Doc ID 1566935.1)." At this moment,[5] a dedicated note for R12.2 is not available, but must be similar. Here I'll pay most of the attention to the virtualized deployment of e-Business Suite R12.2 on ODA.

Plan for Your Unique Environment

One of the settings to be careful at is the number of CPU cores you choose to enable and license by generating the license keys in My Oracle Support. If you set the initial core count too high, it's not possible to reduce it in bare metal configurations without assistance from My Oracle Support. It's better to start with a lower setting that can be increased later if needed.

---

[4]The same vendor supports all components of the system.
[5]October 17, 2013.

Plan the memory allocations to each component carefully, especially on the Original ODA. It's required to leave 8G of RAM for the Dom0. An averagely sized R12.1 application tier, running forms, self-service applications and concurrent managers, might require 16G of RAM (be aware that R12.2 requires more memory compared to R12.1). This leaves up to 72G for each ODA Base. The memory settings can be changed later if needed, but in case of R12.2 deployment on the original ODA, you need to make sure 96G of total RAM will be sufficient because there are no hardware upgrade options available for an ODA.

The storage configuration options are quite limited and can cause one of the unavoidable roadblocks in the path of installing e-Business Suite fully on ODA. There are two options where files accessible to the virtual machines can be stored:

- The free space on the two mirrored system disks (available space is 250G on the Original ODA and 300G on the X3-2). These disks can be used to store VM virtual disk images for boot, root, and swap volumes, but are too slow to host the e-Business Suite file system because it would significantly impact the maintenance operations, especially patching and backups of e-Business Suite.

- The Oracle ACFS file system shared from the ODA Base domain. It can be mounted on virtual machines using NFS, and then used as the shared application tier file system for both application tier nodes. The performance is much better than on the internal system disks. The ACFS volume resides in the +RECO ASM disk group, which also stores archived logs and backups if no external storage is used.

The Oracle Appliance Kit versions up to 2.7 do not provide many storage configuration options for the ODA (you can choose the backup location and ASM availability mode only) the available disk group sizes might not be suitable for all deployments. Table 11-1 shows the problematic configurations marked in bold and underlined.

Table 11-1. *ASM Disk Sizes Based on Chosen Storage Configuration Options*

Backup location / ASM availability	+DATA / +RECO size Original ODA	+DATA / +RECO size X3-2
Local / High	**1.6 T** / 2.038 T	2.4 T / 3.056 T
Local / Normal	2.4 T / 3.057 T	3.6 T / 4.585 T
External / High	3.2 T / **0.438 T**	4.8 T / **0.657 T**
External / Normal	4.8 T / **0.657 T**	7.2 T / **0.985 T**

You can see the disk size split between +DATA and +RECO is not optimal for e-Business Suite configurations. It's not uncommon to see e-Business Suite application tier file systems as large as 300G (including the concurrent manager logs and outputs). Also, two to three days history of archived logs can easily fill 250G to 350G of space in a relatively busy system; therefore, based on these very rough estimations, I wouldn't feel comfortable planning anything less than 1T for the +RECO disk group. And, the database size can grow quickly to 1T to 1.5T, which leaves you with the only option for storage configuration on the Original ODA—the local backup location setting with normal redundancy ASM disk groups, which provides 2.4T of space for the database and 3.057T of space for the shared ACFS volumes, backups, and the archived logs. The situation on the X3-2 is slightly better, but still the "external backup location" setting probably doesn't provide enough space in the +RECO disk group to comfortably choose these options for a long-term e-Business Suite platform. Your situation will definitely differ from this, but I hope I managed to outline the importance of storage planning for e-Business Suite deployments on an ODA. The storage configuration can't be changed later, so careful planning is extremely important.

The application tier installation on an ODA is only possible if it's deployed as a virtualized platform, which became available with the release of Oracle Database Appliance Kit (OAK) version 2.6. The virtualization on the ODA is a relatively new feature, so it is expected to see many changes in this area, but in OAK version 2.7, there are still many limitations in the virtualization options that you have to be aware of before deciding to use ODA for application tier VMs. These are the limitations that make the deployment of e-Business Suite on ODA more complicated:

- Virtual disk images can be stored on the ODA server nodes' system disks only, because the built-in Oracle VM Server (OVS) Repository is located there. The problem is that it's based on two RAID 1 hot swappable disks that provide 250G of space on the original ODA and 300G of space on X3-2. It might be possible to move the virtual disk images to NFS storage by customizing the VM configuration files to get a better performance from the external NFS; however, your goal here is to deploy e-Business Suite fully on ODA. Therefore, you're leaving the system disks in the original OVS repository location and you're mounting the ACFS volumes on the Application tier VMs to provide a shared storage file system for e-Business Suite.

- Virtual machines can be created from VM templates only. Oracle Appliance Kit Command Line Interface (*oakcli*) does not provide a way to install a VM from an installation media (DVD or CD, or their images). This means you have to use the available VM templates or assemblies from Oracle Software Delivery Cloud. Alternatively, it's also possible to build and use your own VM templates using the Oracle VM Template Builder in case you have access to Oracle virtualization platform elsewhere.

- There is no native load balancing solution available for virtual machines on ODA. And it's not possible to migrate VMs from one ODA node to another, which introduces additional availability constraints that need to be worked around. You'll use two application tier VMs configured with Linux *keepalived* to add an additional virtual IP address with a failover functionality for user connections to the e-Business Suite front-end services.

Configure the Local File System on the Database Server

The fresh installation process of R12.2 does not support installation to the ODA's ASM disk groups because of their database compatibility settings, so there's no other choice but installing the database on a file system. The e-Business Database tier requires 90G of disk space. The installation media downloaded from Oracle Software Delivery Cloud requires 25G[6] and the unpacked staging area for R12.2 installation requires another 25G. All summed up, it's 140G. Listing 11-2 shows a typical sizing of ODA Base file systems. It's clear there's not enough free space for a fresh installation.

Listing 11-2. Sizing of ODA Base File Systems

```
[root@s1 ~]# df -hP
Filesystem           Size  Used Avail Use% Mounted on
/dev/xvda2           55G   17G   36G  32% /
/dev/xvda1           91M   40M   47M  46% /boot
/dev/xvdb1           92G   26G   62G  30% /u01
tmpfs                40G  606M   39G   2% /dev/shm
/dev/asm/acfsvol-352 50G  166M   50G   1% /cloudfs
```

Additional free space is available on the /OVS file system on the management domain (Dom0) of the virtualized ODA. It's been reserved here for future use by VMs, as displayed in Listing 11-3. Note the available 202G of disk space in /OVS.

---

[6]The figures are calculated by downloading only the files needed for fresh installation. Files required for installation of the Vision database are not included.

Listing 11-3. Sizing of Dom0 File Systems

```
[root@ovs-host1 ~]# df -hP
Filesystem         Size  Used Avail Use% Mounted on
/dev/md1           19G   2.1G  16G  12% /
tmpfs              2.0G     0  2.0G   0% /dev/shm
/dev/md3           429G  205G 202G  51% /OVS
/dev/md0           99M    53M  41M  57% /boot
none               2.0G  144K 2.0G   1% /var/lib/xenstored
```

You'll borrow some of the available space from Dom0 to create a temporary, 100G virtual disk image for your needs. If you can use NFS to access the installation media, you don't need the whole 140G. The commands given in Listings 11-4 to 11-6 need to be performed on the Dom0 and the ODA Base on one of the ODA's physical servers to add a /u02 mount point on ODA Base. In the following examples, I'm adding the space to the ODA Base on the first node of the ODA.

Listing 11-4 explains how to create an empty virtual disk image file on Dom0 using the dd command. Please note the total size of the file in bytes is the multiplication of bs and seek parameters, and you need to adjust the parameters for your needs.

Listing 11-4. Creating an Empty 100G Disk Image File u02.img on Dom0

```
[root@ovs-host1 oakDom1]# pwd
/OVS/Repositories/odabaseRepo/VirtualMachines/oakDom1

[root@ovs-host1 oakDom1]# dd if=/dev/zero of=u02.img bs=1k seek=102400k count=0
0+0 records in
0+0 records out
0 bytes (0 B) copied, 2.2717e-05 seconds, 0.0 kB/s

[root@ovs-host1 oakDom1]# ls -lptr u02.img
-rw-r--r-- 1 root root 107374182400 Aug 25 07:57 u02.img
```

The ODA virtualization platform is based on Oracle VM. Although it's a specially adjusted configuration of Oracle VM that runs on ODA, it still contains the Oracle VM server management command-line tool *xm*. Listing 11-5 explains how to use *xm* on Dom0 to attach the empty virtual disk image to the ODA Base VM as device /dev/xvdd.

Listing 11-5. Attach the u01.img As a Block Device /dev/xvdd on ODA Base

```
[root@ovs-host1 oakDom1]# xm block-attach oakDom1 file:/OVS/Repositories/odabaseRepo/
VirtualMachines/oakDom1/u02.img /dev/xvdd w
```

Attaching the disk image to the VM is an online operation. Please note the vm.cfg file for ODA Base is not changed, and if the VM is bounced, the new device will not be automatically attached. Listing 11-6 shows how to partition the new device, how to create the file system, and how to mount it on ODA Base.

Listing 11-6. Partition the Block Device, Create the File System, and Mount It on ODA Base As /u02

```
[root@s1 ~]# fdisk /dev/xvdd
Command (m for help): n
Command action
   e   extended
   p   primary partition (1-4)
p
```

```
Partition number (1-4): 1
First cylinder (1-13054, default 1):
Using default value 1
Last cylinder or +size or +sizeM or +sizeK (1-13054, default 13054):
Using default value 13054
Command (m for help): w
The partition table has been altered!

Calling ioctl() to re-read partition table.
Syncing disks.

[root@s1 ~]# mkfs.ext3 /dev/xvdd1
Writing inode tables: done
Creating journal (32768 blocks): done
Writing superblocks and filesystem accounting information: done

[root@s1 ~]# e2label /dev/xvdd1 /u02
[root@s1 ~]# mkdir /u02
[root@s1 ~]# mount LABEL=/u02 /u02
```

A different approach needs to be taken to increase the available space in the bare metal configuration of ODA. It utilizes Linux Logical Volume Manager (LVM) to manage the disks. The steps to adjust the configuration are outlined in My Oracle Support note "How to customize available disk space for installing your Application on the Oracle Database Appliance (ODA) (Doc ID 1457717.1)."

Create a Virtual Machine for the Application Tier

Before starting the installation of the e-Business Suite, you have to create one of the planned application tier machines. The second VM will be cloned from the first one after the installation is completed. Alternatively, you may also choose to create two VMs (once on each ODA node) and use R12.2 Rapid Install to deploy the environment using a shared application tier file system. The example described here does not cover this scenario.

The easiest way to create the VM is to download the templates from Oracle Software Delivery Cloud.[7] I'm using the latest available Oracle Linux 6 update 4 x86_64 templates[8] to build the VMs. Make sure to download the paravirtualized template because it allows full use of Xen features to reduce the amount of needed hardware virtualization.

Once the template is downloaded and uncompressed, the Oracle virtual assembly file (in my case, it's OVM_OL6U4_x86_64_PVM.ova) needs to be placed in /OVS directory on Dom0 on the first node of the ODA, from where it will be loaded into the OVS repository. Listing 11-7 shows the commands to import the VM template into the OVS repository, after which the new VM is cloned from the template and sized to your needs. In the end, the new VM is started.

Listing 11-7. Creating the VM from Template

```
[root@s1 ~]# oakcli import vmtemplate oel6u4 -assembly /OVS/OVM_OL6U4_x86_64_PVM.ova -repo odarepo1
Imported VM Template

[root@s1 ~]# oakcli clone vm oevm1 -vmtemplate oel6u4 -repo odarepo1
Cloned VM : oevm1
```

---

[7]https://edelivery.oracle.com
[8]Oracle Linux 6 Update 4 template (OVF) - Paravirtualized x86_64 (64 bit), part number V38315-01.

```
[root@s1 ~]# oakcli configure vm oevm1 -maxvcpu 4 -vcpu 4
Configured VM : oevm1. The settings will take effect upon the next restart of this VM.

[root@s1 ~]# oakcli configure vm oevm1 -network "['type=netfront,bridge=net1']"
Configured VM : oevm1. The settings will take effect upon the next restart of this VM.

[root@s1 ~]# oakcli configure vm oevm1 -os OL_6
Configured VM : oevm1. The settings will take effect upon the next restart of this VM.

[root@s1 ~]# oakcli configure vm oevm1 -memory 12G -maxmemory 24G
Configured VM : oevm1. The settings will take effect upon the next restart of this VM.

[root@s1 ~]# oakcli start vm oevm1
Started VM : oevm1
```

At this moment, the new VM doesn't have an IP address, so you have to open the VM console by executing `oakcli show vmconsole oevm1` (this requires the graphical environment to be configured and the DISPLAY setting correctly pointing to a running virtual desktop) for the new VM to complete the initial configuration. Listing 11-8 shows the configuration values provided to the wizard. Be careful choosing the system host name, because e-Business Suite R12.2 does not support `<Oracle SID>_<hostname>`[9] values longer than 22 characters.

Listing 11-8. VM Configuration Wizard

```
Entering non-interactive startup
Starting OVM template configure:  network: System host name, e.g., "localhost.localdomain".:
oevm1.odalab.com
network: Network device to configure, e.g., "eth0".: eth0
network: Activate interface on system boot: yes or no.: yes
network: Boot protocol: dhcp or static.: static
network: IP address of the interface.: 10.177.0.61
network: Netmask of the interface.: 255.255.0.0
network:  gateway IP address.: 10.177.0.1
network: DNS servers separated by comma, e.g., "8.8.8.8,8.8.4.4".: 8.8.8.8,4.2.2.2
authentication: System root password.:
```

The VM templates starting with Oracle Linux 6 update 4 have been built using the minimal installation of the operational system, which means you have to install quite a number of RPMs to meet the requirements of e-Business Suite. The VM template has been preconfigured with the public yum repository and I found it very beneficial to allow the Internet connectivity from the ODA, at least during the setup phase, to speed up and simplify the configuration of the VM.

My Oracle Support note "Oracle E-Business Suite Installation and Upgrade Notes Release 12 (12.2) for Linux x86-64 (Doc ID 1330701.1)" contains an up-to-date list of all requirements for e-Business Suite R12.2, which includes the list of RPMs and the library patches; make sure to install them all. Additionally, you might consider upgrading the VM to the latest OL6 level and install the 11gR2 preinstall package because it delivers most of the required RPMs and settings; moreover, as you'll use the NFS-mounted ACFS volume, you'll need some NFS-related RPMs too. See Listing 11-9 for the additional RPMs I installed and for the commands I ran to start the NFS services and disable the firewall.

---

[9]The hostname doesn't include the domain name.

Listing 11-9. Additional Configuration to the Requirements Listed on MOS Note 1330701.1

```
[root@oevm1 ~]# yum upgrade
[root@oevm1 ~]# yum install portmap
[root@oevm1 ~]# yum install oracle-rdbms-server-11gR2-preinstall
[root@oevm1 ~]# chkconfig rpcbind on
[root@oevm1 ~]# chkconfig nfs on
[root@oevm1 ~]# chkconfig iptables off
[root@oevm1 ~]# service rpcbind start
[root@oevm1 ~]# service nfs start
[root@oevm1 ~]# service iptables stop
```

Use ACFS for the Application Tier Files

Using ACFS is the only way to configure a shared application tier file system without introducing external dependencies. Virtualized ODA is configured with a single 50G ACFS volume, which is mounted on both ODA Base VMs as /cloudfs. The 50G size is not sufficient for R12.2 implementations because the disk space requirement for the e-Business Suite dual file system is 64G, so it has to be increased. My Oracle Support document "ODA (Oracle Database Appliance): How To Resize CloudFS (Doc ID 1437717.1)" explains how to add and resize the ACFS volumes on ODA. Listing 11-10 shows the steps to execute as the *grid* user on the ODA Base to increase the /cloudfs from 50G to 150G.

Listing 11-10. Resizing the /cloudfs

```
[grid@s1 ~]$ . oraenv
ORACLE_SID = [grid] ? +ASM1
The Oracle base has been set to /u01/app/grid
[root@s1 ~]# df -hP /cloudfs
Filesystem               Size  Used Avail Use% Mounted on
/dev/asm/acfsvol-352    50G  166M   50G   1% /cloudfs

[grid@s1 ~]$ /sbin/acfsutil size +102400m /cloudfs
acfsutil size: new file system size: 161061273600 (153600MB)

[grid@s1 ~]$ df -hP /cloudfs
Filesystem               Size  Used Avail Use% Mounted on
/dev/asm/acfsvol-352   150G  369M  150G   1% /cloudfs
```

Once you have resized the ACFS volume based on your needs, it's just a matter of mounting it to the VM server using NFS. It might seem a straightforward task to add the volume to the ODA Base server in the /etc/exports file and /etc/fstab file on the VM, which would allow you to mount the file system successfully, but you have to make sure the mounted file system remains accessible, even if one of the ODA Base VMs goes down. Thus, a smarter solution is required.

First of all, you need to make sure each ODA Base VM can act as the NFS server for any of the application tier nodes (you have only one of them at the moment, but you know the IP address of the second one already). I'm adding one entry for each application tier VM to both ODA Base nodes in /etc/exports, as displayed in Listing 11-11.

Listing 11-11. /etc/exports on ODA Base VMs

```
[root@s1 ~]# cat /etc/exports
/cloudfs 10.177.0.61(rw,sync,no_root_squash,fsid=1)
/cloudfs 10.177.0.62(rw,sync,no_root_squash,fsid=1)
```

This configuration allows you to mount the /cloudfs to the application tier servers from any of the ODA Base VMs. You can also use virtual IP addresses on the ODA Base VMs for the NFS mounts to make sure you can mount NFS volumes, even if one of the ODA Base VMs is down and the virtual IP is relocated to the remaining node. Listing 11-12 shows the /etc/fstab entries for both application tier nodes that are used to mount the volumes from ACFS.[10]

Listing 11-12. /etc/fstab Entries for the Shared NFS Mount on Both Application Tier VMs

```
[oracle@oevm1 ~]$ grep cloudfs /etc/fstab
s1-vip:/cloudfs   /cloudfs    nfs      rw,intr,bg,hard,timeo=600,wsize=32768,rsize=32768,nfsvers=3,tc
p,nolock,acregmin=0,acregmax=0 0 0

[oracle@oevm2 ~]$ grep cloudfs /etc/fstab
s2-vip:/cloudfs   /cloudfs    nfs      rw,intr,bg,hard,timeo=600,wsize=32768,rsize=32768,nfsvers=3,tc
p,nolock,acregmin=0,acregmax=0 0 0
```

One has to be aware that this is not really a highly available solution for the NFS-mounted ACFS volumes on the application tier VMs. Our testing shows the mounted file systems can and will still hang after a virtual IP relocation happens on the DB nodes. You thus have to be ready to take action to recover the services on application tiers too.

Configure the Virtual IP for the Application Tier

The virtualized ODA platform does not support VM migrations from one physical server to the other, which means you need to have two application tier VMs—one on each physical server—to ensure the availability of e-Business Suite if one of the servers becomes unavailable. As there's no load balancing solution provided for VMs either, the best you can do is use an external load balancer to route the traffic to the application tier VMs you'll configure on the ODA. The e-Business Suite–specific configuration for using load balancers is explained in "Using Load-Balancers with Oracle E-Business Suite Release 12.2 (Doc ID 1375686.1)."

In this chapter, you'll find out how to use Linux *keepalived*[11] software to improve the availability of e-Business Suite if an external load balancer is not available. *Keepalived* is available on the Oracle Linux 6 public yum repository.

In this scenario, a very simple configuration that only manages a virtual IP address will be used. The virtual IP address will be mounted on one of the servers and will be configured as the web entry point for the e-Business Suite front-end services, this way providing an Active/Passive configuration from an end-user perspective.

You'll have two application tier nodes in the configuration—*oevm1* and *oevm2*—and the virtual IP 10.177.0.60 will be assigned hostname *oevip*. Listing 11-13 provides the commands for the installation of *keepalived* and shows the content of its configuration file. No configuration changes to *keepalived* will be needed after cloning the second application tier node.

Listing 11-13. Linux keepalived Installation and Configuration

```
[root@oevm1 ~]# yum install keepalived
[root@oevm1 ~]# vi /etc/keepalived/keepalived.conf
[root@oevm1 ~]# cat /etc/keepalived/keepalived.conf
vrrp_instance VI_1 {
interface eth0
state BACKUP
NOPREEMPT
virtual_router_id 1
```

---

[10]The recommended mount options are listed in My Oracle Support note "Sharing the Application Tier File System in Oracle E-Business Suite Release 12.2 (Doc ID 1375769.1)."

[11]Find more information about keepalived at www.keepalived.org.

```
virtual_ipaddress {
10.177.0.60
}
[root@oevm1 ~]# service keepalived start
Starting keepalived:                                        [  OK  ]
```

This simple configuration ensures the virtual IP address 10.177.0.60 is assigned to one of the servers running this configuration. State *BACKUP* means there is no preferred server for the virtual IP address. *NOPREEMPT* instructs the server not to try to grab the virtual IP address at the startup if the IP is already assigned to another server. This will ensure bringing up the VM after the failure doesn't cause downtime for the front-end services. Listing 11-14 shows how to check if the virtual IP address was allocated to the server (if *keepalived* is used the outputs of ifconfig don't report the virtual IP address as assigned to any of the interfaces).

Listing 11-14. Checking the Virtual IP Address Is Assigned to the Application Tier Node

```
[root@oevm1 ~]# ip addr list dev eth0
2: eth0: <BROADCAST,MULTICAST,UP,LOWER_UP> mtu 1500 qdisc pfifo_fast state UP qlen 1000
    link/ether 00:16:3e:29:ea:12 brd ff:ff:ff:ff:ff:ff
    inet 10.177.0.61/16 brd 10.177.255.255 scope global eth0
    inet 10.177.0.60/32 scope global eth0
    inet6 fe80::216:3eff:fe29:ea12/64 scope link
        valid_lft forever preferred_lft forever
```

The are many other configuration options for *keepalived,* and for the production use one should consider adding settings to monitor the application URLs so that the virtual IP would always be located on the node the application services are actually running on. One should also set the passwords for the communication between the *keepalived* servers to reduce the risks of someone stealing the virtual IP address, or even adding a *haproxy* package to configure true software load balancing solution for e-Business Suite.

Installing the e-Business Suite

Having prepared the ODA, it is time to perform the actual installation. This is done in two parts. First install the database tier, then install the application tier. The hardware configuration and virtualization layer you have configured on the ODA is transparent to the e-Business Suite installation process, and it does not introduce any complications specific to deployments on ODA.

The Database Tier Installation

From the e-Business Suite database tier installation point of view, the database server on ODA is just a Linux machine and the installation process doesn't differ from the one described in the *Oracle E-Business Suite Installation Guide: Using Rapid Install, Release 12.2 (12.2.0).*[12] As the ODA is a preconfigured system, you can skip most of the preinstallation tasks. However, the following steps still need to be performed:

1. Download the installation media from Oracle Software Delivery Cloud and stage the installation on an attached NFS share or local file system /u02, which was created in the previous step, on ODA Base.

---

[12]Available from otn.oracle.com documentation section, http://docs.oracle.com/cd/E18727_01/index.htm.

2. Check if any Rapid Install StartCD patches[13] have been released. Install the latest available patch to resolve any known issues with the original StartCD included on the freshly downloaded installation media.

3. Don't create a new OS user and group. You'll use user "*oracle*" and group "*dba*" for the installation. Create the Oracle Base directory for the e-Business Suite installation on the new file system.

```
[root@s1 ~]# mkdir /u02/prod
[root@s1 ~]# chown oracle:dba /u02/prod
```

4. ODA Base is fully capable of running a 11.2.0.3 database because it's built for this purpose, but additional packages are needed to run the Rapid Install. Follow My Oracle Support note "How to Download Linux RPM's Directly on the Oracle Database Appliance (ODA) (Doc ID 1461798.1)" to configure *odarpm* tool and use it to download and install the following additional RPMs: libstdc++-devel.i386, gdbm.i386, libXp.x86_64 and libXi.i386. For each package, execute the following commands (this example shows the download and installation of libstdc++-devel.i386 package; the same needs to be executed for other packages too):

```
[root@s1 ~]# cd /opt/oracle/oak/odarpm
[root@s1 odarpm]# ./getrpm libstdc++-devel
libstdc++-devel-4.1.2-54.el5.i386.rpm
RPM libstdc++-devel has been downloaded in this directory /opt/oracle/oak/pkgrepos/rpms/
[root@s1 odarpm]# rpm -ivh /opt/oracle/oak/pkgrepos/rpms/libstdc++-devel-4.1.2-54.el5.
i386.rpm
Preparing...                ########################################### [100%]
   1:libstdc++-devel        ########################################### [100%]
```

Now, before you start the Rapid Install, make sure you write down the hostname and domain name for the prepared application tier VM, and choose the base path on the shared /cloudfs volume you want to use for the application tier file system. This information will have to be provided to the installation wizard on the database tier. The configuration details will be saved in the database and will be retrieved later when the installation is started on the application tier servers.

The Rapid Install wizard requires a graphical environment to be configured and the DISPLAY variable to be set to an available virtual desktop, which can be launched locally or remotely. In the figures to follow, I use VNC to provide the graphical environment. The installation of R12.2 requires two port pools to be provided because it includes a dual application tier file system needed for e-Business Suite online patching; all the other port numbers are derived from the port pools. The installation described in this chapter uses port pools 11 and 12. Don't choose port pool 0 on ODA because it will cause a port conflict with ODA's default database listeners.

Figure 11-2 shows the Rapid Install wizard input values for the installation of e-Business Suite R12.2 database on ODA. Note how /u02 (the temporary file system created in previous steps) is used as the location for all files.

---

[13]At the time of writing, no Rapid Install (StartCD) patches were available for R12.2. Once released, they will be noted in My Oracle Support note "Oracle E-Business Suite Release Notes, Release 12.2 (Doc ID 1320300.1)."

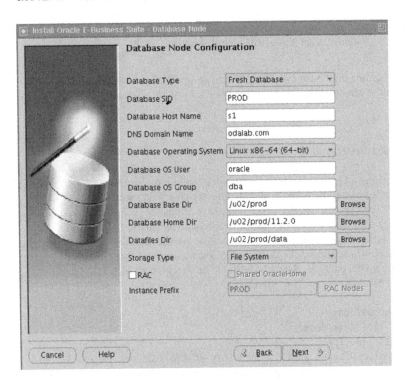

Figure 11-2. *Rapid Install parameter values for the database tier*

Figure 11-3 shows the Rapid Install wizard input values for the installation of the e-Business Suite R12.2 application tier on the prepared VM. Note how the NFS-mounted ACFS volume /cloudfs is used for the installation of all application tier files.

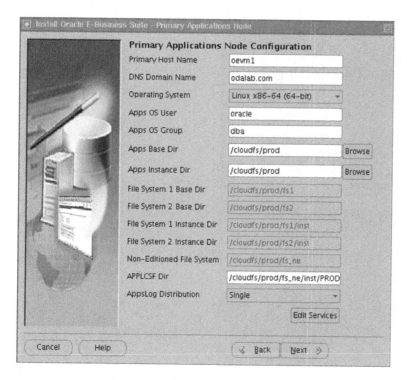

Figure 11-3. *Rapid Install parameter values for the application tier*

The Application Tier Installation

The current version of the Rapid Install Wizard (12.2.0.46) has a bug in the prerequisites checks on Oracle Linux 6. The bug does not allow the installer to start. The following file in the staging area needs to be changed to avoid the bug: `startCD/Disk1/rapidwiz/jlib/webtier/Scripts/prereq/linux64/refhost.xml`. The value "`<VERSION VALUE="6"/>`" needs to be replaced with "`<VERSION VALUE="oracle"/>`".

The installation process of the e-Business Suite application tier on ODA-based virtual machines is exactly the same as on any other type of server. The configuration settings for the Rapid Install have been saved in the database during the installation of the database tier. You need to start the Rapid Install on the application's VM after completing the installation of the database. The configuration parameters don't need to be entered manually anymore; all you have to do is point the wizard to the new database where the parameters have been saved, as shown in Figure 11-4. The wizard will load and validate all the settings before starting the installation process.

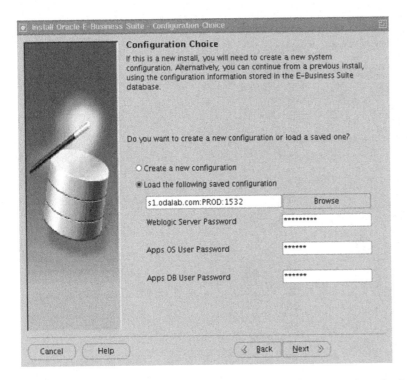

Figure 11-4. *Retrieving the application tier installation parameters from the database*

The installation should complete successfully, but there are still a few post installation tasks listed in My Oracle Support documents "Oracle E-Business Suite Release Notes, Release 12.2 (Doc ID 1320300.1)" and "Oracle E-Business Suite Installation and Upgrade Notes Release 12 (12.2) for Linux x86-64 (Doc ID 1330701.1)" that need to be completed before proceeding with the finalization steps of e-Business Suite configuration on ODA. These tasks are as follows:

1. Patch AS 10g (10.1.2) Oracle Home (Doc ID 1330701.1).

2. Apply the mandatory fs_clone fix—Patch 17064510:R12.TXK.C.

3. Run the AD Administration Maintain Snapshot option to Create the Snapshot (Doc ID 1320300.1).

4. Apply Consolidated Seed Table Upgrade Patch 16605855:12.2.0.

5. Apply the 12.2.2 AD and TXK Release Update Pack (Doc ID 1560906.1).

6. Apply the 12.2.2 Suite-Wide Release Update Pack (Doc ID 1506669.1).

At this moment, you have a fully functional e-Business Suite system. It's definitely not ready for production use yet because you still have to integrate it into the ODA so that you will be able to use all the good features that ODA is able to provide. The next section of the chapter addresses the tasks that you need to perform to finalize the configuration.

Finalizing the Configuration

You've just completed the installation of e-Business Suite on ODA, but it's still far from being properly configured for running your production environment. The database resides on one of the ODA nodes on its local disks (ASM and RAC are not used). The application tier has no server redundancy. In this portion of the chapter, you'll find out how to finalize the configuration of your new e-Business Suite system to use both server nodes, ASM, RAC, and two application server virtual machines to ensure the best possible availability.

Create a New 11.2 Oracle Home

The R12.2 installation process delivered an 11.2.0.3 database home that was installed in a temporary mount point that you created on the local disks in one of the ODA nodes. This configuration is fully capable of running the e-Business Suite database, but it's not recommended, as the goal is to minimize any nonstandard changes to the ODA. In this section, you'll find out how to create an ODA-compatible 11.2.0.3 Database Oracle Home and how to adjust it for e-Business Suite.

Creating a new Oracle Home is a very simple process on ODA. Executing the oakcli create dbhome command creates a new database home on both ODA database nodes simultaneously. You'll also need to provide the version of the database home you want to install.[14] The tool will ask you to enter root, oracle and sysasm passwords and will spool lots of output; and in the end, it will print out the name of the freshly created Oracle Homes:

```
[root@s1 ~]# oakcli create dbhome -version 11.2.0.3.7
...
INFO: 2013-08-25 12:58:43: Installing a new home: OraDb11203_home3 at /u01/app/oracle/
product/11.2.0.3/dbhome_3
...
SUCCESS: 2013-08-25 13:05:21: Successfully created the database home OraDb11203_home3
```

It's also important to change the permissions of the Oracle binary in the new Oracle Homes on both DB nodes to allow the database access to the ASM disks. Log on as the grid user on both nodes and run the setasmgidwrap utility as explained in Listing 11-15.

Listing 11-15. Fixing the Permissions of the Oracle Binaries

```
[grid@s1 ~]$ . oraenv
ORACLE_SID = [grid] ? +ASM1
The Oracle base has been set to /u01/app/grid
[grid@s1 ~]$ $ORACLE_HOME/bin/setasmgidwrap o=/u01/app/oracle/product/11.2.0.3/dbhome_3/bin/oracle
```

The next step in the preparation process is the installation of the Examples CD on top of the new Oracle Home. This is a specific requirement for e-Business Suite, and it has to be completed manually. The version of the new Oracle Home is 11.2.0.3.7, so you need to install the Examples CD content from the installation package of Oracle Database 11.2.0.3, which is available from My Oracle Support as patch 10404530. Checking the Read Me information of the patch reveals the exact file ("disk") you need to download—p10404530_112030_Linux-x86-64_6of7.zip. Upload the installation disk of the Examples CD to any ODA Base, unzip it, and run the runInstaller from the examples folder. Again, you'll need the graphical environment to be able to launch the installation wizard. Point the installer to the new Oracle Home and it will install the Examples CD content to both Oracle Homes (one on each ODA server).

---

[14]See My Oracle Support note 888888.1.

The next step is to create the NLS directories by executing the `cr9idata.pl` script on each node. Make sure to set the database `ORACLE_HOME` variable before running the script. Listing 11-16 shows an example.

Listing 11-16. Creating the NLS Directories in the New Oracle Home

```
[oracle@s1 ~]$ export ORACLE_HOME=/u01/app/oracle/product/11.2.0.3/dbhome_3
[oracle@s1 ~]$ perl $ORACLE_HOME/nls/data/old/cr9idata.pl
Creating directory /u01/app/oracle/product/11.2.0.3/dbhome_3/nls/data/9idata ...
Copying files to /u01/app/oracle/product/11.2.0.3/dbhome_3/nls/data/9idata...
Copy finished.
Please reset environment variable ORA_NLS10 to /u01/app/oracle/product/11.2.0.3/dbhome_3/nls/
data/9idata!
```

The last and the most complicated step is the installation of the required database patches. The list of one-off patches can be obtained from My Oracle Support note "Database Preparation Guidelines for an E-Business Suite Release 12.2 Upgrade (Doc ID 1349240.1)." The R12.2 database Oracle Home requires 57 patches; fortunately, not all of them need to be applied manually because patch 16342486 (n-apply bundle patch III for RDBMS 11.2.0.3.0 with eBS Release 12.2) delivers 51 of all the required patches. But the task is especially complex because a PSU is already applied to the new Oracle Home and many of the patches conflict with it.

I found the following approach effective in dealing with all the patch conflicts:

1. Apply the latest OPatch version first (patch 6880880).

2. Install the bundle patch (16342486) as instructed by running `opatch napply -skip_subset -skip_duplicate`. The installation will fail because of the conflicts; however, the outputs will provide useful information about which exact patches conflicts with the CPU patch that's already applied. Listing 11-17 shows the important outputs.

Listing 11-17. Identifying the Conflicting Patches

```
[oracle@s1 16342486]$ opatch napply -skip_subset -skip_duplicate
...
Verifying environment and performing prerequisite checks...
Checking skip_duplicate
Checking skip_subset
These patches will be skipped because they are subset patches of some patch(es) in the Oracle Home:
11071989,12764337,12780983,12845115,12849688,12971775,13036331,13070939,13366202,13466801,13499128,
13528551,13544396,13923995,14398795,8547978,9858539
OPatch continues with these patches:
12942119,12949905,12949919,12951696,12955701,12965899,12985184,13004894,13023632,13040331,13146719,1
3258936,13259364,13366268,13388104,13477790,13495307,13602312,
13808632,14005749,14013094,14207902,14237793,14296972,14598522,14649883,14698700,14751895,14832335,
15967134,16040940,16163946,16342486,4247037
...
Following patches have conflicts: [   16619892    13004894    14727310    13923374    13259364
14598522   16056266    14275605    13696216    13343438    14649883    14751895    15967134    16163946 ]
Refer to My Oracle Support Note 1299688.1 for instructions on resolving patch conflicts.
```

3. Install the bundle patch again, but instruct the *opatch* to apply only the patches that don't conflict with the installed PSU this time. This can be done by subtracting the patches in the "Following patches have conflicts" list from the "OPatch continues with these patches" list spooled by the initial run of the *opatch*. The remaining list of patches should be passed to *opatch* by using the-`id` parameter:

```
[oracle@s1 16342486]$ opatch napply -skip_subset -skip_duplicate -id 12942119,12949905,12949919,129
51696,12955701,12965899,12985184,13023632,13040331,13146719,13258936,13366268,13388104,13477790,134
95307,13602312,13808632,14005749,14013094,14207902,14237793,14296972,14698700,14832335,16040940,163
42486,4247037
```

4. Watch as the installation progresses and applies the patches to both new Oracle Homes.

5. Install the remaining patches from My Oracle Support note 1349240.1. Some of the patches may conflict with the installed PSU again.

6. Check the My Oracle Support note "Database Patch Set Update Overlay Patches Required for Use with PSUs and Oracle E-Business Suite (Doc ID 1147107.1)" to find the replacement patches for the conflicting patches found during the previous steps.

7. Create service requests for Oracle Support if any of the patch conflicts are still unresolved.

There's no point in listing all the patches here because these PSUs are released quarterly, and Oracle tries to keep up the same pace with the new versions of the Oracle Appliance Kit that delivers the new Patch Set Updates to the Oracle Database Appliance. It's also likely the patching requirements of R12.2 database home will change because the Release 12.2 version of e-Business Suite was recently released. The installation of patches in the new home completes this step, and the database can be started from the new home.

Configure the New Oracle Home

AutoConfig manages the configuration of the Oracle Home in an e-Business Suite environment. It is not enough to copy initialization and Net services' configuration files from the existing database home to the new one to start using it. A few additional steps need to be taken to implement the *AutoConfig* in the new Oracle Home. You will use a set of tools delivered by e-Business Suite to clone the configuration of the old home (referenced as the OLD_OH later in the text) to the new home (referenced as the NEW_OH).

Follow the instructions outlined next to implement *AutoConfig* and prepare the configuration files needed for the existing e-Business Suite database:

1. Run the *adpreclone.pl* utility to capture the configuration details of the existing Oracle Home and save them in the $OLD_OH/appsutil directory. Then stop the listener and shut down the database. Here are the commands to execute this step:

```
[oracle@s1 11.2.0]$ . $OLD_OH/PROD_s1.env
[oracle@s1 ~]$ cd $OLD_OH/appsutil/scripts/$CONTEXT_NAME
[oracle@s1 PROD_s1]$ perl adpreclone.pl dbTier
[oracle@s1 PROD_s1]$ ./addlnctl.sh stop PROD
[oracle@s1 PROD_s1]$ ./addbctl.sh stop immediate
```

2. Copy the appsutil directory from the old Oracle Home to the new one and rename the existing database context file because the same filename needs to be used for the new context file. For example:

```
[oracle@s1 ~]$ cp -rp $OLD_OH/appsutil $NEW_OH/
[oracle@s1 ~]$ cd $NEW_OH/appsutil
[oracle@s1 appsutil]$ mv PROD_s1.xml PROD_s1.xml.old
```

3. Use *adclonectx.pl* to create a new context file by using the old one as a template. This utility will launch a command-line wizard that will ask a few questions about the new configuration. Here's an example run:

```
[oracle@s1 appsutil]$ cd $NEW_OH/appsutil/clone/bin
[oracle@s1 bin]$ perl adclonectx.pl contextfile=$OLD_OH/appsutil/PROD_s1.xml.old
Enter the APPS password : notimportant
Target System Hostname (virtual or normal) [s1] : s1
Do you want the inputs to be validated (y/n) [n] ? : n
Target Instance is RAC (y/n) [n] : n
Target System Database SID : PROD
Target System Base Directory : /u01/app/oracle
Oracle OS User [oracle] : oracle
Oracle OS Group [dba] : dba
Target System utl_file_dir Directory List : /usr/tmp
Number of DATA_TOP's on the Target System [3] : 1
Target System DATA_TOP Directory 1 : /u02/prod/data
Target System RDBMS ORACLE_HOME Directory [/u01/app/oracle/11.2.0] : /u01/app/oracle/
product/11.2.0.3/dbhome_3
Do you want to preserve the Display [null] (y/n)  : y
Target System Port Pool [0-99] : 11
New context path and file name [/u01/app/oracle/product/11.2.0.3/dbhome_3/appsutil/PROD_s1.xml] :
/u01/app/oracle/product/11.2.0.3/dbhome_3/appsutil/PROD_s1.xml
contextfile=/u01/app/oracle/product/11.2.0.3/dbhome_3/appsutil/PROD_s1.xml
```

4. A new context file was created in the previous step, but the configuration files still need to be prepared by running *AutoConfig*. Normally, *AutoConfig* connects to the database too, but at this moment, you're unable to start it because the configuration is still missing. You need to run a subset of all *AutoConfig* actions (called the "Instantiate phase") that will prepare the configuration files, but will not attempt to apply the configuration to the database. Specifying the run=INSTE8 option to the *adconfig.pl* utility allows you to do this. When the configuration is ready, the new environment file can be sourced and the listener can be started from the new Oracle Home, as in the following example:

```
[oracle@s1 bin]$ perl adconfig.pl contextfile=$NEW_OH/appsutil/PROD_s1.xml run=INSTE8
[oracle@s1 bin]$ . $NEW_OH/PROD_s1.env
[oracle@s1 bin]$ cd $NEW_OH/appsutil/scripts/$CONTEXT_NAME
[oracle@s1 PROD_s1]$ ./addlnctl.sh start PROD
```

5. The initialization file for the database does not exist yet. You need to create it from the old server parameter file and adjust it for the new Oracle Home manually. First, create the new initialization parameter file as follows:

```
[oracle@s1 PROD_s1]$ sqlplus / as sysdba
...
Connected to an idle instance.
SQL> create pfile from spfile='$OLD_OH/dbs/spfilePROD.ora';
File created.
```

6. Adjust the initialization parameter file $NEW_OH/dbs/initPROD.ora to replace all references to the temporary file system you've been using for the old Oracle Home with appropriate paths in the new configuration. The following are the parameters you need to adjust:

```
*.diagnostic_dest='$NEW_OH/admin/PROD_s1'
*.log_archive_dest_1='LOCATION=+RECO'
*.utl_file_dir='/usr/tmp','$NEW_OH/appsutil/outbound/PROD_s1'
```

7. You also need to set the verified initialization parameters for ODA. These settings are set by default when a new database is created using the ODA's *oakcli* utility. The parameters have been specifically tuned for ODA, and the e-Business Suite database has to use them too. Here are the parameters and their values:

```
*._disable_interface_checking=true
*._gc_undo_affinity=false
*._gc_policy_time=0
*._enable_numa_support=false
*._file_size_increase_increment=2143289344
*.compatible='11.2.0.3.0'
*.db_recovery_file_dest='+RECO'
*.db_create_file_dest='+DATA'
*.db_create_online_log_dest_1='+REDO'
*.db_block_checksum=full
*.db_block_checking=full
*.db_lost_write_protect=typical
*.filesystemio_options=setall
        *.use_large_pages=only
```

8. The last step that finalizes the implementation of *AutoConfig* managed configuration in the new Oracle Home is starting the database and running *AutoConfig*. Also, because the initialization parameter file has been prepared, it can be converted into a server parameter file, as in the following example:

```
[oracle@s1 PROD_s1]$ sqlplus / as sysdba
...
Connected to an idle instance.
SQL> create spfile from pfile;
File created.
SQL> startup
...
```

```
Database opened.
SQL> exit
[oracle@s1 PROD_s1]$ ./adautocfg.sh
Enter the APPS user password:
...
AutoConfig completed successfully.
```

The preceding eight steps complete the configuration of the new Oracle Home for your e-Business Suite database; however, you need to remember that the new Oracle Home has a different set of patches installed on top of it, at least because it contains a Patch Set Update. You have to complete all the post-installation tasks for the patches installed to the new Oracle Home. Most of the patches are the same in the old and new Oracle Homes, therefore it's best to compare the lists of installed patches and execute the post-installation tasks for the ones that are not present in the old Oracle Home. Listing 11-18 shows how to extract nicely formatted and sorted lists of patches that are easy to compare, and identify the differences in each Oracle Home.

Listing 11-18. Extracting the List of Installed Patches

```
[oracle@s1 ~]$ cd $ORACLE_HOME/OPatch/
[oracle@s1 OPatch]$ ./opatch lsinventory | grep "^Patch   " | awk -F ":" {'print $1'} | sort
Patch  12942119
Patch  12949905
Patch  12949919
Patch  12951696
...
```

Once you have compared the installed patches in both Oracle Homes and executed the remaining post-installation, the configuration of e-Business Suite with the ODA's natively created Oracle Home is completed.

Migrate to ASM and RAC

Migration to ASM and RAC is quite a complex change that can be implemented in a number of ways, including a manual reconfiguration of the database. However, that would require much time and it is relatively easy to miss something or make an error in the process due to the large number of items to address. Instead, it is good to automate the migration.

My Oracle Support note "Using Oracle 11g Release 2 Real Application Clusters and Automatic Storage Management with Oracle E-Business Suite Release 12.2 (Doc ID 1453213.1)" lists the *RCONFIG* utility as one of the tools that can be used to automate the RAC conversion. An additional benefit of *RCONFIG* is the fact it can move the database to ASM as part of the operation. This is why the tool is especially useful in our situation.

One deficiency of *RCONFIG* is its inability to work with user-defined Oracle listeners. Therefore, before you run the utility, make sure the following standard configuration is present:

- Local_listener parameter is not set in your database.

- Remote_listener parameter is set to '<scanname>:1521' (i.e. 'scan.odalab.com:1521').

- The scan listeners are started.

- The default listener (one named "LISTENER") is started on each ODA Base node.

- And your DB is properly registered with the default listener on the same server that the DB is running on and with the scan listeners on both nodes.

Execute the steps explained in the document "Using Oracle 11g Release 2 Real Application Clusters and Automatic Storage Management with Oracle E-Business Suite Release 12.2 (Doc ID 1453213.1)" to convert the database to RAC and migrate to ASM. Listing 11-19 shows the XML file that I prepared as input into those steps.

Listing 11-19. Example Contents of an rconfig XML Input File

```
[oracle@s1 ~]$ cat PRODtoRAC.xml
<?xml version="1.0" encoding="UTF-8"?>
<n:RConfig xmlns:n="http://www.oracle.com/rconfig"
           xmlns:xsi="http://www.w3.org/2001/XMLSchema-instance"
           xsi:schemaLocation="http://www.oracle.com/rconfig rconfig.xsd">
    <n:ConvertToRAC>
    <n:Convert verify="YES">
          <n:SourceDBHome>/u01/app/oracle/product/11.2.0.3/dbhome_3</n:SourceDBHome>
          <n:TargetDBHome>/u01/app/oracle/product/11.2.0.3/dbhome_3</n:TargetDBHome>
             <n:SourceDBInfo SID="PROD">
           <n:Credentials>
             <n:User>sys</n:User>
             <n:Password>password</n:Password>
             <n:Role>sysdba</n:Role>
           </n:Credentials>
         </n:SourceDBInfo>
         <n:NodeList>
           <n:Node name="s1"/>
           <n:Node name="s2"/>
         </n:NodeList>
         <n:InstancePrefix>PROD</n:InstancePrefix>
         <n:SharedStorage type="ASM">
           <n:TargetDatabaseArea>+DATA</n:TargetDatabaseArea>
           <n:TargetFlashRecoveryArea>+RECO</n:TargetFlashRecoveryArea>
         </n:SharedStorage>
       </n:Convert>
    </n:ConvertToRAC>
</n:RConfig>
```

The process will take a while to complete, because the data files need to be copied to ASM. Once completed, the database will be started and the required CRS resources will be registered.

The e-Business Suite configuration for RAC is still missing at this time, so it has to be prepared. The steps are outlined in the same document (1453213.1), but I find the document hard to follow because it tries to explain multiple options on how e-Business Suite can be configured on RAC at the same time. You need a configuration that uses srvctl to manage the database and the custom user-created listener, and the e-Business Suite needs to be aware of the SCAN listener. Following are the verified steps for this particular configuration.

1. Create a new appsutil.zip package on the applications server oevm1:

```
[oracle@oevm1 ~]$ . /cloudfs/PROD/fs1/EBSapps/appl/APPSPROD_oevm1.env
[oracle@oevm1 ~]$ . $RUN_BASE/EBSapps/appl/APPS$CONTEXT_NAME.env
[oracle@oevm1 scripts]$ $AD_TOP/bin/admkappsutil.pl
Starting the generation of appsutil.zip
Log file located at /cloudfs/prod/fs1/inst/apps/PROD_oevm1/admin/log/MakeAppsUtil_10221301.log
output located at /cloudfs/prod/fs1/inst/apps/PROD_oevm1/admin/out/appsutil.zip
MakeAppsUtil completed successfully.
```

2. Set the environment variables and clean up the existing configuration (if such exists) on both database nodes. (The Oracle SID will be different on each node). For example:

```
[oracle@s1 ~]$ export ORACLE_HOME=$NEW_OH
[oracle@s1 ~]$ export LD_LIBRARY_PATH=$ORACLE_HOME/lib:$ORACLE_HOME/ctx/lib
[oracle@s1 ~]$ export ORACLE_SID=PROD2
[oracle@s1 ~]$ export PATH=$PATH:$ORACLE_HOME/bin
[oracle@s1 ~]$ export CONTEXT_NAME=${ORACLE_SID}_`hostname -s`
[oracle@s1 ~]$ export TNS_ADMIN=$ORACLE_HOME/network/admin/${CONTEXT_NAME}
[oracle@s1 ~]$ mv appsutil appsutil.old
[oracle@s1 ~]$ mv $TNS_ADMIN ${TNS_ADMIN}.old
[oracle@s1 ~]$ rm $ORACLE_HOME/network/admin/*.ora
```

3. Create the new Net services' configuration files on both database nodes. The configuration files will only include pointers to the *AutoConfig*-managed configuration files that do not exist at the moment, but will be created later. For example:

```
[oracle@s1 ~]$ echo "IFILE=${ORACLE_HOME}/network/admin/${CONTEXT_NAME}/tnsnames.ora" >
$ORACLE_HOME/network/admin/tnsnames.ora
[oracle@s1 ~]$ echo "IFILE=${ORACLE_HOME}/network/admin/${CONTEXT_NAME}/listener.ora" >
$ORACLE_HOME/network/admin/listener.ora
[oracle@s1 ~]$ echo "IFILE=${ORACLE_HOME}/network/admin/${CONTEXT_NAME}/sqlnet.ora" >
$ORACLE_HOME/network/admin/sqlnet.ora
```

4. Extract the new appsutil.zip on both database nodes (the file is already accessible because the application tier is located on the /cloudfs). You also need to copy the JRE from the old database Oracle Home into the extracted appsutil directory, as shown next:

```
[oracle@s1 ~]$ unzip -q -d $ORACLE_HOME/ /cloudfs/prod/fs1/inst/apps/PROD_oevm1/admin/out/appsutil.zip
[oracle@s1 ~]$ rsync -az s1:/u02/prod/11.2.0/appsutil/jre $ORACLE_HOME/appsutil/
```

5. Create the new database listener. Use "LISTENER_<SID>" as the listener name and set the port according to the primary port pool you chose for the e-Business Suite (in this example, the port pool is 11, so the listener port is 1532 (1521+11)). This needs to be run on one of the DB nodes only. For example:

```
[oracle@s1 ~]$ srvctl add listener -l LISTENER_PROD -o $ORACLE_HOME -p  1532
[oracle@s1 ~]$ srvctl setenv listener -l LISTENER_PROD -T TNS_ADMIN=$ORACLE_HOME/network/admin
[oracle@s1 ~]$ srvctl start listener -l LISTENER_PROD
```

6. Adjust the local_listener parameter so that both database instances register to the local listeners:

```
[oracle@s1 ~]$ sqlplus / as sysdba
SQL> alter system set local_listener='s1:1532' sid='PROD1';
System altered.
SQL> alter system set local_listener='s2:1532' sid='PROD2';
System altered.
```

7. Clean up the current configuration in the database. Execute the following commands, which need to be run from only *one* of the DB nodes.

```
[oracle@s1 ~]$ sqlplus apps
SQL> exec fnd_conc_clone.setup_clean;
PL/SQL procedure successfully completed.
```

8. Generate the new database context file on both database nodes by running the *adbldxml.pl* utility from within the new appsutil directory, as in the following example. Adjust the parameters as needed depending on which database node the utility is executed.

```
[oracle@s1 ~]$ cd $ORACLE_HOME/appsutil/bin
[oracle@s1 bin]$ adbldxml.pl appsuser=apps appspass=***
...
Enter Hostname of Database server: s1
Enter Port of Database server: 1532
Enter SID of Database server: PROD1
Enter Database Service Name: PROD
Do you want to enable SCAN addresses[N]: Y
Specify value for s_scan_name: scan.odalab.com
Specify value for s_scan_port: 1521
Enter the value for Display Variable: s1:0.0

The context file has been created at:
/u01/app/oracle/product/11.2.0.3/dbhome_3/appsutil/PROD1_s1.xml
```

9. Change the s_virtual_hostname and s_db_listener context parameters in both new context files. Use the name of the new database listener, which was created in Step 5 of this instruction list. The following example shows how the values are changed on the first node:

```
[oracle@s1 bin]$ egrep "s_virtual_hostname|s_db_listener" $ORACLE_HOME/appsutil/PROD1_s1.xml
      <host oa_var="s_virtual_hostname">s1</host>
         <DB_LISTENER oa_var="s_db_listener"></DB_LISTENER>
[oracle@s1 bin]$ vi $ORACLE_HOME/appsutil/PROD1_s1.xml
[oracle@s1 bin]$ egrep "s_virtual_hostname|s_db_listener" $ORACLE_HOME/appsutil/PROD1_s1.xml
      <host oa_var="s_virtual_hostname">s1-vip</host>
         <DB_LISTENER oa_var="s_db_listener">LISTENER_PROD</DB_LISTENER>
```

10. Run the *adconfig.pl* utility on both nodes to create the initial configuration:

```
[oracle@s1 bin]$ perl adconfig.sh contextfile=$ORACLE_HOME/appsutil/PROD1_s1.xml
Enter the APPS user password:
...
AutoConfig completed successfully.
```

11. Connect to each of the database instances and change the `local_listener` and `remote_listener` database initialization parameters. Note the `local_listener` parameter requires different values on each node. For example:

```
# on the 1st node
[oracle@s1 ~]$ sqlplus / as sysdba
SQL> alter system set remote_listener='PROD_REMOTE' sid='PROD1';
System altered.
SQL> alter system set local_listener='PROD1_LOCAL' sid='PROD1';
System altered.
SQL> exit

# on the 2nd node
[oracle@s2 ~]$ sqlplus / as sysdba
SQL> alter system set remote_listener='PROD_REMOTE' sid='PROD2';
System altered.
SQL> alter system set local_listener='PROD2_LOCAL' sid='PROD2';
System altered.
SQL> exit
```

12. Source the new environment files and run *AutoConfig* on each node:

```
[oracle@s1 ~]$ . $ORACLE_HOME/$CONTEXT_NAME.env
[oracle@s1 ~]$ cd $ORACLE_HOME/appsutil/scripts/$CONTEXT_NAME
[oracle@s1 PROD1_s1]$ ./adautocfg.sh
Enter the APPS user password:
...
AutoConfig completed successfully.
```

13. The last step, which concludes the configuration of the e-Business Suite database in RAC, is adding an e-Business Specific `ORA_NLS10` environment variable to the CRS service of the database. Execute the following command on any of the database servers:

```
[oracle@s1 ~]$ srvctl setenv database -d PROD -t "TNS_ADMIN=$ORACLE_HOME/network/admin,ORA_NLS10=$ORACLE_HOME/nls/data/9idata"
```

14. Additionally, it's important to know that *AutoConfig* on the database nodes sets the `tcp.validnode_checking=yes`, and `tcp.invited_nodes` lists only the physical and virtual IPs of the database nodes in the `sqlnet.ora` file. This means the listener will accept new connections from the database nodes only. As you'll need to connect to the database from two application servers, too additional nodes need to be added to the `tcp.invited_nodes` by overriding that parameter in the custom include file `sqlnet_ifile.ora`, as shown next. (If you prefer disabling the `tcp.validnode_checking` completely, the best way of doing so is changing the e-Business Suite profile option "SQLNet Access" to *ALLOW_ALL,* and then re-running *AutoConfig* on the database nodes).

```
[oracle@s1 ~]$ echo "tcp.invited_nodes=(s1, s2, s1-vip, s2-vip, oevm1, oevm2)" > $TNS_ADMIN/sqlnet_ifile.ora
```

The configuration of the database tier is completed. Now it's time to test whether the listener and the database can be started from any of the database nodes using *srvctl*. Execute the commands srvctl stop database -d PROD and srvctl stop listener -l LISTENER_PROD to stop the services. Then execute srvctl start listener -l LISTENER_PROD and srvctl start database -d PROD to start the services. Try these commands from one node, and then from the other node. Check the listeners after each test to see how the database instances are registered.

Listing 11-20 shows correctly registered services for one of the SCAN listeners. Please observe the following characteristics of a correct configuration:

- Two services are registered, named *PROD* and *ebs_patch* (*ebs_patch* is used by the online patching feature of e-Business Suite R12.2 to provide the connectivity to the "patch edition" of the database).

- Each service has two registered instances, in this case *PROD1* and *PROD2*.

- Each instance is registered with the virtual address of a database server. There are two such servers in the example, named *s1-vip.odalab.com* and *s2-vip.odalab.com*.

Listing 11-20. Database Services Registered with SCAN Listeners

```
[grid@s2 ~]$ . oraenv
ORACLE_SID = [grid] ? +ASM2
The Oracle base has been set to /u01/app/grid
[grid@s2 ~]$ ps -ef | grep "tns.*SCAN"
grid      19280      1  0 Oct07 ?        00:05:24 /u01/app/11.2.0.3/grid/bin/tnslsnr LISTENER_SCAN1
-inherit
grid      81264  79505  0 15:35 pts/1    00:00:00 grep tns.*SCAN
[grid@s2 ~]$ lsnrctl services LISTENER_SCAN1

LSNRCTL for Linux: Version 11.2.0.3.0 - Production on 22-OCT-2013 15:36:02

Copyright (c) 1991, 2011, Oracle.  All rights reserved.

Connecting to (DESCRIPTION=(ADDRESS=(PROTOCOL=IPC)(KEY=LISTENER_SCAN1)))
Services Summary...
Service "PROD" has 2 instance(s).
  Instance "PROD1", status READY, has 1 handler(s) for this service...
    Handler(s):
      "DEDICATED" established:0 refused:0 state:ready
         REMOTE SERVER
         (DESCRIPTION=(ADDRESS=(PROTOCOL=tcp)(HOST=s1-vip.odalab.com)(PORT=1532)))
  Instance "PROD2", status READY, has 1 handler(s) for this service...
    Handler(s):
      "DEDICATED" established:0 refused:0 state:ready
         REMOTE SERVER
         (DESCRIPTION=(ADDRESS=(PROTOCOL=tcp)(HOST=s2-vip.odalab.com)(PORT=1532)))
Service "ebs_patch" has 2 instance(s).
  Instance "PROD1", status READY, has 1 handler(s) for this service...
    Handler(s):
      "DEDICATED" established:0 refused:0 state:ready
         REMOTE SERVER
         (DESCRIPTION=(ADDRESS=(PROTOCOL=tcp)(HOST=s1-vip.odalab.com)(PORT=1532)))
  Instance "PROD2", status READY, has 1 handler(s) for this service...
    Handler(s):
```

```
      "DEDICATED" established:0 refused:0 state:ready
        REMOTE SERVER
        (DESCRIPTION=(ADDRESS=(PROTOCOL=tcp)(HOST=s2-vip.odalab.com)(PORT=1532)))
The command completed successfully
```

You're ready to finalize the apps tier configuration when the testing of the database startup and shutdown process is completed. At this moment, the e-Business Suite configuration on the application tier server is unaware of the changes in the database tier; that is, Net services and JDBC configuration is still set for a single-node database and needs to be adjusted for the RAC database.

As expected, *AutoConfig* is capable of adjusting the configuration and the process is well explained in the "4.7. Establish Applications Environment for Oracle RAC" section of My Oracle Support note "Using Oracle 11g Release 2 Real Application Clusters and Automatic storage management with Oracle E-Business Suite Release 12.2 (Doc ID 1453213.1)." Here's a quick summary of the steps:

1. Adjust the *tnsnames.ora* and the JDBC URL in the context file manually to allow connectivity to one of the database instances of the RAC-enabled database.

2. Run *AutoConfig* on the applications server to retrieve the configuration information from the database, and then write the necessary changes to the configuration files.

3. Update the JDBC URL from in the Weblogic Server data source.

This concludes the database migration to ASM and RAC. You've made it through the most complicated part—implementing e-Business Suite on ODA. At this moment, you have a fully functional system with two nodes in the database tier and one node in the application tier. The next section of this chapter will show you how to clone the application tier VM and implement the second application tier node using the shared application tier file system.

Clone the Application Tier VM

At this moment, you have only one virtual machine running the e-Business Suite application tier. Fortunately, it's very easy to clone a new VM on the ODA from an existing one, and doing so will give you a VM that is already preconfigured the for the existing environment. Create a VM template from the existing VM, and clone the new VM from the new template. Additionally, you'll have to change the hostname and the IP address. Let's take a more detailed look at how to accomplish this process:

1. Stop the e-Business Suite services. Make sure they are not running during the cloning process to follow.

2. Stop the existing VM (oevm1) by connecting to one of the ODA Base servers and running oakcli stop vm, as shown next. Follow by executing oakcli show vm to confirm when the VM shuts down.

```
[root@s1 ~]# oakcli show vm
    NAME                MEMORY      VCPU        STATE       REPOSITORY
    oevm1               12288       4           ONLINE      odarepo1

[root@s1 ~]# oakcli stop vm oevm1
Shutdown VM initiated for oevm1

[root@s1 ~]# oakcli show vm
    NAME                MEMORY      VCPU        STATE       REPOSITORY
    oevm1               12288       4           OFFLINE     odarepo1
```

3. Connect to the Dom0 as *root* on the same ODA node where the existing VM is configured, and package the VM in a *tarball*. The existing VMs are located in /OVS/Repositories/ odarepo1/VirtualMachines/{VM name} on the first ODA node and /OVS/Repositories/ odarepo2/VirtualMachines/{VM name} on the second ODA node. For example:

```
[root@ovs-host1 ~]# cd /OVS/Repositories/odarepo1/VirtualMachines/oevm1
[root@ovs-host1 oevm1]# ls -lh
total 13G
-rw-r--r-- 1 root root 12G Oct 24 07:09 15574aa1d9f24f57b44bc6045d924cff.img
-rw-r--r-- 1 root root 350 Sep  2 10:03 vm.cfg
[root@ovs-host1 oevm1]# tar -cvzf /OVS/oevm1_clone.tgz ./*
./15574aa1d9f24f57b44bc6045d924cff.img
./vm.cfg
```

4. Copy the tarball to the Dom0 on the second ODA node:

```
[root@ovs-host1 oevm1]# scp /OVS/oevm1_clone.tgz 10.177.0.59:/OVS/
oevm1_clone.tgz                                100% 4700MB  47.5MB/s   01:39
```

5. Once the tarball is copied to the second Dom0, you can import it as a template in the repository on the other node. This step can be executed on any of ODA Base nodes; it doesn't have to be the same node to which you copied the tarball. Here are the commands to execute:

```
[root@s1 ~]# oakcli import vmtemplate oevm1_tmp -files /OVS/oevm1_clone.tgz -repo odarepo2
Imported VM Template
```

6. Create a new VM by cloning the template, and then start it up:

```
[root@s1 ~]# oakcli clone vm oevm2 -vmtemplate oevm1_tmp -repo odarepo2
Cloned VM : oevm2

[root@s1 ~]# oakcli start vm oevm2
Started VM : oevm2

[root@s1 ~]# oakcli show vm
    NAME                          MEMORY     VCPU      STATE        REPOSITORY
    oevm1                         12288        4      OFFLINE       odarepo1
    oevm2                         12288        4      ONLINE        odarepo2
```

7. Both VMs are now configured with the same hostname and IP. You need to change the configuration before both VMs can be started at the same time. I find the easiest way of doing this is by adjusting the configuration files /etc/sysconfig/network and /etc/ sysconfig/network-scripts/ifcfg-eth0, and then bouncing the VM. Additionally, depending on the configuration of the name resolution that you have chosen to implement, the host file may need to be adjusted. Here's an example of what to do:

```
[root@oevm1 ~]# grep HOSTNAME /etc/sysconfig/network
HOSTNAME=oevm1.odalab.com
[root@oevm1 ~]# vi /etc/sysconfig/network
[root@oevm1 ~]# grep HOSTNAME /etc/sysconfig/network
HOSTNAME=oevm2.odalab.com
```

```
[root@oevm1 ~]# grep IPADDR /etc/sysconfig/network-scripts/ifcfg-eth0
IPADDR=10.177.0.63
[root@oevm1 ~]# vi /etc/sysconfig/network-scripts/ifcfg-eth0
[root@oevm1 ~]# grep IPADDR /etc/sysconfig/network-scripts/ifcfg-eth0
IPADDR=10.177.0.64

[root@oevm1 ~]# reboot
```

8. You also want to mount the /cloudfs from the other Virtual IP on the new VM, so you need to adjust your /etc/fstab file and remount the ACFS file system on oevm2. For example:

```
[root@oevm2 ~]# grep cloudfs /etc/fstab
s1-vip:/cloudfs    /cloudfs    nfs    rw,intr,bg,hard,timeo=600,wsize=32768,rsize=32768,
nfsvers=3,tcp,nolock,acregmin=0,acregmax=0 0 0
[root@oevm2 ~]# vi /etc/fstab
[root@oevm2 ~]# grep cloudfs /etc/fstab
s2-vip:/cloudfs    /cloudfs    nfs    rw,intr,bg,hard,timeo=600,wsize=32768,rsize=32768,
nfsvers=3,tcp,nolock,acregmin=0,acregmax=0 0 0
[root@oevm2 ~]# umount /cloudfs
[root@oevm2 ~]# mount /cloudfs
```

9. Lastly, you can start the first VM too because the conflicting configuration has been removed. (See the following example). Once started, you should check that the virtual IP (10.177.0.60 in this example is configured on oevm2) is managed and started on one of the VMs. You can also test how *keepalived* manages the virtual IP by stopping and starting its service (use service keepalived stop and service keepalived start to do it) on the hosts. The IP will always be allocated to one of the VMs the *keepalived* is running on.

```
[root@s1 ~]# oakcli start vm oevm1
Started VM : oevm1

[root@s1 ~]# oakcli show vm
      NAME              MEMORY    VCPU    STATE       REPOSITORY
      oevm1             12288      4      ONLINE      odarepo1
      oevm2             12288      4      ONLINE      odarepo2

[root@oevm1 ~]# ip addr list dev eth0 | grep "inet "
      inet 10.177.0.63/16 brd 10.177.255.255 scope global eth0

[root@oevm2 ~]# ip addr list dev eth0 | grep "inet "
      inet 10.177.0.64/16 brd 10.177.255.255 scope global eth0
      inet 10.177.0.60/32 scope global eth0
```

You have two-application tier VMs now, but only one of them is configured with e-Business Suite. The final step to complete the e-Business Suite application tier configuration on ODA is to enable the services on the second VM. This is covered in the next section.

Configure the Second Application Tier Node

In order to start using the second application tier VM you need to enable the usage of the virtual IP address for the e-Business Suite front-end services. Then you need to add the new node to the application tier configuration.

Usage of the virtual IP address in your configuration simulates the physical load balancer, so from an e-Business Suite configuration perspective you have to implement a load balancer. This is covered by My Oracle Support document "Using Load-Balancers with Oracle E-Business Suite Release 12.2 (Doc ID 1375686.1)." Chapter 2.1 in that document, "Using Hardware Load Balancers with Single Web Entry Point," describes the configuration changes needed for the architecture you are building on ODA. The instructions explain the manual configuration steps to implement the support of a load balancer IP address in e-Business Suite for all front-end services. Follow the instructions to implement such an address.

There is an alternative way to enable the virtual IP—by using the configuration wizards included in the e-Business Suite Oracle Application Manager. The HTTP Load Balancing wizard can be accessed after logging on using the System Administrator responsibility and navigating: Oracle Applications Manager ➤ Dashboard ➤ Site Map ➤ AutoConfig ➤ Launch Wizards. Then click the Enable button.

Figures 11-4 to 11-6 show the most important screens of the configuration wizard for enabling HTTP load balancing. Figure 11-5 shows the first screen, where you have to choose the nodes to enable the load balancing. You have only one node to select at this time. The load balancing settings will be prepopulated when the second node is added to the e-Business Suite configuration.

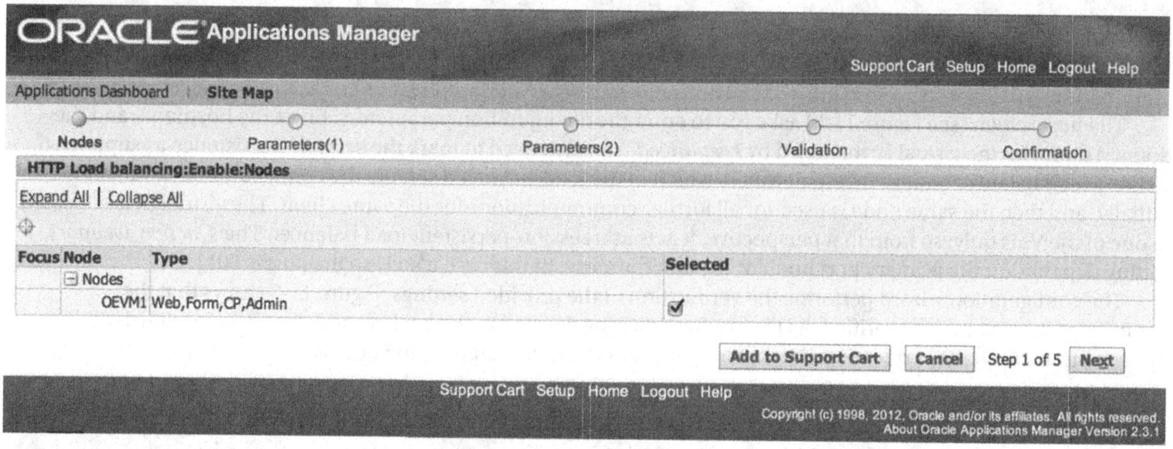

Figure 11-5. *Select the node for the load balancing configuration*

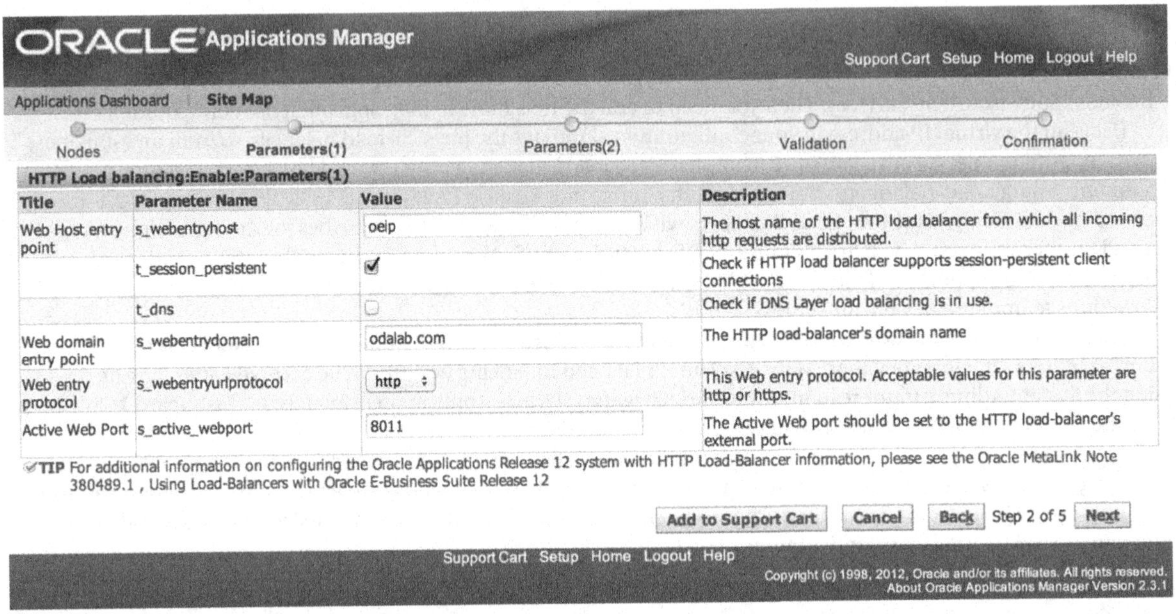

Figure 11-6. *Providing the load balancing configuration parameters*

The next screen (see Figure 11-6) asks you to enter the configuration parameters. Enter the hostname and the domain name for the virtual IP managed by *keepalived*. You also need to mark the session-persistence as supported. This is a load balancer feature that remembers which of the load-balanced servers the connection was routed to initially, and then the same node is used for all further communications for the same client. The virtual IP is allocated to one of the VMs only; so from that perspective, it acts as a session-persistent load balancer. The *s_active_webport* setting depends on the primary port pool for the environment. In this case it's 11, so the port is 8011.

The configuration wizard performs the verification of the provided settings. Figure 11-7 shows that the parameters are successfully verified. As the verification is performed in the background, you'll have to push the Refresh button until the verification checks complete and the status changes to Success.

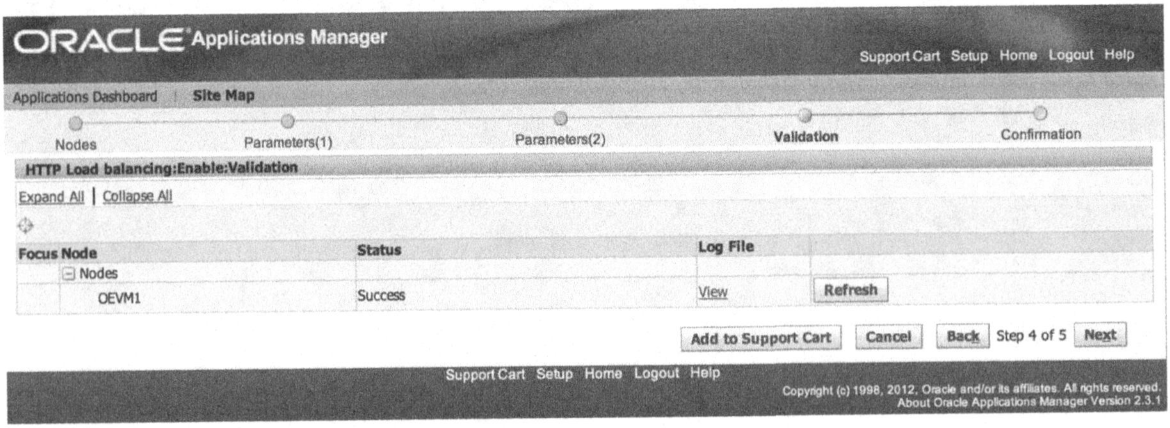

Figure 11-7. *Verification of the configuration parameters*

Submit the changes in the remaining configuration screens until you're presented with the following message: "The configuration options have been saved to the Context File. Now you can run AutoConfig and restart services to make sure these settings take effects."

Run the AutoConfig on the VM as instructed and bounce the services to start using the virtual IP.

The virtual IP has been configured in e-Business Suite. The last remaining step is to enable the services on the second VM. You can do so by implementing the shared application tier file system as instructed in My Oracle Support note "Sharing The Application Tier File System in Oracle E-Business Suite Release 12.2 (Doc ID 1375769.1)." It's a fairly complex process, but my testing shows the instructions are accurate and they deliver the desired configuration.

Revert the Temporary Configuration

A while ago, you added a temporary file system (/u02) to the ODA Base on the first node of the ODA. Since then, the e-Business Suite database has been migrated to ASM and RAC using a natively created database Oracle Home on ODA, thus the temporary configuration can be removed. The following steps will remove the /u02 file system and will restore the Oracle Inventory on the ODA Base where the database was initially installed.

1. Unregister the old Oracle Home from the inventory:

```
[oracle@s1 ~]$ cd /u02/prod/11.2.0
[oracle@s1 11.2.0]$ cd oui/bin
[oracle@s1 bin]$ ./runInstaller -silent -detachHome ORACLE_HOME=/u02/prod/11.2.0
Starting Oracle Universal Installer...

Checking swap space: must be greater than 500 MB.   Actual 19748 MB    Passed
The inventory pointer is located at /etc/oraInst.loc
The inventory is located at /u01/app/oraInventory
'DetachHome' was successful.
```

2. Remove the /u02 from ODA Base. Use fuser to find if any processes are still using the mountpoint and terminate them if any are found. For example:

```
[root@s1 ~]# fuser -m /u02
/u02:              89091ce
[root@s1 ~]# kill -9 89091
[root@s1 ~]# umount /u02
```

3. Remove the partition that you created on the attached block device /dev/xvdd to create the temporary ext3 file system on the ODA Base. Here are the commands to execute:

```
[root@s1 ~]# fdisk /dev/xvdd
Command (m for help): d
Command (m for help): w

[root@s1 ~]# ls -l /dev/xvdd*
brw-r----- 1 root disk 202, 48 Sep 28 18:52 /dev/xvdd
```

4. Detach the block device from the ODA Base. This is a tricky process. If you want to walk the easy path, simply restart the ODA Base and the temporary block device will be removed because it wasn't saved in the configuration for the ODA Base. But if the system is used by other databases, or for some reason bouncing the ODA Base is not an option, then execute `xenstore-ls` to find out the *domain id* and the *vdb id* (the virtual block device id) for the attached block device. The command will spool a lot of output, but if you search for the filename of the attached file (`u02.img`), you'll find a section similar to that in the following example:

```
[root@ovs-host1 oakDom1]# xenstore-ls
...
      51760 = ""
       domain = "oakDom1"
       frontend = "/local/domain/2/device/vbd/51760"
       uuid = "def6fa49-aeb6-eab8-1ed6-2c6007489c9c"
       bootable = "0"
       dev = "/dev/xvdd"
       state = "4"
       params = "/OVS/Repositories/odabaseRepo/VirtualMachines/oakDom1/u02.img"
       mode = "w"
       online = "1"
       frontend-id = "2"
       type = "file"
       node = "/dev/loop4"
       physical-device = "7:4"
       feature-flush-cache = "1"
       feature-discard = "0"
       feature-barrier = "1"
       sectors = "204800"
       info = "0"
       sector-size = "512"
       hotplug-status = "connected"
   ...
```

5. You're interested in finding the correct "front-end" path for the attached device. In this case, the path is "/local/domain/2/device/vbd/51760". The *domain id* in the path is "2" and the *vdb id* is "51760". This information is sufficient for detaching the device from the ODA Base using `xm block-detach` by using the following commands:

```
[root@ovs-host1 ~]# xm block-detach 2 51760
[root@ovs-host1 ~]# xenstore-ls | grep "u02.img"
# no rows retrieved#
```

6. The `u02.img` file is not needed anymore and can be removed.

```
[root@ovs-host1 ~]# rm -vf /OVS/Repositories/odabaseRepo/VirtualMachines/oakDom1/u02.img
removed `/OVS/Repositories/odabaseRepo/VirtualMachines/oakDom1/u02.img'
```

The ODA Base is now restored to its original state.

Post-Installation Tasks

The installation of e-Business Suite Release 12.2 on ODA has been completed. The remaining tasks are not directly related to deploying the system on ODA, but rather to the specific requirements you have for your system, and most of them will be covered during the e-Business Suite implementation project you are running. This chapter mentions a few important steps and references to additional documentation besides the technical configuration of the e-Business Suite on ODA, without which the implementation would not be complete.

Additional Configuration

The list of additional configuration tasks you'll perform in your system depends on the requirements you have for your environment. A typical list of areas to explore include:

- *Integration with other systems*: Includes identity management products (Oracle Access Manager, Oracle Internet Directory), reporting tools (Oracle Discoverer, OBIEE), connected systems using incoming and outgoing database links, custom-built in-house applications, and others.

- *Configuration of the required business functionality*: e-Business Suite is a comprehensive suite of integrated, global business applications. Depending on your plans, you will configure few or many modules included in Oracle e-Business Suite. The R12.2 documentation library contains at least 85 implementation guides for different areas of functionality. You'll definitely need to review at least some of these and you probably will have to make some changes to the existing environment.

- *Tuning of the configuration*: Your environment will likely require some tuning after the initial implementation. This includes sizing the connection pools between application tier servers and the database, tuning the memory parameters of the database and application tier services, sizing the concurrent managers and implementing parallel concurrent processing (PCP), adjusting the session timeouts, and others.

- *Recommended patches*: The e-Business Suite modules are constantly being developed as bugs are fixed and new features are implemented. The Release 12.2 was made generally available in September 2013 and it is not uncommon to see critical or recommended patches to be released soon after a product is released. You should check the "Recommended Patches" reports in My Oracle Support to identify any known bugs and be able to fix them before your system is transferred into production use.

Backups and Monitoring

An important preparation step for going live with ODA is the implementation of a monitoring framework for timely notification about issues. The best way to monitor the ODA hardware is by configuring the Auto Service Request (ASR) support feature that is included in the ODA software bundle. ASR automatically creates Service Requests, provides diagnostic information to Oracle Support, and notifies administrators about hardware faults.

ASR does not provide any monitoring for the database, the VMs, and the e-Business Suite application. You need to implement tools to monitor the software components of the system. ODA supports installation of third-party agents to manage, monitor, backup, replicate, authenticate, or otherwise act on the database, the server, or the environment,[15] thus giving the opportunity to handle the ODA the same way as any other server in your IT infrastructure.

---

[15]My Oracle Support note "FAQ : ODA 2.3 New Features includes Multiple Homes & 3rd Party Agent Support (Doc ID 1415773.1)."

You also need to decide how backups will be taken. The default configuration of the ODA assumes the fast recovery area for the database is used and it's configured to use the ASM disk group +RECO, but this does not cover the VMs and the shared file system for e-Business Suite. You might consider and find it more convenient to use an external NFS-mounted file system for both the database backups and the backups of the e-Business Suite file system; this way, the backups of the whole system would be logically kept together, and if a recovery situation occurs, it would be easier to retrieve the required backups from the same location, compared to extracting them from different locations.

Summary

This chapter explains how to convert the Oracle Database Appliance into an Oracle e-Business Suite Appliance. It proposes a configuration, which allows creating a highly available e-Business Suite system fully configured on a single ODA. The configuration utilizes ASM for the database storage, RAC for the database availability and workload balancing, two virtualized application tier servers for availability of the middle tier services, shared application tier file system on ACFS for simplified management of e-Business Suite, and a virtual IP address for the failover of the front-end services. The nonstandard steps for implementing such configuration are explained in details.

The chapter also outlines the installation process of e-Business Suite Release 12.2 and can be used as a reference for installations and conversions of e-Business Suite into a highly available configuration on any supported hardware. The installation and migration of older releases to ODA are not covered, but the proposed architecture and the configuration steps to prepare the ODA for such architecture are still valid for e-Business Suite R12.1, R12.0, and even 11i.

CHAPTER 12

■ ■■ ■

Oracle Enterprise Manager and the ODA

Oracle Enterprise Manager Cloud Control 12c (referred to hereafter as *EM12c*) is the latest version of Oracle Corporation's end-to-end management tool for both Oracle and non-Oracle technology. Previously known as Oracle Enterprise Manager (OEM) or Oracle Enterprise Manager Grid Control, the tool has been around for quite some time now. The 12c release, though, is a landmark version that makes huge advances in terms of both the breadth and depth of its functionality. In many ways, this release has moved Enterprise Manager from being a database administrator's monitoring tool, to a tool that can be used to manage your entire Oracle data center.

Before you can understand how EM12c can be used in an ODA environment, you really need to have an understanding of the basic architecture of EM12c, so let's start by providing you with an introduction to the basic architecture of EM12c.

Architecture Overview

From an architectural perspective, EM12c is composed of five main parts:

- The Cloud Control console
- Oracle Management agents
- The Oracle Management Service
- The Oracle Management Repository
- Plug-ins

Let's look at each of these in more detail.

■ **Note** A discussion of the licensing for EM12c is beyond the scope of this book. (An entire licensing document is available in the Enterprise Manager documentation at http://docs.oracle.com/cd/E24628_01/license.121/e24474/toc.htm.) However, it's worth noting that, in general, most of the basic functionality described here carries a restricted-use license and therefore is free. This restricted-use license refers specifically to Enterprise Manager, however, and many add-on options do come with license costs. Refer to the licensing documentation for full details.

The Cloud Control Console

The *Cloud Control console* provides the user interface that you use to access, monitor, and administer your computing environment. The console is accessed via a web browser, thus allowing you to access the central console from any location. You can customize the EM12c console much more than in previous releases, allowing you the following options:

- Choosing your home page from various predefined pages (or indeed setting any page you want to be your personal home page)

- Moving regions around on a target home page

- Adding regions that might be of more interest to you than the defaults

- Deleting regions that aren't of interest to you

The graphical user interface (GUI) provides a history of the most recent targets you have visited (the standard browser history is also available). In addition, you can mark pages as favorites and have them appear in a favorites list on the new menu-driven interface. Figure 12-1 shows an example of the default home page.

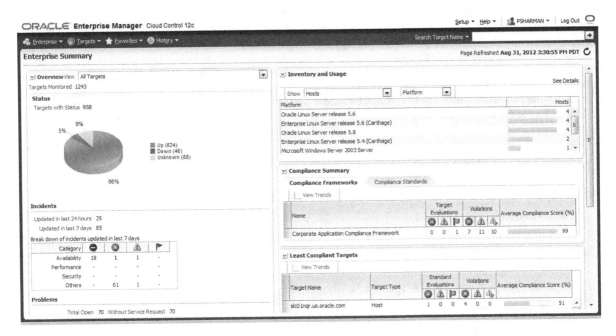

***Figure 12-1.** The new default home page in EM12c*

Oracle Management Agents

An *Oracle Management agent* (usually referred to as simply an *agent* or abbreviated to *OMA*) is generally installed on each host that is monitored in your computing environment. (EM12c also introduces the capability to manage environments remotely in some cases.) These agents are deployed from the console (see Figure 12-2), and then monitor all the targets that have been discovered by the agents. They are used to control blackouts on those targets, execute jobs, collect metrics, and so forth, and in turn provide details such as availability, metrics, and job statuses back to the Oracle Management Service.

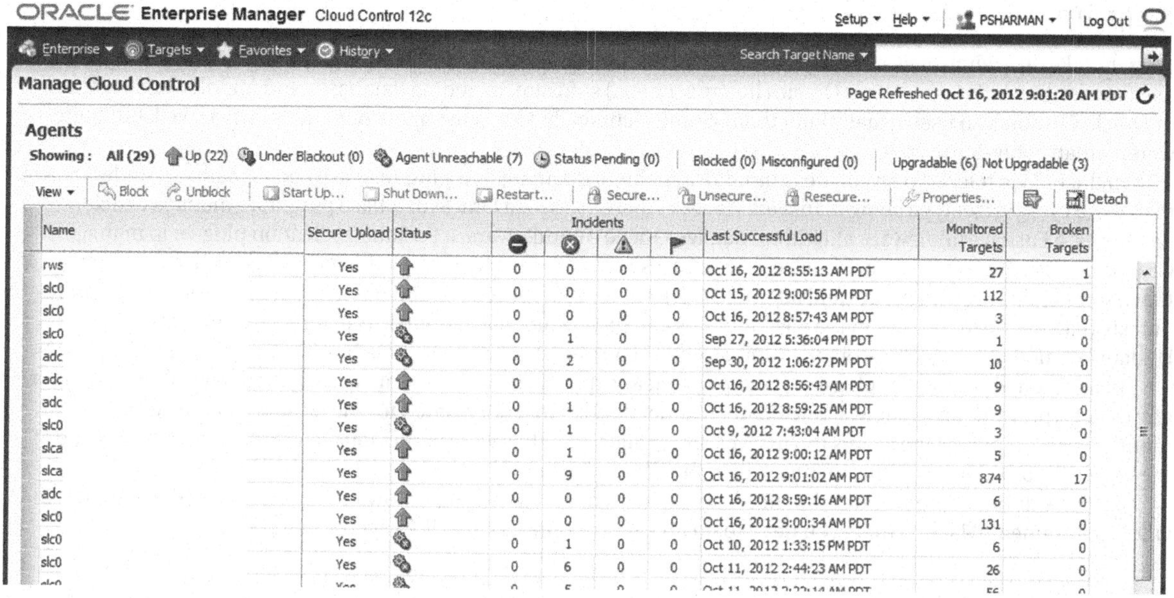

Figure 12-2. *User interface for managing agents within EM12c*

For the EM12c release, agents were completely rewritten from the ground up for greater reliability, availability, and performance (see the upcoming section on plug-ins for details on how this was achieved). The only downside of this change is that you must use an EM12c agent to talk to the EM12c Oracle Management Service. Backward compatibility between 12c and earlier agents was lost because of the number of changes that were made in the new release.

Oracle Management Service

The *Oracle Management Service (OMS)* is a web-based application that communicates with the agents and the Oracle Management Repository to collect and store information about all the targets on the various agents. (Note that the information itself is stored in the Oracle Management Repository, not the OMS.) The OMS is also responsible for rendering the user interface for the console.

The OMS is installed into an Oracle middleware home, which also contains the Oracle WebLogic Server (including the WebLogic Server administration console), an Oracle Management agent for the middleware tier, the management service instance base directory, the Java Development Kit (JDK), and other configuration files. You can install the OMS into an existing WebLogic Server (WLS) configuration if it exists, but usually it is better from an availability perspective to have it installed in a dedicated WLS home.

Oracle Management Repository

The *Oracle Management Repository* (also called the *repository* or *OMR*) is an Oracle database that stores all the information collected by the various management agents. It is composed of database users, tablespaces, tables, views, indexes, packages, procedures, and database jobs.

Unlike the OMS, the installation process for the OMR requires that a database already exists for the repository. This means you need to have created the database somewhere in your environment prior to installing the OMS. Again, it is typically recommended for the repository to be created in a dedicated database.

Plug-ins

Plug-ins take on a whole new meaning in EM12c. In earlier releases, plug-ins were largely system-monitoring utilities used to monitor and manage non-Oracle (heterogeneous) software, including databases and middleware. Partners or Oracle Corporation itself usually built them. Some technically savvy customers built their own as well, but there weren't many plug-ins overall.

In the EM12c release, a few of these monitoring plug-ins remain, but plug-ins have been greatly expanded to include every target type being managed. As such, there is now an Oracle database plug-in to manage Oracle databases, a Fusion Middleware plug-in to manage Oracle's middleware, a Fusion Application plug-in to manage Oracle's applications, and so on. Because new releases of the Oracle software will include plug-ins used to manage that software, this means EM12c (and later releases) will be able to monitor and manage those releases much more quickly than has been the case in the past. Plug-ins can be downloaded, applied, and deployed using the new Self Update functionality available from the Cloud Control console (if you have sufficient privileges to use it).

In addition, this modular plug-in architecture means that an agent is no longer configured to be able to monitor any target type. Now, an agent will download only the plug-ins that are needed for the targets that the agent is monitoring. This means the agents themselves are smaller than they were in previous releases. This change is one of the biggest improvements in the architecture of the EM12c release.

So that's the basic architecture you need to understand. Now let's look at how EM12c can be used to manage an ODA environment. The first thing you need to do for this, of course, is install an agent.

Agent Installation

Agent installation on an ODA machine is not all that different to agent installation on any other machine. First you need to add the hosts, and then discover the targets that are available on the hosts. In this example, I will walk you through the installation of agent software on a two-node ODA from Enterprise Manager Cloud Control 12c.

Adding the Hosts

To add the hosts, start Enterprise Manager Cloud Control 12c and select Setup ➤ Add Targets ➤ Add Targets Manually. Do this as shown in Figure 12-3.

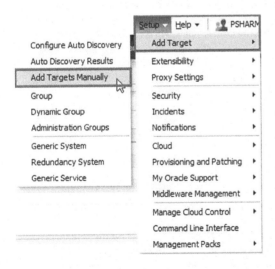

Figure 12-3. *Choosing to manually add a target*

On the Add Targets Manually page, select Add Host Targets if not already selected, and then click the Add Host button, as shown in Figure 12-4.

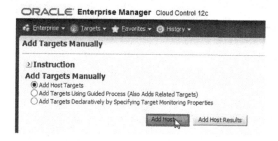

Figure 12-4. *Starting the Add Host Targets Manually wizard*

On the Add Host Targets : Host and Platform screen, click the Add button, as shown in Figure 12-5.

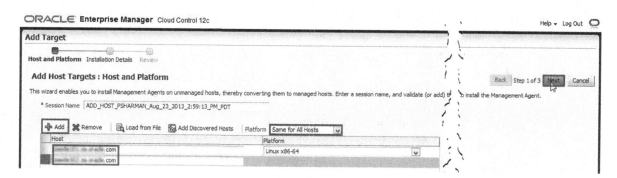

Figure 12-5. *Step 1 of the Add Host Targets Manually wizard, adding hosts*

Select the hosts from the search window, select the platform, and set platform to "Same for all hosts" and click Next, as you can see in Figure 12-6.

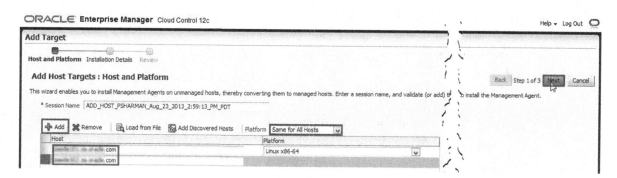

Figure 12-6. *Step 2 of the Add Host Targets Manually wizard, selecting host names and platforms*

Enter the appropriate values for Installation Base Directory and Instance Directory (or accept the defaults), as shown in Figure 12-7.

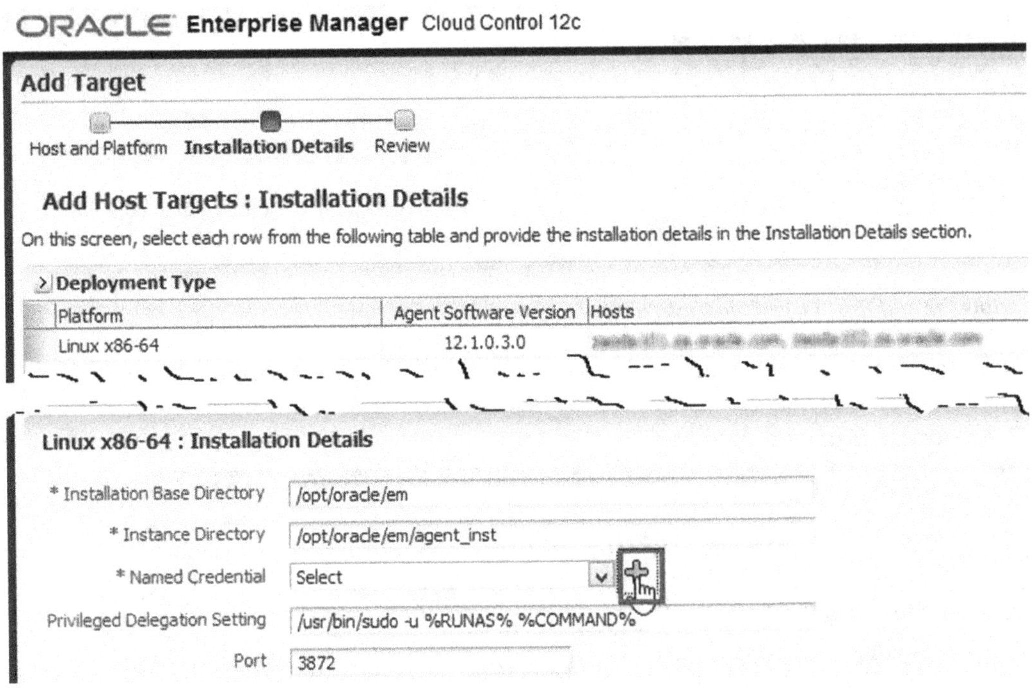

Figure 12-7. Step 3 of the Add Host Targets Manually wizard, selecting installation details

If a named credential already exists for these hosts, select that named credential or click the "+" sign (as shown in Figure 12-7) to create a new one. Enter the username and password for the owner of the agent software. If that username has sudo privilege, set the run privilege appropriately or leave it at None if it doesn't, as you can see in Figure 12-8. Click OK.

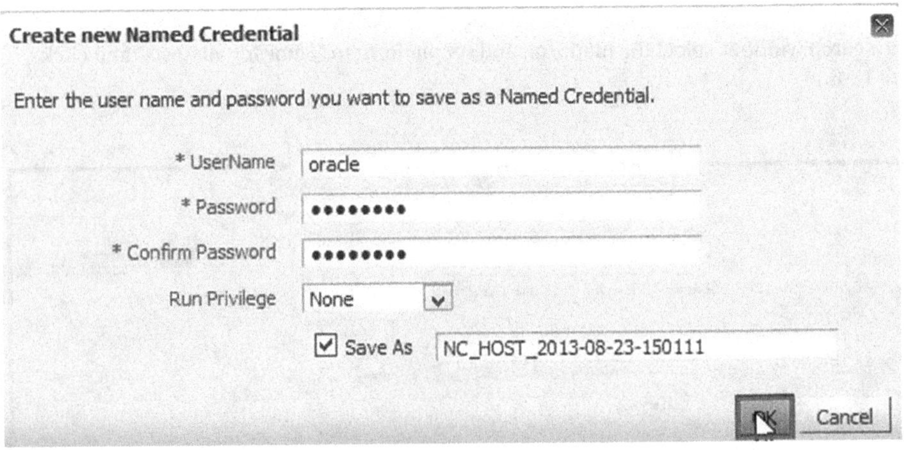

Figure 12-8. Creating a New Named Credential

When you are returned to the Add Host Targets: Installation Details page, click Next to move to the Review page, as shown in Figure 12-9. Review the information that you have provided. If it is correct, click Deploy Agent.

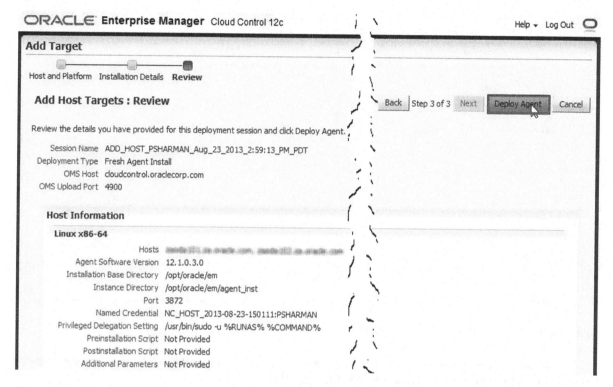

Figure 12-9. *Step 4 of the Add Host Targets Manually wizard, reviewing the details and deploying the agent*

The agent installation will now start. The screen should auto-refresh for you until the installation either completes or hits a problem.

Running the root.sh Script

One problem you might encounter is the user account not being set up to run the sudo command. Such is the case in Figure 12-10. If you encounter this problem, then you must run the root.sh script manually.

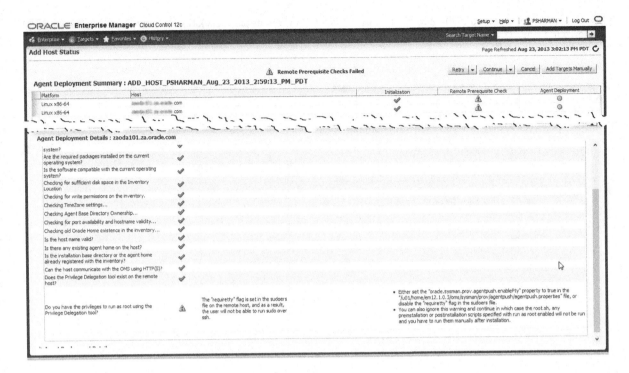

Figure 12-10. *Warning to run root.sh script manually*

You can proceed from this point, and run the root.sh script later. To proceed, click on the down arrow next to Continue and choose Continue, All Hosts, as seen in Figure 12-11.

Figure 12-11. *Continuing after the warning to run root.sh*

Finally, Figure 12-12 shows the installation completing with a reminder to run root.sh on all nodes.

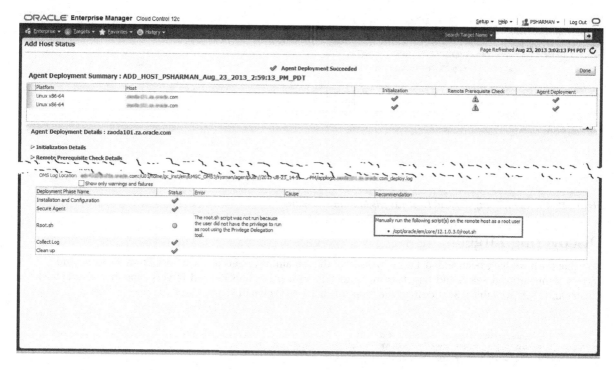

Figure 12-12. *A final reminder to run root.sh on all nodes*

Log onto each host as root and run the relevant script. For example:

```
[root@node1 ~]# /opt/oracle/em/core/12.1.0.3.0/root.sh
Finished product-specific root actions.
/etc exist
Finished product-specific root actions.
[root@node1 ~]# ssh node2
root@node2's password:
Last login: Fri Aug 16 10:50:11 2013 from node1
[root@node2 ~]# /opt/oracle/em/core/12.1.0.3.0/root.sh
Finished product-specific root actions.
/etc exist
Finished product-specific root actions.
```

As shown in Figure 12-13, return to the installation and click Done to complete the Add Host Targets Manually wizard.

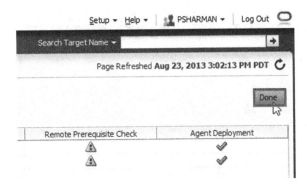

Figure 12-13. *Completing the Add Host Targets Manually wizard*

Discovering Targets

Now that the hosts have been added, I want to discover the remaining targets on each host. From the same Add Targets Manually page, select Add Targets Using Guided Process (Also Adds Related Targets), and then select Oracle Cluster and High Availability Service from the drop-down list, as shown in Figure 12-14.

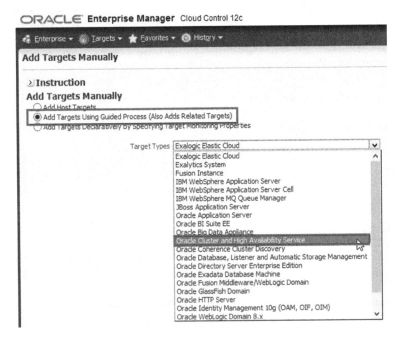

Figure 12-14. *Starting the Add Targets Using Guided Process wizard to add Oracle Cluster and High Availability Service*

Next, click Add Using Guided Process ... to start the wizard. This will take you to the first step in the wizard—Add Cluster Target: Specify Host, as seen in Figure 12-15. Either search for the first node using the magnifying glass or simply type the host name into the Host field and click Continue.

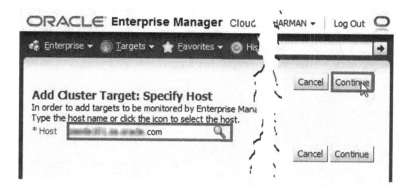

Figure 12-15. *Step 1 of the Add Targets Using Guided Process wizard, specifying the host name*

If the cluster is configured correctly, the installation process should automatically discover the cluster name and other values, along with populating Selected Hosts with both host names. If it hasn't, populate these fields and then click Add, as seen in Figure 12-16.

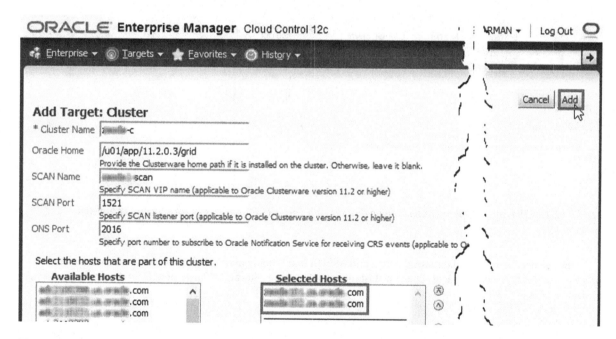

Figure 12-16. *Step 2 of the Add Targets Using Guided Process wizard, specifying the cluster details*

Figure 12-17 shows the Add Target: Cluster screen, which will be seen while the target addition is in progress.

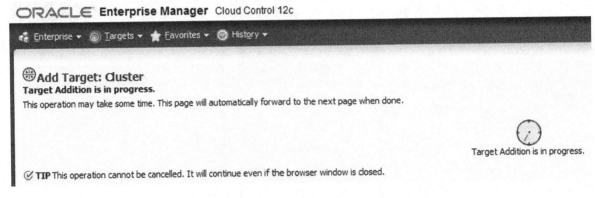

Figure 12-17. *The Add Target: Cluster wizard showing the progress toward making an addition*

Once the cluster has been added, you will be taken to the screen seen in Figure 12-18, which shows that the cluster details have been saved. Click OK.

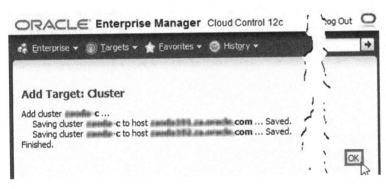

Figure 12-18. *The confirmation screen showing that the Add Target Using Guided Process wizard completed successfully*

Now we need to add the database, listener, and ASM (if that is being used). Again, we can do this via the guided process, but this time select Oracle Database, Listener and Automatic Storage Management from the target types list, as shown in Figure 12-19.

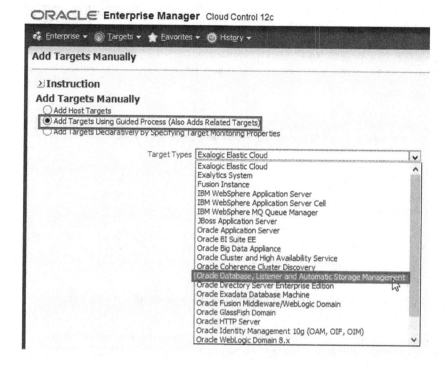

Figure 12-19. Starting the Add Targets Using Guided Process wizard to add Oracle Database and related targets

Now click the Add Using Guided Process... button to move to the Add Database Instance Target page. As shown in Figure 12-20, either search for or simply enter the host name for the host that the database runs on, and then click Continue.

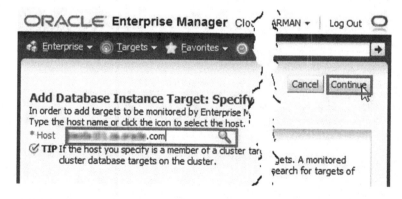

Figure 12-20. Step 1 of the Add Oracle Database and related targets wizard, specifying the host name

The host is recognized as being part of a cluster, so in Figure 12-21, we choose to look for databases on all hosts in the cluster to add to Enterprise Manager, and then click Continue.

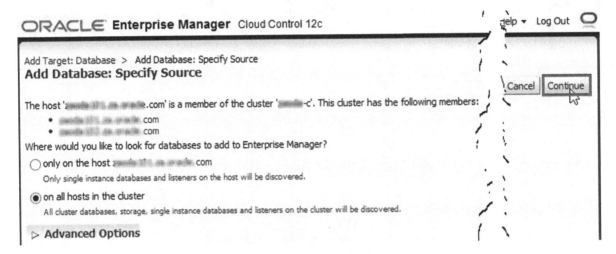

Figure 12-21. *Step 2 of the Add Oracle Database and related targets wizard, searching for databases on all nodes of the cluster*

Again, the target discovery process screen appears. Once the targets have been discovered, you will be taken to the screen shown in Figure 12-22. Here you will need to configure the monitoring credentials, so click the Configure button for the first database.

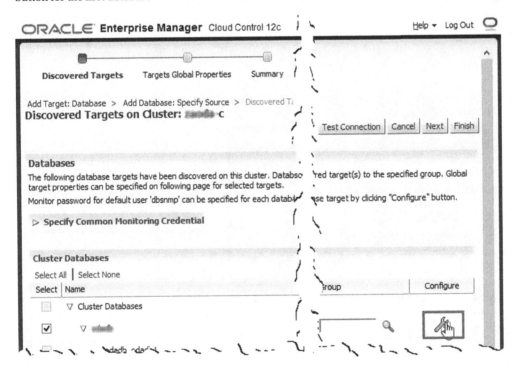

Figure 12-22. *Step 3 of the Add Oracle Database and related targets wizard, configuring the first discovered database*

As shown in Figure 12-23, enter the password for the DBSNMP account and click the Test Connection button.

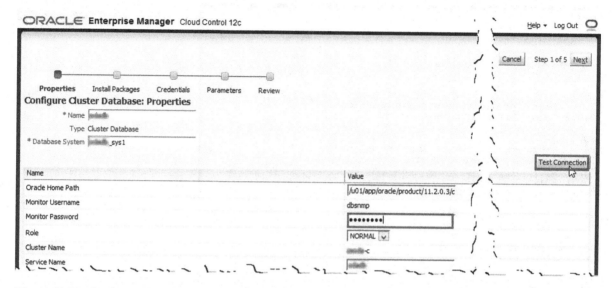

Figure 12-23. *Configuring and testing the DBSNMP account*

You should see a "Success" message like that shown in Figure 12-24, so click Next (or go back and correct the password if you entered an incorrect value).

Figure 12-24. *Screen showing that the connection test was successful*

This will bring up the Configure Cluster Database: Review screen, where you can simply click OK.

Repeat this process for any other databases that were found as part of the discovery process, as well as the listener and ASM. Once all targets have been configured, click the Finish button. You'll be brought to a Summary page from which you should click the Save button. Then a progress page will appear before you are forwarded to the Target Configuration Results page (Figure 12-25), where you simply click OK to finish the process.

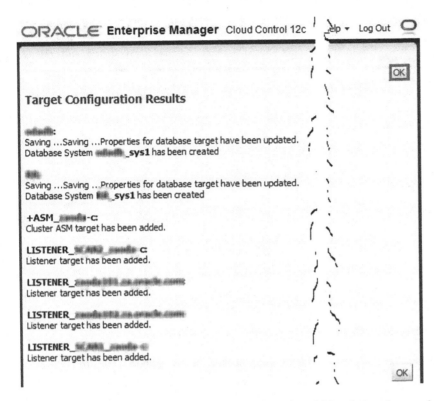

Figure 12-25. Target Configuration Results page from the Add Oracle Database and related targets wizard

This completes the installation and configuration of the agents on the ODA environment, so now I can monitor all these targets as I would any other Oracle database environment.

Summary

This chapter provided a quick overview of the Oracle Enterprise Manager architecture and how to push agents to an ODA for monitoring. Monitoring an ODA from Enterprise Manager behaves and is done the same way as any other database version. By monitoring the ODA with Enterprise Manager, the complexity of the ODA can be simplified and easier to resolve issues as they occur. Enterprise Manager should be the first choice for monitoring this entry-level engineered system.

Index

■ P, Q

Get the eBook for only $10!

Now you can take the weightless companion with you anywhere, anytime. Your purchase of this book entitles you to 3 electronic versions for only $10.

This Apress title will prove so indispensible that you'll want to carry it with you everywhere, which is why we are offering the eBook in **3 formats** for only $10 if you have already purchased the print book.

Convenient and fully searchable, the PDF version enables you to easily find and copy code—or perform examples by quickly toggling between instructions and applications. The MOBI format is ideal for your Kindle, while the ePUB can be utilized on a variety of mobile devices.

Go to www.apress.com/promo/tendollars to purchase your companion eBook.